"For fifty years Geoff Thomas has been my mentor and friend. His weekly emails recounting details of encounters and observations are often priceless. If I were forced to list my top five preachers, his name would be there. As a young Christian at Aberystwyth University in Wales, I found that his mentorship and care for me proved definitive. I would not be where I am today without his guiding, supportive hand. He has preached all over the world, met thousands of people and kept extensive diary-like notes of his conversations with them, remained in one church for over a half century, and influenced generations of preachers. That he should write a self-deprecating autobiography is a measure of the heart of this man. His autobiography is a window into the evangelical/Reformed church of the last seventy years and more. I predict that this book will be widely read and talked about for years to come."

—Derek W. H. Thomas, senior pastor of First Presbyterian Church of Columbia, South Carolina

"For some time now, Geoffrey Thomas has been in the habit of sending out occasional letters that reflect on God and the gospel, his travels and life, and people and movements in the Christian world. They are gems. Well, reading these autobiographical reflections is like receiving an 'eleventy' of these letters at one fell swoop! This volume of reminiscences is enthralling, winsome in its wisdom, and a fabulous window on God's work in one influential life. Geoffrey Thomas has indeed had a profound influence for good in the Christian world, and especially among those people who are Reformed in their theology and vision of church life. It was Geoff's recommendation to a Baptist elder in Belfast in 2000 that led to my being involved in Ireland, both the North and Eire, for two decades now—and I thank God for the author of this book and the fruit of Geoffrey Thomas's ministry and life."

—Michael A. G. Haykin, professor of church history, The Southern Baptist Theological Seminary

"Biographies and autobiographies usually make for fascinating reading. This volume will not disappoint. Yet it is more than the story of one faithful man's ministry in 'Aber' for fifty years. The reader will gain perspective on the twentieth century as Geoff weaves his own story into the religious climate in Wales either side of World War II. The recovery of historic biblical Christianity is portrayed through his eyes. There are also delightful cameos of his professors at Westminster Seminary, of men who were his friends and had a formative influence on him, and also of some who were converted to Christ under his preaching ministry. The author has been candid and is very aware of his shortcomings but at the same time very conscious of divine mercy and grace that sustained him for those fifty years."

—Austin Walker, former pastor of Maidenbower Baptist Church, Crawley, UK

"By the time Geoff Thomas began his long ministry in Aberystwyth, the tide had gone out, leaving the churches in Wales high and dry. The higher critical movement had robbed us of the gospel. I arrived in Aberystwyth in 1968, was converted, and was called to preach but lacked any models or mentors. I learned to preach by listening to Geoff and by devouring the books he recommended. And I saw firsthand how the ascended Christ uses a local church for the advancement of His kingdom in the world.

With disarming frankness, Geoff looks back over a lifetime of faithful, fruitful gospel ministry and shares with us the influences that shaped him and the highs and lows of pastoral ministry. He speaks about his own mistakes and failures with refreshing honesty and self-deprecating humor. But at the same time, there is no mistaking the high view he has of the call to full-time ministry. 'What a marvelously privileged life we lead,' he says of the gospel minister.

This book is full of so many rich, instructive brief bios of teachers and colleagues in ministry—some relatively unknown, some household names in the evangelical world. Of particular interest are the vivid little cameos of the Westminster faculty. What a privilege to have such teachers. How vital it is for a lifetime of ministry to set yourself up with the best possible theological education. And how blessed are we who came under the influence of this man and his ministry."

—David N. Jones, Hobart, Tasmania, Presbyterian Church of Australia

"I was under the ministry of Geoff Thomas during my doctoral studies at the university in Aberystwyth. His book is a magnificent work of autobiography. It provides the reader with a fascinating account into the life, upbringing, and influences on this well-loved and respected pastor and preacher who for over fifty years was a minister in Aberystwyth. This autobiography also provides fascinating glimpses into life at Westminster Theological Seminary in the early 1960s and into the church scene in Wales during the twentieth century, as well as the establishment of a couple of confessional Christian churches in Mid Wales in both the Welsh and English languages."

—Jean-Marc Alter, school teacher and contributor to the *Oxford Dictionary of National Biography*

"You can hear Geoff Thomas as you read this book. There is a generosity of spirit that gushes through the written word as it flows in his preached words—a love for his Lord, for people, for the church, for his Baptist form of Calvinistic Methodism, for Wales, for Aberystwyth, for the people of Alfred Place. The anecdotes about and insights into his esteemed teachers at Westminster Theological Seminary are a treat. His openness about his own perceived failings and the troughs and peaks of his long ministry at Alfred Place, Aberystwyth, are lessons in honesty. We learn about many much-loved people and a multifaceted pastoral ministry. Read it, be challenged, and be refreshed."

—Mostyn Roberts, minister at Welwyn Evangelical Church

"A man who has ministered for fifty years in a single congregation and remains as enthusiastic for the ministry as when he first began is a man who needs to write his autobiography. For those who know Geoff, this book will fill you with thankfulness to God for him and for his influence. For those of you who don't know Geoff personally, it will be an introduction to one of the most remarkable ministers I've ever known. I'm delighted he has written his story."

—Paul Levy, minister at the International Presbyterian Church, Ealing, London

"This is a lively and engaging account of the life and ministry of one man, but it also sheds fascinating light on the state of Christianity in Wales and beyond in recent times. It demonstrates the value of faithful biblical preaching in bringing people to Christ, in building up believers in the faith, and in challenging the widespread godlessness in both the church and society at large."

—Gwyn Davies, elder in the Aberystwyth
Welsh Evangelical Church

"This personal account of Pastor Geoff's life makes for a thoroughly enjoyable read, containing a bright array of personal and historical anecdotes written in a warm and lucid manner. There is openness and honesty, the confession that not all has been as it could have been—a feature so helpful to those of us whose ministries have witnessed relatively little fruit. The brief biographical and irenically written sketches provide flashes of fascinating insight; the tracing of historical associations serves to deepen the understanding of evangelicalism, especially here in Wales. Geoff is eager that Christ be glorified, and especially through good theology. This account of his life as a minister of Christ's gospel serves to do this. It has been a joy and a privilege to have read this book and it comes with a warm recommendation."

—Gareth Williams, minister, Bala Evangelical Church,
and lecturer at Union Seminary

"Geoff Thomas—one of Wales's best-known preachers during the twentieth and early twenty-first centuries. He pastored a church in Aberystwyth for fifty years, influenced many of us, preached in congregations and conferences around the world, and has written helpful books and many articles. Godly, wise, interesting, funny, and good company! And now his life story is in print. It is everything I was expecting and more. The story is fascinating, and the way it is written, a real page-turner. This deserves a wide audience. Geoff is one of the true servants of the Lord Jesus."

—Alun Ebenezer, headmaster of
Fulham Boys School, London

"Geoff is like Boris. He doesn't need a surname. If a fellow pastor tells me that Geoff is preaching or that he has had a letter from Geoff, I don't need to ask which Geoff. For countless Reformed Christians and especially pastors, there's only one Geoff. He has mentored us, encouraged us, inspired us, and befriended us. He has taught us to preach by preaching to our minds and hearts. He has counseled us through tangles we've gotten ourselves into. He has driven hundreds of miles to speak at our little meetings. We owe him more than I can say. And here it is at last—Geoff Thomas's autobiography. All you ever wanted to know about Geoff's forebears, his upbringing, his conversion and call to the ministry, his heroes, his teachers, his love for the US, that extraordinary half century of ministry in Aberystwyth, and so much more beside. Geoff's memoirs are fascinating, moving, self-deprecating, Christ-honoring, and at times gloriously indiscreet. Thank you, Geoff."

—Stephen Rees, minister at Grace Baptist Church, Stockport

"A year or so after Dr. Martyn Lloyd-Jones had delivered his Westminster seminary lectures 'Preachers and Preaching,' I asked him for his opinion of Westminster. He paid high tribute to the quality of its scholarship and teaching and to the way in which its professors had upheld the Reformed faith in the face of considerable opposition. But his concern was that 'they are not producing preachers.' I interjected, 'But what about Geoff Thomas?' He replied, 'Yes, he is a preacher, but he comes from a different tradition.' In this fine autobiography we can see the outworking of that tradition and ways in which it has been enriched from other tributaries to produce a Reformed pastor and teacher whose appeal has extended far beyond his native Wales. Geoff was converted in Welsh evangelicalism as a teenager at a time when nonconformity as a whole was suffering from the debilitating effects of liberal theology. More recently, however, a number of congregations were being blessed by the emergence of a generation of younger preachers who, encouraged by the ministry of Dr. Lloyd-Jones, had discovered something of the biblical strength of an older dissent. The university Christian unions were being strengthened at the same time. Geoff's own thinking was undoubtedly sharpened by his years at Westminster Seminary after his graduation from Cardiff. At Westminster he was profoundly influenced by the Scottish Highland theology and piety of Professor John Murray. But he came back to Wales, still a Baptist, and was called to his only pastorate at Aberystwyth in the heart of the principality. There he served, supported by his beloved Iola and their three daughters. Calls to preach came from far and wide, and he was at home among conservative Presbyterians as well as among Reformed Baptists, ever ready to minister to small groups as well as to large congregations. How we thank God for the help and encouragement that he has given to us. Now in retirement from his pastorate and living in London with Barbara, his second wife, he continues to serve the wider cause with God-given energy."

—Robert W. Oliver, pastor emeritus at the Baptist church,
Bradford on Avon, and church history lecturer
at the London Seminary

IN THE SHADOW
OF THE ROCK

IN THE SHADOW OF THE ROCK

An Autobiography

Geoffrey Thomas

Reformation Heritage Books
Grand Rapids, Michigan

In the Shadow of the Rock

Reformation Heritage Books
3070 29th St. SE
Grand Rapids, MI 49512
616-977-0889
orders@heritagebooks.org
www.heritagebooks.org

Printed in the United States of America
22 23 24 25 26 27/10 9 8 7 6 5 4 3 2 1

Library of Congress Cataloging-in-Publication Data

Names: Thomas, Geoff, 1938- author.
Title: In the shadow of the rock : an autobiography / Geoffrey Thomas.
Description: Grand Rapids, Michigan : Reformation Heritage Books, 2022.
Identifiers: LCCN 2021049491 (print) | LCCN 2021049492 (ebook) | ISBN 9781601788672 (hardcover) | ISBN 9781601788689 (epub)
Subjects: LCSH: Thomas, Geoff, 1938- | Baptists—Wales—Clergy—Biography.
Classification: LCC BX6495.T419 A3 2022 (print) | LCC BX6495.T419 (ebook) | DDC 286/.1092 [B]—dc23/eng/20211130
LC record available at https://lccn.loc.gov/2021049491
LC ebook record available at https://lccn.loc.gov/2021049492

For additional Reformed literature, request a free book list from Reformation Heritage Books at the above regular or email address.

In thanksgiving to God,
and in the sweetest memory of
my first wife, my dearest Iola,
and as a joyful dedication to
my lovely present wife, my Barbara.

“The Shepherd leads the flock in the shadow of the Rock.”
—*Frances Ridley Havergal*

Contents

Preface

Why did Augustine of Hippo in Roman North Africa write his autobiographical work, *Confessions*? What was the reason John Bunyan, while serving a twelve-year prison sentence in jail in Bedford, England, penned his autobiography, *Grace Abounding to the Chief of Sinners*? Why did George Whitefield choose, at age twenty-six, to publish his *Journals*, other than "for the Benefit of the Orphan-house in Georgia."[1] For what purpose did John Wesley publish his vast *Journal*? Why did C. H. Spurgeon tell his own life story? What provoked Elisabeth Elliot to publish the diary of her first husband, Jim Elliot? And why did Dr. Martyn Lloyd-Jones cooperate fully with Iain H. Murray in the writing of two volumes of his life?

Surely none of them did it for 100 percent completely spiritual reasons; we are too corrupted by sin to hit that target in anything. But they believed that their personal dealings with God and the impact of their lives on the people around them could be helpful for readers. How right they were.

Certainly none of them made that choice for purely carnal and self-promoting reasons, but as in everything they did—and that we do—there's a mixture of the flesh *and* the Spirit. "Vanity of vanities…all is vanity" (Eccl. 12:8). Even the holiest things we have done have some pollution of sin.

---

1. *George Whitefield's Journals* (Edinburgh: Banner of Truth, 1960), 33.

It was Spurgeon who made the best defense of the reason for writing about himself: "Whether this arises from egotism or not, each reader shall decide according to the sweetness or acidity of his own disposition. A father is excused when he tells his sons his own life-story, and finds it the readiest way to enforce his maxims; the old soldier is forgiven when he 'shoulders his crutch, and shows how fields were won.' I beg that the license which tolerates these may, on this occasion, be extended to me."[2]

I wrote these chapters as an extension of my ministry and my vocation to proclaim the truth of the gospel of Jesus Christ and that I might further the end of the calling I believe I had received from God to explain the message of Christianity and to make known the whole counsel of God. And in this, as in all else, there is some success and some failure. These are bigger illustrations and smaller statements of important truths that I have believed all my Christian life.

2. C. H. Spurgeon, *Lectures to My Students* (London: Passmore and Alabaster, 1875), v–vi.

CHAPTER 1

Dad

I wanted that word *Dad* to be the very first because increasingly over the years I have felt that I never honored Dad as I should have. Harry Eastaway Thomas was the finest and most loving father to me, his only child. He took his first breath at a most significant time for Christians in Wales. Dad and his twin brother, Bryn, were born in Dowlais in South Wales on Sunday, October 30, 1904.

Harry and Bryn Thomas, before Christmas 1904

The Significance of the Year 1904 for Wales

Dad once told me that someone had revealed to him that was the day the 1904 Welsh revival started. When Dr. J. Gresham Machen came to Wales to speak for R. B. Jones in Tabernacle Baptist Church in Porth in the Rhondda Valley in 1927, Machen was struck by the conversation of the preachers he met there. He noted that they saw the past as bifurcated by the 1904 revival—what the condition was before that event and then after. So it was with this person, whoever he was, who upon hearing the birthdate of my father, immediately linked it to the revival that exploded to worldwide attention during that year. It was an international hope in the churches that a revival in the "Land of Revivals" would be a harbinger of a new global work of God.

The Welsh Revival

No single spiritual starting pistol can be fired to begin a true awakening. However, a series of gatherings and the activities of certain personalities throughout a period of growing spiritual intensity can signify an unusual work of God. Meetings that impact the listening world and begin to draw genuine fascination are held in the cities and in the countryside. The year my father was born, in the dawn of the twentieth century, was a time of worldwide anticipation that the future was to be a mightily productive period of growth and influence for each nation and for their churches. Such confidence was certainly true in Wales, where church membership grew until the year 1907 (though after that time, in every subsequent year until today, the numbers of those attending church were to continually decrease).

But another vital religious movement was pouring into Wales and affecting all of Europe in the early years of the century. Its fulcrum was Germany, and it displayed a very different rationalist approach to Christianity, a cerebral movement that would capture every major seminary in Wales without exception. It influenced every denomination in the principality, its denominational papers, its city-center prestigious congregations, and most of its countryside pulpits. The movement demeaned theological truths of the confessions of faith and shrank Christianity to a message of the universal fatherhood of God and the brotherhood of man with Jesus Christ set forth as merely the special exemplary man. What "hair shirts" three of my uncles—who all became ministers—were to wear from taking on board those teachings, declension, and indifference.

The excesses of the 1904 revival in Wales as well as its enthusiasms assisted this new religious ideology that was to take heavenly life out of the religion in Wales, leaving churches that were an ever-shrinking moralistic rump. The humanistic voice was saying that Wales was (as was every nation in the world) being presented with just two stark choices for the future. There was the theology and methodology of Charles Grandison Finney and his manufactured religious excitements: "Get up from your pew now and confess your sins before us all and be filled with the Spirit!" Or there was the bleak alternative that the majority chose of submitting to the cerebral moralistic teaching, in the name of "education," of the new and increasingly popular rationalistic religion, a powerful movement that called itself Christianity. Of course, a third way—unrecognized by the media or by cultural and religious establishments but vitally important—was the unostentatious holy alternative still manifest in hundreds of village bethels and city congregations where the great hymns are sung, fervent prayer is made, holy lives are lived, and men called by God are preaching the whole counsel of God, doing what our Lord did in Galilee when He sat to preach in a synagogue: He opened the Book and found the place and spoke in the power of the Spirit.

From such gatherings, blessed by awakening ministries of the Word of God, many true converts were begat from above. And in the years before and after 1904, many of the King's champions were preaching not in word only but by power and the Holy Spirit and with much assurance. I am referring to those hundreds of pulpits where the historical biblical Christianity of the 1823 Confession of the Calvinistic Methodists or the faith once given by the apostles and summarized in the 1689 Confession of the Baptists or so beautifully set forth in the Thirty-Nine Articles of the Church of England was being believed and proclaimed. Where these truths were being preached, the seed of that Word created fruit, and those "children of the revival" (the many truly converted in 1904 and 1905) were choice Christians whom it was a privilege to meet. They kept experiential religion alive in the chapels for the next decades. The men taught the young people, prayed in the prayer meetings, gave sacrificially to support the cause, became the deacons and elders in their churches, rejoiced whenever they heard messages that exalted Jesus Christ, and urged men and women and children to repent and believe on Him.

An example of this ministry happened on the day of my father's birth, Sunday, October 30, 1904, in a west Wales village called Newcastle Emlyn, Carmarthenshire, in Bethel Calvinistic Methodist Church. A sermon was preached by seventy-five-year-old Evan Phillips, who had been the minister for forty-four years in that church, the only congregation he was ever to pastor. In Newcastle Emlyn, a preparatory school was also connected with that church, which had been set up by the Calvinist Methodist denomination so that young men who left the pits, farms, shops, steel mills, and tinplate works to prepare for the ministry could improve their education (most of them having left school at thirteen years of age). This would provide twelve months' adjustment to the later years of lectures at the Trefeca Theological College or the Calvinistic Methodist Theological College in Aberystwyth. One of the men just beginning his training at this school was twenty-six-year-old Evan Roberts, who six months earlier had been working as a colliery blacksmith.

Evan Phillips, the old preacher there in Newcastle Emlyn, had a son who became a prominent ophthalmologist in London and an elder in the Charing Cross Welsh Calvinistic Methodist Church. He led the adult Sunday school class where the lively theological discussions stimulated the understanding of the gospel in a medical student named Martyn Lloyd-Jones. Dr. Phillips had two sons, who were close friends with Martyn, and one beautiful daughter, Bethan. The family claims Bethan received twenty-seven proposals of marriage—the first and the twenty-seventh both from Martyn Lloyd-Jones! They were married in 1927.

Evan Phillips was alleged to be one of the great preachers of the Victorian period; his entire ministry was through the Welsh language. He lived through two conspicuous Welsh awakenings, one in 1859 and then the 1904 revival. His sermons were said to be "fresh and sparkling" by some who heard him often. He did not preach long sermons, and on the Sunday that Dad was born, Phillips was preaching in Bethel. His text was John 12:23, "The hour has come that the Son of Man should be glorified," to a congregation that heard him with gripping attention.

It was an awakening ministry and, thus, not unique. In nearby New Quay, powerful preaching from a minister named Joseph Jenkins resulted in Christians going out from that beautiful seaside village to evangelize in the surrounding churches. In September 1904, meetings took place close by in Blaenannerch, with the notable evangelist Seth Joshua preaching mightily each evening while prayer meetings took place in the mornings. Farms and villages were visited in the afternoons by students from the school in Newcastle Emlyn and church members. The students had abandoned classes to attend all these meetings, and Evan Roberts was so stirred by the events surrounding the ministry of Seth Joshua that he got permission for the following week to leave school and return to his church at Loughor, a village halfway between Swansea and Llanelli, to report there to his family, friends, and congregation of the exciting and encouraging events in Blaenannerch, New Quay, Newcastle Emlyn, and west Wales. Those meetings in Loughor were the catalyst of what was to become identified as the 1904 Revival. Wales was soon to be made aware of the fact that there was a religious stirring taking place within the principality, and the press began to send reporters to cover the meetings led by the young Evan Roberts. A daily column in the *Western Mail* soon appeared reporting on the previous evening's events.

Bethania, Dowlais

My father's parents had met one another in my grandfather's home community of Pontarddulais, a village between Swansea and Llanelli. The Thomas family was a prominent clan in that community. My grandfather, Philip Henry Thomas, was a cousin of the poet Edward Thomas, whose first poems were brought out under the family name, Edward Eastaway. So Dad was named Harry Eastaway Thomas. *Harry* was also the name of Harry Evans, the musician and beloved organist in Bethania, Dowlais. As a boy I was embarrassed at his middle name, "Eastaway," and even the name Harry seemed so old-fashioned in the 1940s. Giving an unusual middle name to all the Joneses and Thomases and Williamses and Evanses that filled

Wales was unexceptional. When I was in junior school one morning, our teacher had to record the full names of all our fathers, and we were instructed to call them out to him one by one. Gales of laughter were heard at the revealing of the outrageous middle names most of them bore. I dreaded my turn, but there was no escape, and red-faced, I was greeted with another explosion of mirth as I called out "Harry Eastaway Thomas!" Why couldn't he have had a nice Welsh middle name?

Dad's mother came from Beulah in Breconshire. She was raised in the Welsh-speaking home of a God-fearing man, some of whose notebooks I possess. He sent his daughter to Pontarddulais to a cottage industry where a man taught half a dozen young women to become milliners—that is, hat makers. The daughter and this man married and moved to the steel town of Dowlais and opened a milliners in a shop called Bradford House with Grandpa Thomas working behind the counter as manager. She rather intimidated me.

Philip Henry Thomas, Geoff's grandfather, his wife, and children.

They attended Bethania, a Welsh Congregationalist chapel, the largest church building in the town. With a thousand people in the beautiful auditorium on many Sundays, it was one of the largest Congregational churches in the world, certainly in Europe, with six hundred of the congregation being actual church members. It had been four years since the church had had a minister, with many people waiting for one to be appointed before they joined. So, with the call to its pulpit in the summer of 1904 of the eloquent and academically qualified Peter Price, over a hundred men and women joined the church—which Price referred to as a "revival." Soon in that congregation the two conflicting religious movements emerging in Wales clashed, and both were severely injured by the collision.

As a boy attending that church, I would listen to the old men speaking of the early days of the twentieth century and the personalities in Bethania's congregation. I remember one man being described as coming straight from the steel furnaces to the midweek prayer meeting still dressed in his leather apron, and there he would stand and pray publicly with heavenly unction. So in the summer of 1904, the congregation at Bethania had its new minister, and soon the little Thomas twins, Bryn and Harry, were taken at the end of the year to be baptized by him.

Peter Price

On January 23, 1905, Evan Roberts himself held a meeting in Bethania, and my grandfather had to come to some conclusion about him and what took place. An air of excited anticipation was present in the chapel; Bethania was full long before the appointed time, with an estimated two thousand people present and overflowing into a packed adjacent Sunday school room. The services of Roberts were not like those mighty meetings of Seth Joshua in Blaenannerch, when a verse from Scripture would be opened up and explained and applied to the congregation, and people urged to repent and trust in Jesus Christ, having heard of His divine nature and saving work. There was by choice no one evidently in charge of these 1904 meetings of Evan Roberts. Various people stood in turn and faced the congregation and exhorted them. A man in the gallery might rise to his feet and exhort his fellow steelworkers to come out on the right side. "Many have come to Him in Dowlais," someone else announced to a response of shouts of praise. Hymn after hymn was sung. Prayers, experiences, testimonies, appeals, exhortations, solos, duets, or recitations of a verse or a hymn followed in rapid succession from all over the congregation. Men, women, children, and ministers would be on their feet speaking or singing. A group of women always accompanied Roberts to his meetings, and one by one they would exhort people around them to take their stand for Christ, or they would lead the congregation by choosing and singing a hymn or a solo. Roberts said a few words from the pulpit, but then he walked up and down the aisles and spoke personal words of encouragement to various people. He urged and invited people who had accepted Christ to stand up and confess Him there and then. Each one who did so was greeted with cries of "Thanks be to God!" The meeting was held in both Welsh and English.

My grandfather had to judge whether what he was seeing was a remarkable work of the Spirit of God or human manipulation or a mixture of both. His minister, Peter Price, barely six months in Bethania, observed it all, taking it all in, and he was someone who came to his own agitated conclusion, though he lacked the theological and spiritual judgment to do so. He decided to let everyone in Wales know his opinion of the revival, expressing his disquiet in a lengthy letter to the chief Welsh daily paper, the *Western Mail.* It proved to be a long and devastating attack on Evan Roberts and his kind of meetings:

> Before Evan Roberts visited Dowlais, we had the holy fire burning brightly—at white heat; and at my own church alone we could count our converts during the last five or six months by the hundreds. But what happened when Evan Roberts visited the place? People came from all parts anxious to see the man, to understand something of the movement, and to get some of the fire to take home with them. I suppose that most of them did see the man; but I doubt whether they understood the

> movement—even the mock movement. They had no chance to understand the true movement, nor had they a chance of catching any of the true fire, for it wasn't there. I will say that with much effort Evan Roberts, together with his co-operators (and, evidently, they understand one another thoroughly, and each knew his or her part well and where to come in), managed, by means of threats, complaints and incantations. They reminded me of the prophets of Baal, to create some of the false fire. But never in my life did I experience such agony—the whole procedure being utterly sacrilegious. I should say that Evan Roberts must have seen and felt that he was a failure at Dowlais; but to cover the circumstance of failure, there appeared in the paper, after he had proved himself so, a prophecy concerning certain misgivings of his as to whether he ought to have undertaken a mission to Dowlais....
>
> Evan Roberts had no controlling or constructive influence over the real Revival,... but was out of touch with it.... This [real] Revival...was the result of spiritual forces that had been quietly at work for years.... Evan Roberts was...the embodiment of the...rubbish...the waves of hysteria...and psychic manifestations...which were looked upon as necessary adjuncts to a successful meeting,... and became at last, in the estimation of the press and the public, *the* characteristic marks of the Revival.[1]

There was certainly some truth in his extreme response, particularly his unhappiness with the absence of preaching from the Scriptures during the Evan Roberts's meetings. Peter Price finally signed the letter thus: "Peter Price (BA Hons), Mental and Moral Sciences Tripos, Cambridge (late of Queens College, Cambridge)."[2]

The next five years in Bethania, as in many other congregations in Wales, were ones of friction and division as the rise of the social gospel and the methods advocated by Finney came into conflict. There was no unity of the Spirit, no bonds of peace. Those

1. *Western Mail,* January 31, 1905.
2. *Western Mail,* January 31, 1905.

who "entered into the blessing" (as was the popular phrase used), exhorted their fellow church attenders to believe and be saved. They were met with resentment and opposition, and many throughout Wales left to form new evangelical churches or moved to join such congregations. It was the time of the birth of the Apostolic Church, whose headquarters were at Pen-y-groes in Carmarthenshire. This was the first Pentecostal denomination.

At Price's farewell meeting in Bethania, Dowlais, on October 15, 1910, only two of the twelve deacons made an appearance. A local preacher was asked to preach the next Sunday evening, but just as he was to announce his text, a woman stood up and asked the entire large congregation whether the deacons were going to be allowed to remain sitting in the "big seat." The service stumbled on, with a suddenly arranged, lengthy, acrimonious members' meeting following. People even came in from the streets to eavesdrop and watch the bitter arguments. A final vote decided that all the deacons could be permitted to sit in the big seat. Where now were all the claims from all sides that the Spirit was present reviving their particular convictions and labors in Bethania?

When Peter Price left Bethania, he moved back to North Wales where he pastored a church but spent much of his energy organizing various educational courses and speaking at political meetings. This was the fruit of the social gospel. Price was a pacifist, and he published a couple of booklets on this theme in the Welsh language.

F. B. Meyer

F. B. Meyer, the Baptist preacher and writer, considered himself to be a leader of evangelical Christianity in England and Wales. In early 1905 he was invited to preach in Bethania, Dowlais. He caught a train there to the Dowlais Top station and wandered slowly through the main street of the little community. My grandfather was in the milliner's shop and saw through the window that F. B. Meyer was looking at the products on display. It was over an hour before the service was due to start, so Grandpa went out, introduced himself, and invited the preacher in to make himself comfortable. F. B.

Meyer entered and sat in the front room, and after a few minutes, baby Harry, in a hidden crib, made a cry. "Oh, you have a baby!" the preacher observed. Three minutes or so later, Uncle Bryn cried from another hidden crib. "Ooh, you have two!" said F. B. Meyer.

When he had returned to his home, he sent to my grandparents a sepia photograph of himself. Dr. Martyn Lloyd-Jones was no admirer of Meyer, who, in his judgment, considered himself to have tastes superior to others whom he looked down on. For example, he considered that Lloyd-Jones's congregation in Charing Cross did not sing at a meeting in which he was the invited preacher but rather "shouted" the hymns, and he told them so: "I said 'sing,' not 'shout.'" Can you imagine an Englishmen telling a congregation of Welshmen that they were shouting? When I told Dr. Lloyd-Jones that Meyer had sent a photo of himself to my grandparents, Lloyd-Jones shook his head. "Typical!" he commented.

So Meyer came to evaluate firsthand the Welsh revival. He listened to the reports, he preached that evening, and finally he put his seal of approval on Evan Roberts and his meetings.

A Sad Children's Talk

My father passed the scholarship at eleven years of age and went to Cyfarthfa Grammar School, though he never spoke about it. He had to leave at fourteen or fifteen years of age. He had no delight in his education there. He was deaf in one ear, which came about through an art lesson in junior high school. He had been drawing something that was misunderstood by the teacher, who promptly hit him savagely on his ear; it resulted in deafness in that ear for the rest of his life. There was no money to pay for his further education, so he joined the Great Western Railway as a clerk where he remained for the next forty-five years. How the mines, buses, railways, and town halls' civil service profited from these thousands of intelligent, moral, reliable nonconformists. What a workforce they supplied! Dad told me that he would love to have been in a more challenging profession, such as becoming a pharmacist, and he certainly had the ability to do so.

Harry Eastaway Thomas, Geoff's father, in his office.

In his twenties Dad became a deacon in Bethania and was the church treasurer for years. I was the only child in the church for Lord's Day evening services, and I would stand near Dad in the big seat as the deacons talked, opened the envelopes, and entered the amount the members gave in a large ledger. The usual amount per person was two shillings (ten pence), though the better off would give half a crown (twelve-and-a-half pence).

Dad was a most moral man. I never heard him utter a swear word. People of his generation could not even say the word *homosexual*—or even knew what it meant.

Dad understood the religion he heard for years from the Bethania pulpit, and he put it into practice. What that religion of his was became neatly illustrated by a rather pathetic and embarrassing providence for me. I would go with my mother to High Street Baptist Church in Merthyr, where she had attended all her life, and her parents before her. It was English speaking, as neither Mam nor I spoke a word of Welsh. The new minister, G. H. Williams, like most ministers was expected to give a ten-minute children's address every Sunday morning. We children sat in the front two pews, the boys on one side and the girls on the other. Then Pastor Williams had an idea that he would ask some of the children to give the children's talk, and the first one he asked was me—there really was no other child capable of this task, as I was the only one who returned to church on Sunday evenings. I was fearful of standing in the pulpit and speaking to the whole congregation, but my father told me it would be all right and that he would write a story for me to give. He had, I suppose, heard it in a Sunday sermon in Bethania and approved of it as being the heart of the Christian message. So, this is what I read:

> A farmer needed a new laborer to work on his farm. He interviewed three men. He asked each one what they could do. The first man told him that he could cut hedges, and plough, and thatch. The second man told him that he with his dog could be a good shepherd to the sheep, and he could milk the cows and make butter. When he asked the third man what he could do, the man simply said, "I sleep well on windy nights." He was the man who got the job, because he worked hard at whatever he was asked to do and was weary with the toil at the end of the day. The moral of this story is, "If a job is worth doing, it is worth doing well."

Then I hurried out of the pulpit before the smiling faces of the congregation to return to sit with the other boys in the front pew. No other child was ever asked to address the children—nor should they have been.

That story illustrates the kind of religion that now gripped too many of the pulpits of Wales. It was no longer the plight of man in his sin, to be redeemed by the life and sacrifice of the Son of God, to be applied to us sinners by the life-giving and indwelling Holy Spirit in a new birth, and then living a new life each day that showed itself in good works and love for one's neighbor. The new Christian message was that we showed we were Christians by our good lives, and when we get to heaven, God will let us in because we had behaved decently. Who needs church and preaching and the Bible if doing things well is the key to eternal life? Who needs the righteous life of the incarnate Lord of glory and the atoning death of the Lamb of God if we look at life as a series of jobs to be done as sons and husbands and fathers and workmen, doing what we must do well and sleeping with a good conscience every night, whether we know Christ or not? I cringe with embarrassment today as I think of reading that story to a Baptist congregation.

Fond Memories

Of course, Dad was enormously competent in all he did. He had beautiful handwriting. He always had a spotlessly clean handkerchief in his top pocket. He ate his food like a gentleman, cutting his bread into smaller pieces and putting the butter on it. I never saw anyone else doing it his way, and yet he never taught me even how to hold my knife. I held it like a pen, and think I still do. (The headmaster once, as he wandered around the school dining room, told me off for cutting my meat and vegetables like that.) Dad was able to make anything out of wood—a piano stool, a chicken shed, a cricket bat and wickets.

My father had a pleasant baritone voice and sang in a choir. He also could play the piano. Any hymn tune you set on the piano rack, he could immediately sight-read and play. When I complimented him, he said, "You should have seen my mother. She could play from a tonic sol-fa copy and then immediately transpose the tune higher or lower." He also played the violin. I heard him once as part of a local orchestra in Ystrad Mynach playing a piece by Mozart, his glasses perched on the end of his nose.

Dad was a good gardener, specializing in kidney beans and dahlias. He also kept chickens until one night he forgot to close the hencoop door and a fox got them.

Then too, my father was a good sport. One evening just before Guy Fawkes Night, the national evening of bonfires and fireworks, we had three fireworks, and Dad decided to light them. He put one on the wall outside the kitchen window and lit the blue touch paper, and we watched it through the window. But a gust of wind blew it off the wall, and it failed to light. So Dad decided we would not waste another firework like that. He put it in the grate of a large fireplace, where there was no fire burning at that time, and lit it. He switched off the electric light, and we watched in the darkness as the brief burst of sparkling began, followed by an enormous explosion in the confined space of the kitchen, enough to make one's ears ring. When the light was switched on, we could not see one another for a moment across the kitchen as a thick cloud of soot hung in the air. Then, as silent as a fall of snowflakes, it landed on every surface. A quarter inch of soot was deposited on the floor, table, chairs, shelves, oven, sink, lampshade, towels, bread bin, saucepans, and even the dog's bed. We looked silently at one another. It was time for me to take my book to bed and leave my patient parents to clean it up, later adding it to the stories of family mishaps.

Another similar mini disaster was connected to soot six years later. One half-day off work Dad borrowed a set of chimney-sweep brushes from a fellow workman and determined to sweep the living room chimney. He sent the brush up on the first stick, a brush the size and shape of a cycle wheel. He screwed tightly to that rod another rod, and then another, and after ten had gone up sent my mother out to check if the brush could be seen. She came back saying that the brush was about a couple of feet above the chimney top, and so he pulled the brush down, rod by rod. But when he came to the first rod, to his intense dismay no brush was attached to it. He looked into the darkness and reached up, but nothing was there. What could he do?

He envisaged knocking a hole in the chimney breast and finding the brush that way. A handyman friend, Mr. Knock, lived a hundred yards away, and Dad walked over to explain his dilemma. Mr. Knock listened sympathetically and suggested that Dad attach a walking stick to a rod and send that up the chimney to hook over the brush and pull it down. My father did this carefully, tying the stick very securely to the rod, sending up ten rods, and then out went Mam to see if the walking stick had reached the top.

My mother returned to say that it was sticking out above the top of the chimney by eighteen inches. But then when he sought to bring it down, the handle hooked over the edge of the chimney pot and became detached from the rods. Dad, now very disconsolate, unscrewed the ten rods safely enough, but now he was lacking a walking stick as well as a brush. Then the doorbell rang, and at the door was the man who had come to install a TV aerial and attach it to the chimney. (This all happened in June 1955 when I had passed my nine subjects for my general School Certificate of Education. My parents would not let a TV enter the house until I had passed that exam.) So, the engineer put up his ladder and roof ladder, climbed up, and stood at the chimney and looked down, but there was no sight of the brush, though he did toss down the walking stick. Dad was almost in tears. What was there to do now but knock a hole in the chimney breast?

He tried again, cutting a branch off a holly bush from the garden and tying it very securely to the first rod, and then gingerly and with little to lose, pushing the rodded bush firmly up the chimney. My mother went out to inform him that she could see the bush poking out of the chimney top. He pulled them down rod by rod until the holly bush appeared—but no brush.

In desperation he stretched his arm up into the gloom, and his fingers touched a bristle. He pinched it between his fingers, pulled, and there was movement. With a flurry of soot, down came the brush! What relief! The next day he was able to restore the complete set of rods and the brush back to the porter from whom he had borrowed them. It was his first and last attempt to be a chimney sweep.

Dad had much ability and initiative and was so kind toward me, but sadly, he had little concept of God's grace and of Christ's accomplished and applied redemption because he had never been taught these things in the churches he attended.

My Uncle Bryn

Dad's twin brother, Bryn, became a shop assistant but wanted to become a minister and so applied to the Congregational College in Brecon. They interviewed him but concluded that he was not physically robust enough, that his heart was too weak for this profession, and they turned him down, much to his disappointment. But speaking to a friend, he learned that recently a young man had begun his ministry at Bethlehem Forward Movement Church (Sandfields) in Port Talbot. His name was Dr. Martyn Lloyd-Jones, and he had been a heart specialist in London. The friend asked him, "Why don't you write to him and tell him of your dilemma and ask him if he will examine your heart?" Uncle Bryn did this, an appointment was made, and in Sandfields the Doctor examined the patient. Lloyd-Jones concluded that his heart was perfectly sound, and Bryn went with the news to the college, where he was accepted to take the theological course. I once told Dr. Lloyd-Jones of this incident. He had no memory of it at all, as so many people went to see him for similar reasons. Then he paused and asked me, "Well, how did he do?" "He is still alive today," I told him. "Oh, very good," said the Doctor, clapping his hands with delight at a successful diagnosis.

But the theology Bryn Thomas was taught in Brecon was far from New Testament Christianity. He did not preach on the writings of the apostle Paul for years and then a text or two, infrequently and selectively. He had been taught that the simple Galilean gospel of Jesus had been scholastically misinterpreted by Paul. Dad's sister Olive married a man from Bethania named Stanley, who also went to Brecon Congregational Memorial College, along with his brother, Elvert, and they became Congregationalist preachers with those same bereft ideas. Those boys were being confronted with a Hobson's choice—that is, both alternatives facing them being bad. They were asked to choose between the obscurantist man-manipulation of the methodology of Charles Grandison Finney or the dry, cerebral religion of Friedrich Schleiermacher.

Those were not the only alternatives, however. There were hundreds of people, especially among the Presbyterians and Baptists, for whom the climactic aspect of worship at their meeting places, after they had sung their praises and prayed to the living God, was that the Lord spoke to them in the opening up of a passage of Scripture that the preacher announced to them. The preacher often felt guided to that passage by God and had studied it and prayed diligently over his text during the previous week.

Since the Reformation this is how churches in the historical Christian tradition in the United Kingdom responded to God's grace, and in such churches and under such ministries in the opening years of the twentieth century, many ministers knew great unction from God in their sermons to growing and attentive congregations. There was a burst of growth that continued for a couple of years, but then the general trend was decline.

The Aberfan Disaster

My uncle, Stanley Lloyd, was the local minister in Aberfan at the occasion of that infamous and fearful disaster when a coal tip of millions of tons of rocks and slurry hurtled down a mountain and hit an elementary school one morning on October 21, 1966, killing 144 people, including 116 children and five teachers from the school. The school was fifty yards away from Stanley's manse, while his chapel was one hundred yards away, and so the bodies were finally discovered, removed, carried to the chapel, and laid out on each pew and covered with a blanket. A policewoman then admitted parents one by one into the chapel, and they uncovered the faces of the children until their child was identified. What horrors. The chapel was never used again and subsequently was demolished. Tens of thousands of pounds were sent to Uncle Stanley from Congregational churches in England and North America, and he and my father worked out a method of payment, a scale of financial conferment to a parent or grandparent or sibling of any of the children killed at the school, depending on the closeness of the relationship. People lined up at the Aberfan manse to explain their relationship to the deceased and to receive this bestowment. My mother made cups of tea and Welsh cakes for them.

Uncle Stanley led the funeral service a couple of weeks later when members of the royal family attended. The following year, Dr. Lloyd-Jones was invited to preach at a memorial service in Aberfan, and his text was from Paul's letter to the Romans where the apostle declares that the sufferings of this present time are not worthy to be compared to the glory that shall be revealed in us. It was a definitive response to the disaster and greatly appreciated by the Christians there on that unforgettable occasion.

Concluding Reflections

My first two decades I lived in a number of station houses as Dad moved up the grades from becoming a railway clerk to a stationmaster in Abercanaid, Pentrebach, Nelson, and Llancaiach, and finally to stations around Barry. He went to church twice each Sunday and to the prayer meeting in the week, but I am sad to say I cannot remember him or his father or other members of the family reading the Scriptures. He did not grasp the gospel until I became his pastor for the last decade of his life. But I rarely remember him reading any book at all. He read the daily paper. He was vaguely interested in sports.

Dad wonderfully supported me throughout my life and was proud of me; he was delighted that I became a preacher. When something was suggested for him and Mam to do, he was initially and characteristically negative about it and saw only the problems, but then he accepted it, went ahead and did it, and did it well.

The annual two-weeks' holiday was an unmissable feature of every year, generally to a bed-and-breakfast establishment recommended by another railwayman or chapel-goer and frequently on the south coast, places like Bournemouth, Weymouth, New Quay in Cornwall, or Worthing, but occasionally to Jersey in the Channel Islands. With the free passes he got as a railwayman, he grew more ambitious as they began to embrace the continent. In 1950 we went to Interlaken, and a few years later to Menton. Thenceforth, often we went to the continent. By that time of my teens, I had discovered the joy of camps.

One year the family spent a week at a Butlin's Holiday Camp in Filey. We went incognito with some secrecy. It was a working-class place to visit, while we were lower-middle class. I was told not to tell my friends, and on the train journey north, we met a fellow railwayman whom we informed we were traveling to nearby Scarborough, and he told us the same. But as barriers broke down, we each admitted to the other we were actually going to Butlins. It was a grand week for me, like a week at Blackpool or Atlantic City.

We were a middle-class family bettering ourselves, careful with money. We steadily purchased a washing machine, an electric iron, a vacuum cleaner, a refrigerator, a radio, and after the School Certificate exams were navigated by me in 1955, we bought a television. We never had a phone or a car; Dad could not drive. He had little need to, for he had privilege tickets on the trains that went all over South Wales.

Every two weeks he went to spend an evening with his father, Grandpa Thomas, in Aberfan. I wish I had known about Bethania and Evan Roberts and Peter Price then, for I would have gently interrogated my grandfather. Grandpa Thomas lived a declining, sad life. I do not remember any laughter. The century started for him with a beautiful young wife and five children (two of whom died in infancy). They had a maid called Miriam. He had been in a thousand-member congregation amid a rich bilingual culture, with a love for one's neighbor ethic—the front door never needed to be locked at night—and there was a high view of Sunday's sanctity. He was to witness irrevocable decline in the culture and in the chapel with every passing decade until his death in 1957. When my father was born, there were fifty Welsh-language congregations in the Merthyr district, but by 1990 they had all closed. Not a single Welsh-language church survives among the sixty thousand residents of the borough of Merthyr today. Grandpa Thomas and his wife determined that they would not speak Welsh to their twin boys and daughter, and so I grew up in an impoverished, monolingual household, having painfully to learn the language in my teens at school. Grandpa was a victim of theological betrayal and cultural decline. Interestingly, in the last year a charismatic group has purchased the Bethania building after years of abandonment, and now one hears atonement, a supernatural gospel, and conversion and salvation through faith in Christ being spoken of in the old building.

I was one of the few boys in school whose father attended church regularly. My parents voted in the general election, but I had no idea for whom they voted. I suppose Dad as a Welshman was traditionally a supporter of the Liberal Party. He was no socialist, and for Welsh people then the Tories were the party of the establishment, the nobility, the established Church of England and the well-off, so he could not vote for them. But the Liberal Party had been decimated in the 1945 general election. Dad was once asked to stand as a Liberal candidate for the Barry and Vale of Glamorgan constituency in a general election in the late 1950s, but to my intense relief he rejected the invitation.

Dad and Mam moved to Aberystwyth to spend their final years there, and he died on Christmas Day in 1978 in the same bedroom in the house that is now mine—in fact, in the bedroom and the same bed where I often sleep. I think about him and the twenty years we lived together, with that holy mixture of thanksgiving to God for many sweet remembrances of him and for my anticipation of seeing him again in heaven. Yet I also have many regrets I was not a better son and that it has taken time to appreciate him and his gifts. There was much I unconsciously and consciously learned from him. I miss him and am sorry that I ever caused him pain. He made a massive positive contribution to who I am and what I have become today.

Starting with my dad assists me to explain how my life panned out. Dad could have had strong socioeconomic convictions. He could have been politically conscious and followed David Lloyd-George and the Liberal Party or grew excited at Clement Attlee and the Socialist victory of 1945. He could have believed in what the world refers to as "science" and "evolution" though not understanding it, and then how different my life would have been. He could have been a businessman and lived for a product, but there was nothing like that interest in Dad. At the back of his mind there was a Book and a person in that Book whom he valued, in his own way. And he sought to live by that Book, and the people who congregated around that Book were his people, and thus I, with greater focus and stronger convictions, was the same, and I had the privilege of teaching him about the grace of God.

But of course, everyone has some book they unconsciously make reference to and live by. That book they have written in their minds says that man is the measure of all things; that Jesus Christ was important but confused; that the Bible has good things to say but is also muddled and needs to be treated cautiously; that this life is all we have; that there is no heaven, above us only sky, and nothingness after we die; and that everyone has to work out their values and believe in themselves. That is probably something like the book some readers of these words have written in their minds. But the presupposition of my life since I became a Christian has been that the Bible is true and Jesus Christ is the incarnate God. Only by His life and atoning death can forgiveness and eternal life be mine. I got that from Dad but, particularly, from Mam, to whom I must now turn.

CHAPTER 2

Mam

Mam, who was named Elizabeth Francis, was born two years after Dad, on October 21, 1906. She came from farther down the industrial valley, the southern side of the town of Merthyr Tydfil, than my father's home in the northern hills in Dowlais Top. When her brother Lyn Francis was conscripted to join the army in 1938, the sergeant asked him, "And where do you come from, Francis?" "From the bottom of Merthyr, sir," Lyn swiftly replied—to great hilarity. Merthyr had a bottom.

Mam was the second of four children. Edith was the eldest, and then besides Lyn, there was the youngest brother, Bryn, who had learning difficulties. They lived in a small terrace of houses called Westbourne Place, a neat row of ten homes that still stand today, looking modern and well cared for. Bryn was kept hidden away in the back room.

Geoff's mother, Elizabeth Thomas, circa 1929

Grandpa Francis the Marxist

Mam's father, Jack Francis, worked as a ganger on the railway. He had become a card-carrying Socialist, esteeming such men as the Indian political leader Mahatma Gandhi, British Socialist leader Kier Hardie, and American singer Paul Robeson. He had little or no regard for the king and his family; the marriage of Edward VIII to Mrs. Simpson confirmed his scornful royalist apathy. He spoke persuasively to his brilliant oldest grandson, Bobi Jones, about his political views (but never about religion). However, Jack Francis's wife and four children had no interest whatsoever in socialism or any kind of politics and took the normal interest in the royal family's doings, and thus, I grew up in an apolitical environment. Grandpa Francis was also a shrewd businessman. He carefully invested his savings in houses, purchasing three and renting them out. He loaned money at interest to fellow workers. He was able to leave a house to each of the children.

Though Grandpa was Welsh-speaking, he refused to speak in Welsh. I have his Welsh bilingual New Testament. His beloved grandson Bobi became a devoted Welsh speaker and Welsh nationalist, and even when he addressed Grandpa in Jack Francis's first language, the reply would always come in English. "I did hear him once speak in Welsh," Bobi told me. "There was a cobbler in Merthyr, and he would speak exclusively in Welsh to every one of his customers, and on one occasion I walked with Grandpa to pick up a pair of his shoes that he'd had repaired there. The cobbler engaged in conversation with him in Welsh, and Grandpa replied in Welsh, but that was the only time I heard him speak in the old tongue."

So, three of my four grandparents had as their first language Welsh, but none of them spoke it to their children. What an educational loss! I felt it all my life. They were hoping that the next generation would, through our fluency in English, "go far" and become solicitors in Sutton Coldfield or estate agents in Melton Mowbray. In our early years in Aberystwyth, a candidate for Plaid Cymru, the Party of Wales, in the general election was a local man who had gone seventy miles to Swansea University and earned his

PhD there and then became a professor. He returned to the village outside Aberystwyth and was canvassing. He met two villagers sitting on a bench near its post office and introduced himself to them. They knew about him, of course—a local lad who had made good. "What are you doing now?" one of them asked him. "I am lecturing in Swansea at the university," he replied. "Ah," replied the man after a pause, "I'd have thought you'd have gone far!" Merely staying in Swansea, Wales, was a poor attainment for such a bright intellect.

Grandpa Francis during the 1940s occasionally went to church, elegant and courteous, dressed in a morning suit, to High Street Baptist Chapel on Sunday mornings with his son-in-law. I guess he had gone to that chapel ever since moving to Merthyr. His family were originally from Fishguard, Pembrokeshire in West Wales. When I lived in Merthyr and was attending High Street Chapel during the first twelve years of my life, it was Mam and I who sat together at the six o'clock evening service. The Francis family never sat together in a family pew. Perhaps Grandpa Francis had once had a family pew, but the arrival of baby Bryn and his learning difficulties was an "embarrassment." I wonder whether Bryn was ever taken to church.

The custom all over Wales was for wives to stay home on Sunday mornings and prepare dinner for their husbands and children—the costliest and most delicious meal of the week. Thus, everywhere in Wales the main church meetings with the larger congregation were on Sunday nights. I do not remember Grandpa Francis at those evening services but just see him in my mind's eye on Sunday mornings toward the back of the congregation. He was unimpressed with the 1904 revival, unlike his brother-in-law.

R. B. Jones

Jack Francis's wife, Nana Francis, was an exceptionally attractive woman, petite and affectionate. Her maiden name was Beatrice Blanche Bown. Her mother was French, but how her Welsh father met and married her I will never know.

Nana Francis was blessed to have a brother, Oliver Bown, who was a member of the Tabernacle Baptist Church in Porth in the

Rhondda Valley, near Pontypridd. His pastor was a first-rate minister, Rhys Bevan Jones, a native of Dowlais and a mighty preacher. R. B., as he was known throughout Wales, was a thoughtful and intellectual man as well as a godly pastor. He wrote one of the best older books on the 1904 revival, *Rent Heavens*, which he had observed first-hand and wherein he preached throughout 1904 and 1905, especially in North Wales to great effect as well as near his base in the industrial valleys of South Wales. In 1933 he was to have given the Bible readings at the Keswick Convention but died just before that event. Dr Lloyd-Jones admired him, once saying to me, "He was a Puritan." He was responsible for inviting Dr. J. Gresham Machen to preach in his church, where it is certain that Uncle Oliver would have heard him.

R. B. Jones was the leader of evangelical men among the Baptists and was good friends with the leading minister of the Calvinistic Methodists, Nantlais Williams of Ammanford. R. B. was a regular speaker at the annual Ammanford Easter Convention. Rheinallt Nantlais Williams, the son of Nantlais, told me that when he was a little boy, the family accompanied R. B. Jones to the Ammanford station, the convention having ended the day before, and R. B. opened his coat and took out from his large inner pocket a live rabbit. It was a present for his children. What an all-around minister he was!

R. B. established the Porth Bible Institute to train men for the ministry, which after a decade moved to Barry and Cadoxton where it soon became known as the South Wales Bible College. For decades it was highly successful in training men for the ministry. It finally moved to Bryntirion in Bridgend where it has gone through a number of titles and is known today as the Union School of Theology. I have taught a course on the Holy Spirit there.

Uncle Oliver Bown, the Evangelical

Oliver Bown loved to hear R. B. Jones preach. Oliver became a successful antiques dealer with a shop under the railway arches in Pontypridd. He also opened another shop in what became Churchill Way in Cardiff. We bought a fine mahogany grandfather clock from him. But his passion in life was to speak to people about Christ.

He used every opportunity of doing so, even carrying a text on a pole around the streets of Pontypridd. He organized weekly children's meetings and composed hymns—both the words and tunes. If the family went to the seaside in a charabanc holiday trip, somewhere like Mumbles, Swansea, he could not resist the opportunity to address the crowds on the beach. He would get out of his deck chair, clear his throat, look around, and begin, "Ladies and gentlemen, this is such a beautiful sight, the blue sky and the sea, and we know that the Lord God made this world of ours because He loves us so much. He is the one who sent His Son, Jesus Christ, to be the Savior of all who would put their trust in Him." And he would continue on, while his wife sat on her deck chair and the children continued to build their sandcastles.

Oliver's brother-in-law had a farm, Penheoleli, on the mountain overlooking Pontypridd, where the family would gather on holiday Mondays. While the women prepared a farmhouse tea, he and his brother-in-law would lead the men on a stroll up the mountain. It was not long before Oliver would stop them and speak to them as he did on the vacation beaches, and then he would call them to kneel and pray. Bobi Jones can remember one such occasion, and peeping around as the men had bowed their heads in prayer, he caught the eye of Grandpa Francis, the brother-in-law of Oliver, who wasn't praying at all but who roguishly winked at him. On one occasion, Bobi and Oliver were walking together in the countryside, and Oliver addressed the small boy. "Look at this, Bobi. See this patch of ground here—the moss, the lichen, the clover, these little flowers and grasses. God made all of this. Isn't it beautiful?" Then he prayed and gave thanks to God for His creation. Bobi said, "It was very powerful."

I once asked Dr. Lloyd-Jones if he knew Oliver Bown. There were few people in Welsh Christianity he did not know. "Oh, yes," he said, "with that deep 'Amen'—and that boxer." I was interested to know more about this pugilist and how he had become a Christian and the dynamics of the relationship with my uncle. One afternoon I spent with Uncle Oliver's daughter and some of his family in Crickhowell, and I asked them who this particular boxer was who was a companion of Oliver. I was astonished to learn it was a dog whose breed he admired, which he kept and took to church with him.

Uncle Oliver regularly preached in the open air on the steps of the fountain in Merthyr on Saturday nights. If he noticed Dad walking Mam home at the conclusion of a date, creeping by on the other side of the street, he would instantly call them over and give Dad a handful of tracts to distribute, and Mam would join in the circle of singers. Dad wanted to take Mam around the corner to her home in Westbourne Place, not spend this time in street evangelism!

Mam's Trust in Christ

On Friday nights Uncle Oliver held children's meetings that were attended for some years by Mam and her sister, Edith. They sang an opening chorus of doggerel that Oliver had written:

> Come to the gospel meeting held in the gospel hall.
> Come every Friday evening. Come, and welcome all!
> The meeting is at half past six, and it finishes at half past seven.
> Come to the gospel meeting. Learn the way to heaven.

There he spoke to them for years of the love of God in Jesus Christ. Mam would listen intently to the gospel message, and at some time at the end of the First World War, she received grace to surrender her life to Jesus Christ. She "gave her heart" to Him quite artlessly. Should she not believe what her loving uncle was telling her about Jesus Christ? Were either of them—Jesus or Oliver—deluded or crazy? That was unbelievable. So she gave her life to Christ in a simple act, and thus, at one midweek evening in High Street Baptist Church in Merthyr, she was baptized and became a church member. She was an excessively self-effacing woman. Her decision not to be baptized on a Sunday but quietly during the week demonstrated her feelings of modesty and inadequacy, that she was certainly not good enough to be baptized on a Sunday before everyone in church. She would be baptized on a Tuesday or Wednesday evening with a small group of family and church members.

Mam went with the young people taking services in the workhouse, led by her uncle. The impoverished elderly women sang the Sankey-type hymns earnestly. They were all Welsh-language speakers and pronounced these English words with a thick Welsh accent that Mam could perfectly imitate. One song written by a woman in Philadelphia was on the presence of the Savior:

"Fear not, I am with thee,"
Blessed golden ray
Like a star of glory
Lighting up my way.

Its chorus is,

He'll never, no never, no never leave us alone.
What never? No never. He never will leave us alone.

She tried the "scholarship" at eleven years of age and passed for Cyfarthfa Grammar School, the only one in her family to have that advanced education. There Mam spent three or four of the happiest years of her life—often later talking about it, describing the teachers she'd admired, the French she had learned, the Shakespeare sonnets she had memorized, the school's annual concerts, and especially, the "stunt" afternoon at the end of the year when the female staff would tease and parody the girls' behavior. Thirty years later in my boys' grammar school we never had such relaxed freedom in relationship with the staff. While they lived in Merthyr, she kept returning to the school's annual concerts, taking me with her. I loved attending, thinking I was getting a taste of my future.

Changes

Mam emerged from the trauma of a world war and the more subterranean distress of the pandemic that followed as a young disciple of Christ. Young men came back from the war as existentialists, cynics, believers that life had no high purpose, and people who proceeded to distance themselves from the intellectual and moral constraints of their parents' Christianity. In Wales it was a time of restless rootlessness, a fruitless search to replace Christianity which had been rejected by many. Women displayed, or had displayed to them, a new independence. They drove cars, flew airplanes, and smoked. Merthyr people read of this as the mores of cosmopolitan London clashed with small towns in sociocultural strife. Mam disdained all of that.

In the 1920s Mam had to leave Cyfarthfa School at fourteen or fifteen years of age. By the final year in school, she was in the top three in every subject, but there was no money to pay for her education. She began a silent decade about which she said little. She was not enjoying good health, and she felt she would not live for much longer. But Mam was to outlive everyone in her family, dying in her late eighties.

But what was Mam's early life like?

Family Life

Jack Francis, her father, ran a scheme whereby people gave a small sum of money each week, and then at the end of the year, their savings was returned to them just before Christmas. My grandfather gained a small amount of money in interest from this enterprise. So, during that decade Mam was employed by her father to knock on doors and collect these small sums of money, recording the amounts in the book she kept and in one the savers kept. This gave her the experience to have been a schoolteacher or a bank clerk.

Mam and her sister, Edith, were two attractive girls, who went to all the special Christian meetings organized and advertised in the borough of Merthyr—and there were many of them throughout the 1920s. There were generally two Baptist churches in all the small towns in South Wales, one that was more middle-class and bourgeois in its moral emphases, and another, less posh perhaps, that was evangelical and evangelistic and Bible-believing. In Merthyr, the conservative church was Park Baptist Church, and in Dowlais, it was Hebron Baptist. Aunt Edith soon married a boy from their High Street church named Sidney, who was serious and spiritually minded. His mother lived in Cefn Coed y Cymer and walked twice a week the couple of miles to the High Street Chapel, never missing a prayer meeting. Her son, Sid, and Edith moved to Cardiff, where Sid worked in a draper's shop, Hope Brothers on St. Mary Street.

The sisters' brother Bryn—the boy with learning difficulties—was becoming a burden to his parents, Jack and Beatrice. They felt they could not look after him any longer, and he was accepted to live the rest of his life in Hensol Castle, a large home for people with learning disabilities, twenty-four miles away near Llantrisant. Mam was appointed by the family to break the news to Bryn that he was going to be moving away from the home to live. It broke his heart when she told him what was going to happen. "No, no, I don't want to go. I want to stay here with you. Please! No! No!" and Mam wept with him. But the parents had hardened their hearts, and from that time, Bryn lived in Hensol Castle. Yet each week for the next thirty years, one of the family would take his or her turn to visit him on a Wednesday afternoon. Later, when I drove Mam there, this old man before me lying in that bed—my uncle Bryn—appeared to me as the spitting image of his father as I remembered him twenty years earlier. When Bryn saw Mam, his beloved sister, he shouted out with joy, "Bess! Bess! Bess!" and Mam's face lit up with delight. The other men gathered round. She was like a queen there with her courtiers. She always took magazines for him to look at (his "books") and a dish of trifle and custard with which she fed him.

The sisters went to all the special evangelical meetings in the Merthyr borough. In one of these they came across the Jeffreys brothers, George and Stephen, the founders of the Elim Pentecostal movement, and there was some attraction. But then Mam met Harry and his twin brother, Bryn Thomas, and their group from Dowlais. A number of those young men were attracted to Mam, but she found Bryn too intense. Dad longed to marry her, though she was reluctant. "I am not a well woman. I do not feel I have long to live. I would be a burden to you. I could not make you a good wife," she pleaded. He pleaded in turn, "I will take care of you and look after you. You will not be under any extra pressures at all. You will never be a burden to me." He succeeded, and they married in 1932 and went on honeymoon by train to New Quay, Cornwall. Weddings took place

The wedding of Harry and Elizabeth Thomas (1932)

on Saturday mornings; there would be a small reception and a meal, and then at two o'clock in the afternoon the honeymooners had to catch the Great Western Railway, which put detonators on the track to celebrate the departure of the newly marrieds from Merthyr station. The bangs of the Saturday wedding detonators became a feature of the day for those living in station house.

When Dad and Mam returned, they moved into 1 Pembroke Place, Penydarren, Merthyr, which they bought for £400. There I was born on October 15, 1938. Mam's parents, Jack and Beatrice Francis, soon moved to be nearer to her, purchasing a house in the next

Geoff at six months old

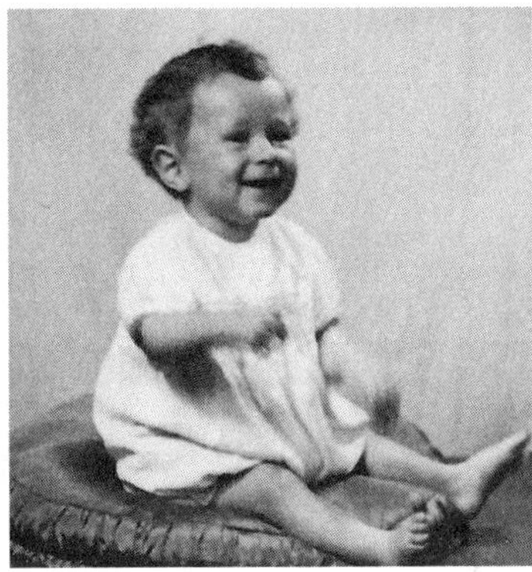

Geoff at a year old

street, 44 Brynglas Street. Mam and I were in that house in 1941 when the telegraph boy got off his bike, knocked on the door, handed the telegram over to Nana, and rode away. She returned, ashen faced, to the kitchen. It was obviously about her son Lyn, who was in the army in North Africa that was fighting General Rommel. I was sitting on my chamber pot with the book I usually read when they sat me on the potty. With trembling hands, Mam and her mother opened the telegram. It told them that Lyn Francis had pneumonia and was in hospital seriously ill. They collapsed, weeping, into one

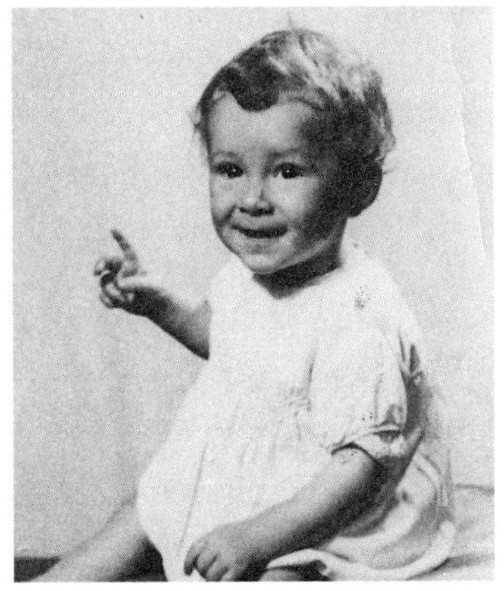

Geoff at 15 months old

Geoff at 18 months old

another's arms. I had never seen people crying, and I buried my head in the book. The next morning the whole episode was repeated. The telegraph boy got off his bike and knocked on the door. Another telegram was handed over, which was brought in and opened, as again I sat on my potty reading my book. The telegram said that Lyn Francis was much better and out of hospital. Once again, the two women fell into one another's arms and wept, and again I buried my head in my book.

Each morning Dad got the bus from Penydarren to his work as a booking clerk for the Great Western Railway at Merthyr station. He returned for lunch and then went back to the station for the afternoon. In the winter, the kitchen was the one room kept warm. Dad began the day by clearing out the ashes from the dead fire of the previous night, keeping the lumps of coal that had turned to coke on one side. He would put newspaper at the bottom of the grate and then a criss-cross of wood on top of the paper and finally coal and the pieces of coke on top of the wood. He would light the paper and put up a metal blower he had made across the fireplace so that all the draft was going underneath, through the paper and wood. He would seal the blower with a big sheet of newspaper, and we would watch that it did not catch fire. Then he washed and shaved next to my mother, who was making tea, toast, eggs, and bacon for us. Then he would attach his collar and tie with special studs, and off he would walk down the hill to the bus stop in front of one of the derelict cinemas erected all over the South Wales valleys in the financial bubble of the 1920s of Hollywood and "going to the pictures." At that bus stop, the same eight people would be standing, waiting for the 8:30 morning bus, and whenever Churchill had addressed the nation, the first question on the lips of the men and women was "Did you hear Churchill speaking last night?"

My mother and I remained in that one warm kitchen all day—as we usually did, especially in the winter months—until bedtime. We would listen to the radio on our Rediffusion set, for which we paid one shilling and eight pence a week, and which offered us two stations—the BBC Home Service or the Light Programme. Some afternoons Mam would bake a cake, and every day she would prepare dinner at one o'clock (we never called it lunch) and a light supper at six. She shopped on Saturdays in Dowlais market where the farmers brought their produce so we could go further than our ration books allowed. She often came back with a skinned and gutted rabbit, which she called "underground chicken"; I loved its taste.

Mam normally sang hymns as she did her chores. Among her favorites were "Master, Speak! Thy Servant Heareth," "How Sweet the Name of Jesus Sounds," and "Jesus Shall Reign Where'er the Sun." I was speaking to my friend Brian Dicks when we were about fifteen years of age, and he said to me, "Your mother is remarkable, isn't she?" I said cautiously, "Yes?" "The way she sings hymns all the time." I thought to myself, *His mother doesn't sing hymns!* I had thought that every mother sang hymns.

Mam sang me to sleep many nights. She sang children's hymns to me and then some of the popular songs of the day. For example, just before Christmas she would sing "Jingle Bells," but she did not know the words, and so she made them up, and the last line would be, "And off to sleep we go." Or she would sing the classic song of the '40s "(There'll Be Bluebirds Over) The White Cliffs of Dover," and again, it had her own words: "And Geoffrey will go to sleep in his own little bed again. There'll be bluebirds over the white cliffs of Dover. Tomorrow, just you wait and see."

The greatest sadness to strike my mother came in September 1936. She was pregnant with her first child, and the day of its appearance had come. The midwife called round in the morning, but there had been no movement in Mam's womb. With her stethoscope the midwife could hear a heartbeat; that was enough. Then she examined Mam, and the lively kicking baby in her womb was full of movement. "No need to ask if this one is okay," she said to Mam. But later that day the little girl arrived, alas, stillborn. How mysterious are God's ways, past finding out. Here was a God-fearing woman who loved Jesus Christ, tender, modest, and humble-spirited. She would have raised this girl to love and serve God, and yet my sister was born never to breathe her first breath. Every anniversary of that birth and death was a dark day for Mam, and especially on the girl's twenty-first anniversary. I was the poorest, poorest sympathizer to comfort her—she would put her arms around me and hug me and shed tears, but I was as stiff as a poker.

What I would have given to have had a sister! Now they are together in heaven, my sister and my mother, and I will see them one day, and each will be as holy and loving and full of every grace as Jesus Christ. And I am promised in the Scriptures that because of all Jesus Christ has done, then I shall be like that too. "Because I live," He has said, "you shall live also," and live like Him, my ego and vanities and lusts all removed, "de-sinned" forever. It often seems an unbelievable prospect to me as ego seems to have such a grip on me. Yet the triumph of Christ means that I shall see Him as He is, and I shall be finally satisfied with His likeness.

Then one day I brought Iola home to meet her, the girl who was to be my bride for fifty-two years, the mother of our three daughters. Mam adored her, the daughter she never had, and Iola cared for her through those final years of Mam's Alzheimer's. She watched her granddaughters grow and marry and become themselves mothers, and this blessed and happy family proved a precious comfort to her in her advanced years.

On Sundays, father and mother went to their different churches—Dad, to Bethania Welsh Congregationalist in Dowlais, and Mam, to High Street English Baptist. I initially went in the mornings to a nearby chapel in Penydarren called Williams Memorial Chapel. I just remember being there by myself. Surely, I was too young for that! Mam was home cooking the dinner. Then once a month in the evenings Mam and I would join Dad in Bethania. I loved singing the Welsh hymns, especially joining, with my piping treble, the men's parts with the tenors and basses. I could not understand the words, yet I was able to pronounce them accurately. Then we would walk back to Bradford House with Grandpa and Grandma Thomas through the quiet town, rarely seeing a car. We would greet people walking home from the Methodist, the Presbyterian, or the Baptist churches, and the men would raise their hats and bow to those families and be acknowledged in return: "Nos da [Good night], Mr. Thomas." We would support their big meetings, and they would support ours with no sense of competition or failure to recognize that we were all mere Christians meeting in different places—temporarily. It was sad that we did not all agree on every point so that there was just one congregation in that important town, but the dividing issues were mainly twig-and-leaf points. There were also nonnegotiable trunk-and-branch doctrines, and that was when the knives came on to the table, with the resulting chapel splits.

I adored Mam. I remember one Christmas when I was nine I went to Woolworth's in Merthyr and bought for her, for twelve pence, a big glass teddy bear full of brightly colored perfume. She was very appreciative—as she was for everything. I love the little boy that did that. How can a nine-year-old give anything that truly expresses his utter dependence and love for Mam?

CHAPTER 3

The Town Where I Grew Up

Merthyr was the fourth largest town in Wales after Cardiff, Swansea, and Newport. When I was growing up, seventy thousand people lived in the borough. The ruins of the steel mills and the coal tips surrounded it. There were grand areas in the town and fine homes where classy, smartly dressed girls lived around the Thomastown Park and the Walk. I dreamed of one day marrying a posh, pretty girl—and I did! I always longed to get married, to have my own wife and children in our own home. That was my only ambition. I never met any of those posh girls socially until, at eleven years of age, I spent a single year at the Merthyr County Grammar School. That was my solitary experience of being in a mixed class of girls and boys before beginning at university near my twentieth birthday.

I believed I gained status from living in such a significant town as Merthyr, with two grammar schools, two large parks, many churches, a fine football team, a superb Carnegie library, and a host of factories, especially Hoovers in Pentrebach where its washing machines were made. The town had a bustle, personalities, and a social conscience. I once saw a boy without shoes on a wet night, and two women had noticed, one pointing it out to the other, frowning, concerned. Real poverty existed among a few who lived near the river in an arched tenement. We boys called the rough children who lived there the "archies" and kept them at a distance. There was a determination in the town's citizens to deal with poverty and bad housing. I remember walking around the first block of prefabs that were set up on a landscaped tip. They seemed small on the outside, but inside was everything the archies could dream of. So, I was born and raised for twelve years in a place that had a strong local sense, where my family on both parents' sides were well known. This gave me a sense of rootedness but also a capacity to value landscape and facilities from the accessible richness of this community's heritage.

Penydarren

Penydarren was a square mile of terraced houses on the edge of the town surrounded by allotments and the countryside. During the war, the blackout was observed, being strictly enforced by the part-time Air Raid Precaution, short men with their steel helmets and long coats who delighted in any chance of displaying their new authority. They hammered on your door if the curtains were not drawn tight. Why should Britain fear the Nazi threat with such men to protect the country! When a German bombing raid appeared overhead, the siren would sound its warning, and after the raid was over and the skies empty, it would sound the "All Clear." Very few bombs, however, were ever dropped on Merthyr. We were twenty-four miles from the docks of Cardiff; there were no munitions factories in the borough. The few bombs dropped were those on the return journey to Germany by pilots who had missed their targets and needed those lethal incendiaries to be dumped as soon as possible. These landed on the moors. After the first diligent risings from bed and headings for a safe spot in the house, such as under the staircase, people resorted to turning over in bed, said a prayer and went back to sleep. I knew one house that did have an air-raid shelter, and we envious boys used it occasionally as a den. We sat in it and found some things to talk about like "What shall we call ourselves? The Chieftains? The Rovers? The Spitfires? The Killers?" But we never found anything actually to do in the den. It was to the parks that we were drawn for activity.

The peace of the home at 1 Pembroke Place was a little broken by the arrival of an evacuee, Victor Noble from Hastings. He was a boy my age and height, but not waiflike and skinny as I was. He was stocky, and he cleared his plate quickly at every meal. The first day I took him to school, he was my "property." He sat next to me in my class in Penydarren Infants School. I would not part from him in case he chose to be a friend of someone rather than me. That attraction for Victor disappeared more speedily than it came. I must have seen him as a rival, an interloper on our trio, Dad, Mam, and me. So I blotted him out of my life. I have no memories of him whatsoever, and after nine months, back to Hastings he went for the remainder of the war with most of the other evacuees who returned to their homes. My cousins Bobi and Keith Jones were evacuated from Cardiff; Keith came and stayed with us for a long time, but he was almost eight years older than me, and we lived different lives.

When I was five, I began two years in the Penydarren Infants School. In the first year we were all put to bed in the afternoons under brightly colored blankets. Once a month we all were taken to the clinic and stripped to the waist, and wearing black goggles, we sat in a semicircle facing a large bright light that shone on our bare chests for half an hour.

In the Infants School we sat in rows on the floor for the morning assembly, and there I saw the prettiest girl I had ever seen in my life. I smiled at her and this blonde, curly haired girl smiled back at me. Her name was Victoria Wright. I went home that afternoon and said to my mother, "Mam, I'm in love," and described my dream to her. Of course, she was tickled pink. I never spoke to the girl; in fact, I never met her, though occasionally riding my bike through Galon Uchaf where she lived, I would look around to see if I could spot her, but I never did.

At Christmas when I was six, a railway man, at Dad's request, made me a red scooter. It was my pride and joy. I would take it to the top of the hill and soar down in the middle of the road. "See bird, I fly!" There were scarcely any vehicles on the streets. But I lost my beloved scooter. There was a gang of boys whom I scarcely knew, but I longed to belong to them. The herd instinct is mighty powerful. I had my scooter, and we went along the lake path in Cyfarthfa Park. Then they decided to go into the woods, so I dropped my scooter in the grass and went into the trees with them, but fifteen minutes later when I returned, someone had taken my scooter, and I never saw it again. I still can feel that sense of loss.

That same magic Christmas I was given an Indian suit that perhaps my mother had made. It was fawn canvas with a fringe down each side and along the sleeves. I also had a feather headdress, or war bonnet. I loved this costume, too, and wanted more people to see how scary and impressive I looked. "Can I go out on the street?" I asked. "Yes, as long as you put your Beau Brummell coat on," Mam responded. I didn't like that at all. Can you imagine Hiawatha in a Beau Brummell coat? There was momentary deadlock. "Can I put the Indian suit *over* the Beau Brummell coat?" That was quite satisfactory, and it filled up my puny body. So out went Hiawatha into Pembroke Place, but then there was another problem. Christmas Day afternoon, and where was everyone on this cold, gray day? They were all around a coal fire sleeping after their Christmas dinner. No one was shocked to see Hiawatha in Penydarren because nobody did see him.

I was cocooned in the love of my parents. They sacrificed so much for me. Food was rationed in those years, but I was given the best. They put margarine on their bread, while I had butter; they put saccharine in their tea, but I had sugar; they ate liver, and I had meat—anything to the end that I would be a healthy boy. I got all the childhood ailments: sore throat, croup, rubella, mumps, measles, whooping cough, chicken pox. You name it, I always seemed to have been ill. Then I contracted pneumonia, which was a killer, and it cast a shadow over the home. I lay weak and barely conscious in my bed, and Dad and Mam sent for a specialist from Cardiff. I think I remember him putting something over my ears. He charged them a week's wages—five pounds—and was driven back to Cardiff. I think I was prescribed phenobarbitone. They prayed. I improved. And if they had protected me savagely before this time, I was hyper-protected afterward.

I adored my Dad. I remember a silly tiff I had with him one lunchtime when I was four or five. On his returning to work, he said goodbye to Mam and me, but I refused to say goodbye to him because of something I had imagined he had done. "Oh, Geoffrey," said Mam, "fancy you not saying goodbye to Dad." Immediately convicted, I flew to the door and stood on the pavement waving, and I shouted after him, "Goodbye, Dad! Goodbye, Dad! Goodbye...." But he was deaf and could not hear me and walked on down to the bus stop. I slowly re-entered the home guilty.

It was then very fashionable to have one's tonsils removed; the procedure was quite *de rigueur*. And so one day a little bus picked me up and drove a few of us silent and fearful children to Merthyr General Hospital. I waited with the others, and then my name was called out, and into the operating theater I went. I lay on the table, and someone put the chloroform pad over my mouth and told me to count to ten. I cried out in my fear, "I am counting..." but off I went into unconsciousness. I woke lying on the floor alongside a stainless-steel saucer to be sick into. The bus took me back home, and I lazed around for a day or two but was forbidden to go to the May Bank Holiday Fete and Gala in Cyfarthfa Park, which I never missed—and for a change, it was a sunny day. There was always one stunt on the stage as the climax of the afternoon. A man would dive into a flaming pool, or someone would ride smaller and smaller bicycles, while we boys would collect pop bottles and return them to the booth to be given two pennies for every bottle we returned. Riches.

Most of what I really needed to know I learned in the first years of my life in Penydarren. Who made me? Almighty God. What else did God make? He made the universe. Where do we learn about God? In the Bible. Why does the world groan? Because man has fallen and rejects God. How can I be forgiven for my sins? Through the life and death of the Lamb of God. How should I live? By taking my turn and letting others have their turn, and by keeping one day special when I worship God. How can I know God? Through His Son, Jesus Christ, especially through His holy Book, the Bible. What must I do to be saved? Believe on the Lord Jesus Christ.

Merthyr Tydfil

When I was seven, we moved from Penydarren down the hill a mile to the very heart of Merthyr. It meant for Mam that she could get back to High Street Baptist Church again every Sunday night, and for me that I went three times every Sunday. The Sunday school was held at half past two in the afternoon. It was the chapel that Mam had attended at my age, and we sang the same hymns from the same hymnbooks with which she had been familiar, and some of the same leaders were leading the meetings in the same rituals.

The world is very beautiful
And full of joy to me;
The sun shines out in glory
On everything I see.
I know I shall be happy
While in this world I stay,
For I will follow Jesus
All the way.

And

The fields are all white,
And the reapers are few.
We children are willing,
But what can we do,
To work for our Lord in His harvest?
We'll work by our prayers
And the pennies we'll bring,
By small self-denials,
The least little thing
To work for our Lord in His harvest.

The infants in their rooms were encouraged to be generous toward the support of missionaries. They were exhorted to give "ship halfpennies" to them, called so because missionaries went to India, Africa, and South America on ships, and there was a sailing ship on every halfpenny coin.

The advantage of High Street Baptist for me was that it was a credible worshiping community. I saw adult baptisms for the first time. When a member was killed in the war on a battleship, a group of sailors in dress uniform from his crew came to the chapel on a Sunday night, and a plaque was unveiled commending him as we all stood in respect to him and his family. One night a strange man and his children came, and they sat in the pew in front of me. Their father wept and wept, burying his head in his hands throughout the whole service. His wife had died that week. I never saw the family again.

The minister suggested that along with a harvest thanksgiving with fruit and crops and vegetables laid out before the congregation, they should attempt an "industrial" harvest. All the factories and manufacturers in the borough of Merthyr were invited to put on display their products on the tables of the big seat between the pulpit and the people. So, before us quite incongruously was a shop window of washing machines, fluorescent lightbulbs, car batteries, a large lump of coal, a bar of steel, and packets of underwear, and in the congregation these smartly dressed strangers sat, the factory owners and managers. It was never repeated. But for getting people in at a service, the innovation was judged a success.

The move from Penydarren to the middle of town brought a big change to Dad too. He was no longer a mere booking clerk at the town station. He became the stationmaster of the first two village stations down the line from Merthyr, one on the Newport line, and the other on the Cardiff line, at Abercanaid and Pentrebach. The Merthyr stationmaster owned his own home, and so the station house was empty, and we moved in, Grandpa and Nana Francis joining us. We even kept lodgers, though I was not to rcfer to them as "lodgers" but as "paying guests." Our relationship with a number of them was much more family than lodgers.

Junior School at Abermorlais

The next step up in schooling after infants was junior school at Abermorlais. I walked across the Glebeland, passing H. Samuel's Jewellery Shop, and then turned up the lane to look at the Merthyr blacksmith shoeing the horses that pulled the rubbish carts and delivered barrels of beer to the pubs. Then I went past the Chinese laundry and on again, turning right and passing the Salvation Army and the health clinic and up the slope to the school. There I stayed for dinner at the cost of four pence a day, but I rarely ate it. I would give it to the boy next to me. Mam asked me to pop home, and so after dinner (I gave the semolina pudding to the other boys, too), I walked home and stood in the kitchen of the station house and enviously watched the family eating a delicious meal. Coming home from school at 4:00 p.m., I had to dodge a gang of Roman Catholic boys who were going home to the Brecon Road area from the Catholic school. They were a tough group and would hit me if they caught me, but I would see them coming and would run like a deer.

At seven years of age, I had Mr. Rees as my first teacher. He was wonderful. He once asked the class who could spell "Wednesday." My hand shot up, and he asked me to come to the front and write it on the board. When I came to writing the *D*, some in the class laughed, and Mr. Rees frowned, "Hush, hush!" Then he praised my spelling. Those rare moments of public success are never forgotten!

Geoff aged 7 years

Geoff aged 8 years

We thirty boys were stuck together for five years. I was generally second in the class, behind a boy called Geoffrey Lewis, who was the son of a French teacher, nicknamed "Bugsy," from Cyfarthfa School. That Geoffrey became a medical doctor in Leicester—he went far.

The teacher when I was eight was Mr. Daniels, who was teaching at his first school and whose brother was a Baptist minister. Then we had Mr. Evans for three long years. But each afternoon for almost an hour, the whole class went into the yard to play. Mr Evans always was the pitcher, and we all fielded. The ball was hit all over the yard,

1949, Dad, Mam, and Geoff aged 10

but not through the high metal fence. That was the best part of those final years in junior school. I enjoyed swinging the bat, but rarely did I connect.

Mr. Evans used the cane to keep order, and I got caned and complained to my parents about it—no doubt exaggerating. To my horror I learned that my mother had gone to Abermorlais and had complained to Mr. Lewis, the headmaster, that Mr. Evans was spanking me too much. Mr. Evans also spoke to me about it and protested how infrequently he had given me some strokes of his cane across my hand. I see myself now as a fussy only child.

The headmaster of Abermorlais was an imposing figure. Mr. Lewis liked me and gave me special duties: I took notices around to the schoolteachers, I returned his books to the town library and paid his fines, I took letters to houses where the children had ceased attending school, and I would accompany boys down the hill to the clinic if they had fallen and cut their knees. A boy in a class a year younger than mine had fallen down, and he had been someone I had looked at with overwhelming pity because his mother had died. Imagine life without Mam! He pleaded with me not to take him down to the clinic. They'd put iodine on the wound, and it would sting. "Please don't take me!" he cried. "I have to," I said. "Mr. Lewis has sent me." He looked at me and made his final plea: "My mother is dead!" Ouch! Down the hill we silently went, and I looked on fascinated as the nurse tenderly put the lint over the wound and stuck it in place with the roll of plaster. It did not hurt at all, to my relief.

I had such a memory at that time, I could have been stretched and learned so much. There was a huge cupboard in one classroom, and one day when the teacher was not there, I opened the door and looked inside. It was full of books in the Welsh language, but we never were taught a word of Welsh. In fact, there was no preparation for the grammar school to which a third of us would be entering at eleven years of age. I remember one day Mr. Lewis came into our classroom and wrote the words of the Welsh national anthem on the blackboard: "Mae hen wlad fy nhadau." We sang them, and I instantly remembered them and always will.

The best class was Singing. We had a superb music teacher. Once a week we would sit on the wooden floor, and he would play the piano while we sang the songs he had taught us. What songs! He taught us none in Welsh, but he did teach us a Latin song:

Gaudeamus igitur Juvenes dum sumus	Let us rejoice While we are young
Post jucundam Juventutem Post molestam Senectutem Nos habebit humus	After the pleasant frolics Of being young After old age In its troubles The earth will cover our bones

I know the Latin still. It appeared first in 1782, and the following century Johannes Brahms took it and put it in the closing movement of his "Academic Festival Overture." Our teacher also taught us John Masefield's "Sea Fever," to the stirring tune written by John Ireland.

> I must go down to the seas again, to the lonely sea and the sky.
> And all I ask is a tall ship and a star to steer her by.
> And the wheel's kick and the wind's song and the white
> sail's shaking,
> And a grey mist on the sea's face, and a grey dawn breaking.

I am stirred each time I hear it sung today. We sang Thomas Moore's Irish patriotic song:

> The Minstrel-boy to the war is gone,
> In the ranks of death you'll find him;
> His father's sword he hath girded on,
> And his wild harp slung behind him.

We sang old nursery rhymes like "A Carrion Crow Sat on an Oak" and classic songs like Vaughan Williams' "Linden Lea." What singing lessons! Imagine the boys playing in the playground and unconsciously singing songs like these. Signing is a significant part of education.

The day began with the regulation religious exercise. We would get out of our desks and stand in the aisle and repeat the Lord's Prayer. Two boys in our class were Jews, and they stood with us but did not pray aloud. One boy was named David Joseph, and on one occasion in 1950, I went to his house for his birthday party. They had a refrigerator, and we were given ice cream. It was the first home I had seen that had a refrigerator.

I once saw David Joseph and a friend going to the synagogue on Saturday morning. Going to a service every Saturday! "How horrible!" I thought. What a religion! I am so glad that I don't belong to a group that worships on a Saturday. Saturday was for fun and the pictures and riding on your bike. On Friday we would chant, "Saturday tomorrow, buy a penny gun. Fill it full of powder and make the bobbie run!" There were other gruesome rhymes seemingly passed on from one generation to another. One began, "Never laugh when a hearse goes by, or you will be the next to die!"

There were impoverished boys in the school. My mother would give me an apple or an orange to eat during eleven o'clock playtime, and one boy with very thick glasses who lived in one of the poor houses in the Georgetown area would ask me for my stump. I would tell him, "I eat it right down to the stump." "Never mind, give me the stump," he would say, and he would eat the lot, pits and all. The same with the orange. He would eat the very peel from the orange that I gave him. He had no breakfast when he left his house for Abermorlais School.

We played soccer at playtime, kicking a stick about. Sometimes someone would bring an old tennis ball to school, but the playground was on a hill surrounded by iron railings topped with a spike, six feet high, and sooner or later the ball would go through the railings and into the bushes. Then one of the agile boys would climb up those railings, balance on the top, and jump down into the bushes on the other side and search for the ball. No one did that for a stick.

But there were also children at Abermorlais School like me from the whole range of the middle classes. What were we? How would you classify us as a family? Lower-middle class? Our member of Parliament was the Socialist S. O. Davies, who had been a theological student in a Congregationalist ministerial college and so had made an easy transition to the Labour Party. Once he had been accepted as the Labour candidate for Merthyr, he had one of the largest parliamentary majorities in the British Isles, and initially he sent his son to our school in Abermorlais. The boy seemed to me to be there for scarcely a single term. He was a gangling loner. I was once standing in the schoolyard looking around when I suddenly decided to move off. I'd run barely a yard when I heard a thump behind me. I stopped, turned around, and saw the son of the MP [member of Parliament] spread-eagled on the ground. He had decided to jump onto me, but as he took off, I had decided to move, and he fell flat on his face. I just walked away. His father, like so many Socialist members of

Parliament, soon sent his son to a private boarding school in England. He, too, went far.

On just one occasion we had a student trainee teacher who taught in our class for a few weeks, and things brightened up in those happy days. He taught a poetry lesson, which we had never had. We all turned to the page on which was the poem "Widecombe Fair."

Tom Pearce, Tom Pearce, lend me your gray mare,
All along, down along, out along lea,
For I want to go down to Widecombe Fair
Wi' Bill Brewer, Jan Stewer, Peter Gurney,
Peter Davy, Dan'l Whiddon, Harry Hawk.
Old Uncle Tom Cobley and all,
Old Uncle Tom Cobley and all.

Six boys were chosen to stand at the front, each one given one of the names from the poem. We all read the poem aloud, but then, when it came to the companions on their way to Widecombe Fair, each boy individually would say aloud his given name. The boy with his glasses who begged me for my apple stump and orange peel was there with the five others, and he was given the name Harry Hawk. He was most excited at this honor, and he said loudly with a big grin, "'Arry 'Awk," and the whole class grinned back. That was a rare refreshing interruption to very unexciting schooling. My learning primarily came from the Carnegie Library in Merthyr.

I loved the I-Spy books, and I joined the I-Spy Club and wore the badge. I particularly enjoyed *I-Spy Trees* and *I-Spy Dogs*. I had spotted and filled in scores of breeds of dogs and types of trees. Once four of us had gone on a cycle ride into the Brecon Beacons, and when it started to rain we took shelter in a forestry plantation where some lumberjacks were cutting down trees. We started to ask them questions, and then one of them said to us, "Do you know what kind of tree that is?" I said, "Oh, it's a Norwegian Spruce." Again, there is that beautiful moment of insight that one has and never forgets it! There were not many of them in my life, but I had learned about the distinctive characteristics of trees from I-Spy and was a member of the club.

One morning the doorbell of our home at 6 John Street rang, and Mam went to the door. A man from an open-topped car was standing there, introducing himself to her. He asked if Geoffrey Thomas lived there and said he was Big Chief I-Spy. It was very odd and meant nothing at all to her, but she explained that I was in school at Abermorlais and told him when he asked how to get there. An hour later, I was summoned to the headmaster's office and introduced to Big Chief I-Spy. Rats! I wasn't wearing my badge! But he got a badge out and pinned it on my pullover, and then he interviewed me for fifteen minutes and took a photograph of me. The next Saturday, the photo and the interview appeared in the *Daily Express*. It spoke in glowing terms of me. Think of it! He had written that I was "chock a block full of intelligence." No, that was Geoffrey Lewis. He also predicted that one day I could play cricket for Glamorgan. That showed how little he knew me.

This was my illustrious end to my years in Abermorlais Junior School. The day came when Mr. Lewis, the headmaster, came into the classroom and read out the names of the fifteen boys who had passed the "scholarship," later known as the "Eleven-Plus." I and all the boys who passed the exam were going to the grammar school. We were awarded five books; one of mine was *Oliver Twist*, and another was George Borrow's *Wild Wales*. Then we were told which of the two schools in the borough of Merthyr we were going to. I was crestfallen to learn I was not going to Cyfarthfa Castle Grammar School where both my parents had gone but rather to the identical level of the county grammar school. Many of the boys in the class who were selected to go to Cyfartha had no parental link with it, as I had. I was so envious of them and disappointed that bureaucracy could be so rigid and unimaginative. Immediately I had to change my loyalties and colors. I begin exalting the county as the very best school in the whole world, and oh! that pathetic Cyfarthfa Castle School that could not be compared to it.

Thus, I finally fizzled out of Abermorlais and moved on to the next grade of school. From infants to junior, and now the great leap forward, and for the next seven years I attended two grammar schools.

CHAPTER 4

My Schooling and My Church

For passing the scholarship I finally got my bike. That was the Welsh tradition as I had understood it—we boys all waited for the reward for diligence in study. Mine was secondhand with yellow stripes on the bars, but soon I had painted it all black. It had straight handlebars, unlike Raleigh bikes, but it had a Sturmey-Archer three-speed gear. It rode well, but its most important feature was that *it was mine*. I soon learned to repair punctures in the tires with the aid of kitchen forks. Every day I rode it, even once to school, but the boys who scorned my fussy manner removed the valve, letting the air down out of one tire, and it had to be pushed home.

Another gift at that new step up from junior to grammar school was a leather satchel for my schoolbooks from Aunty Kitty. The aunties and uncles of the larger family—or even friends of your parents you addressed as "Aunty" or "Uncle"—were a vital part of social life in South Wales.

Merthyr County Grammar School

So, with that satchel, my cap, and my red and green tie, I was prepared for this big school—one I never wanted to attend but pretended I did. My parents were delighted that I was in a grammar school. I lived out the life of a student that my father would have lived if his family could have afforded it. One day he was walking from Pentrebach station to Abercanaid station along a country road and discovered a dead mole. He put it in a bag and gave it to me to take to school to give to the biology teacher: "She will be interested and dissect it." But I was too shy to approach her; I had no classes with her and did not know her. So, instead, I put it in a rubbish bin, though I did not inform Dad.

The first thing that hit me at the county school was "Jerusalem," the majestic hymn tune written by Hubert Parry to those strange words of William Blake that begin, "And did those feet in ancient time…." I had not previously heard the tune or the words—they were not in the *Baptist Hymnal*—but the song was magnificent, and at the first morning assembly how we children sang it! We rivaled the Women's Institute, who still sing it at every meeting. Each of the three terms in the school commenced with "Jerusalem" being sung with full-throated vigor.

So, I expected that was the tradition in every grammar school. I soon was to find out that was not the case, for at the end of my only year in the county school, Dad was promoted to be the stationmaster in Nelson and Llancaiach, and I moved to Lewis School, Pengam, where I discovered that number 11 in the *Students Hymnal*—"And did those feet in ancient time"—was not sung. It was never sung there, and one day I was talking to Dr. Thomas, the music teacher, and asked him why we never sang it. He snarled back his utter contempt for the hymn. He despised it, and while he was music master it would never be sung in this school.

I wonder why. It was not for our evangelical reasons. The tune is stately and majestic with all the hallmarks of a Christian-influenced piece of music. In Aberystwyth we have often sung the tune "Jerusalem" (though some folk disapproved even of that) to Horatius Bonar's words, "O love of God how strong and true."

Streaming children according to their intelligence characterized all grammar schools at the halfway point of the twentieth century. Already many children had been waved goodbye at eleven years of age, as they had been sent off to secondary modern schools, and I never saw them again. Now we grammar school children were again streamed into a top group of the brightest boys and girls in one mixed class, while the other two streams were of a boys' class and a

Geoff aged 15 years

Geoff aged 16 years

girls' class of lesser ability. So, we new kids in the county had to take some exams on our first two days there to weed out the less bright kids. I then went with thirty others to the top-streamed class, where I was surrounded by some educated children, especially girls, most of whom were far better prepared for grammar school than I had been.

We started Welsh classes. Mrs. Jenkins was a formidable teacher. She was confronted with one group of children, who like me, with their English names, did not know a word of Welsh, and another group, at the desks next to us, who came from Dowlais Top where there was a strong Welsh community and who worshiped in Welsh. It was their "kitchen language," spoken every day. Her solution was the only possible one at that time when Welsh-language schools were in their infancy. She went hammer and tongs in both those periods of Welsh language that she had with us each week. We had ten words of vocabulary to learn each lesson. We had the mutations of words in the different modes explained and required. We had to learn the difference between masculine nouns and feminine nouns and which ones took which mutations. We were confronted with the conjugations of the verbs and the lovely tightness of the structure of past tenses in their irregularity. Mrs. Jenkins drove us mercilessly on and on. At first all the homework I seemed to do was my Welsh, just tedious memorization. We were shepherded ad infinitum by force-feeding of vocabulary and verbs in the way French farmers stuff grain down the throats of their geese to make the famous pâté. So differently did my own children acquire the language. And eight of my grandchildren went to Welsh-language schools and easily spoke it as their first language, while the ninth speaks it daily to his mother. The chain momentarily broken by my grandparents' generation was repaired by mine.

But there was a double whammy of getting into a grammar school: one had not only the challenge of learning Welsh but also French. Two languages! And the faint DNA inheritance from the one of my four great-grandmothers who was French did as little to help me as my three Welsh-speaking grandparents' refusal to speak to my parents in that language had failed to prepare me in the streaming wars of grammar school. So, again it was the weary memorizing of conjugations of *avoir* and *etre,* distinctive masculine and feminine nouns, irregular verbs, and the limitless vocabulary. None of that was helped by the fact that I was a fussy boy, used to speaking out and having my questions immediately answered and my fears allayed. In the county in that first year, I was, regrettably, instinctively looking for affirmation most of the time, and there was no one to help me steel myself against it, just the exasperation of teachers and mockery of my peers.

There were other subjects and teachers, of course. A young history mistress's first-year course was to teach us the history of the borough of Merthyr Tydfil from its Celtic origins, through the coming of the Romans, the medieval period, the Reformation, the rise of the industrial movement with coal pits and iron works into the twentieth century. It was quite brilliant. She took us on a trip to see some of the evidences of that around Merthyr, ending in Cyfarthfa Park. We were wandering past the school I had not gone to when Ronald, my former Abermorlais buddy from down the road from the station house, stuck his head out of the school window and waved. I was green with envy, and we began an animated dialogue. "Thomas, be quiet!" she said to me, publicly disgracing me, and Ron was convulsed with laughter.

When I moved on to Lewis School Pengam, the boys in my class mocked this history course when I told them what we had been studying in mighty Merthyr. For them it was childlike and girly.

So, what had they been studying? The ancient Greeks—Sparta and Athens and the Peloponnesian wars. Real history. History for men. Relevant history. But when I spoke to the Welsh teacher at the Pengam school, he was admiring. "That is how in Welsh schools history should be taught," he said.

Then there was a master who had been in school in Dowlais with my father, and he knew who I was. He taught the beginners' course in science, which was fascinating, and woodwork, which was delightful. I did well in those subjects. I also had a sweet encounter with a student teacher of English working for the year's certificate of education, learning his basics for a term or two at the county. He gave us an essay assignment of evaluating a poem, for which he graded me highly.

I was looking for tenderness and affection and patience in my teachers. I suppose I was in fact looking for Christianity. I groan at many memories of my years in grammar school. I found no solace on the sporting field, as I was long and weedy, and team sports was not my forte. Just in the county's final term and my victory in the junior long jump did I find some consolation for a difficult year in which I ended up academically in the middle of the class, a boy who once was at least second in the class. It was all rather good for me, that is, for educating me. It was what I needed, but it was not what I had expected or enjoyed.

Hengoed Tabernacle Baptist Churches

I was delivered from the mixed class in the Merthyr County by a surprising providence when Dad became stationmaster thirteen miles away from Merthyr in Nelson and Llancaiach. The manor house of Llancaiach Fawr was built in 1550 for Dafydd ap Richard to be easily defended during the turbulent reigns of Tudor kings and queens. It is the best example of a semi-fortified manor in Wales. It has been restored and furnished just as it would have been in 1645. Today the staff dress and act as if they were living at that time, using the facilities and materials of the reign of the early Stuarts, and school parties and many Welsh people visit it each week.

Nelson had no station house, but a vacant station house was available over the hill in Hengoed, and in the summer of 1951, the year of the Festival of Britain, we left Merthyr. It was an enormous wrench for me, leaving all that had grown familiar in the eleven long years of childhood in what I considered prestigious Merthyr Tydfil for the uncharted territory of a village in the Rhymney Valley with half a dozen shops. There was no library there in those pretelevision days, but radio had come into its own. The station house was a magnificent independent building, all that a teenager could wish for, with a huge garden leading up to the viaduct crossing the Rhymney River, carrying the railway track that went from Pontypool to Neath Riverside, one of the scenic routes of Wales. In twelve years' time the line was axed along with a third of the country's seven thousand railway stations by Richard Beeching.

When we lived in Nelson, on the other side of the Rhymney River was the railway line that went from Newport to Brecon. One advantage of that was that theological students at the Brecon Congregationalist College could catch the Sunday morning train to the villages and chapels where they were booked to preach. The train arrived in Maesycwmmer just after nine, and they were instructed to call in at our station house in Hengoed and have a cup of tea while waiting for the Tabor Congregational Chapel to open in Maesycwmmer. I was encouraged by my parents to sit in the front room and have a cup of tea with fine theological students like Malcolm Evans, Maldwyn Mundy, Derek Swann, and Gerald Smith and chat to them before they walked back across to the chapel.

There were to be two great advantages, quite unknown to me, from moving to Hengoed, one ecclesiastical and one educational. First there was Tabernacle Baptist Church one hundred yards from our front door, on Raglan Road. Its size and atmosphere were welcoming; its founding theology was responsible for this. Across the valley also in Maesycwmmer stood Mount Pleasant Baptist Church. It originated with a group of local evangelical Christians who first met in 1860 in a wooden hut near the newly erected viaduct. Within thirty years they had built their fine nonconformist chapel that still stands. This was the period characterized by the emergence of those beliefs that Spurgeon dubbed the "Downgrade," when the new theology from Germany, rationalist and antisupernatural, spread rapidly across the British Isles, taking over every seminary and affecting every denomination. Thus began a significant conflict of attitudes and ideals involved in the decline of confessional Christianity—in the Christianity of the Thirty-Nine Articles, the 1823 Confession of Faith of the Calvinistic Methodists, and the 1689 Baptist Confession of Faith—when it was overcome by the spread of the modern spirit in religion whose confidence was in man and political action. Historical Christianity was becoming unpalatable and unreasonable to the self-consciously educated and cultured of Europe. A great spirit and hugely important truths were being deliberately discarded and were being replaced by a vague commitment to human brotherhood and respect for Jesus Christ.

Then in 1904 the revival in Wales was a spark, and it stirred evangelical believers in a great number of congregations to challenge those people in their churches who were being influenced by the new liberalism. What was happening to the preaching of man's ruin by sin and the truths concerning Jesus Christ, the infallible God-man accomplishing redemption by His righteous obedience even to His atoning and completed sacrifice on the cross as the Lamb of God? Where was the preaching of God the Holy Spirit giving the new birth, applying that redemption to favored repentant sinners? Why were these truths marginalized, honored more in token respect than in fearless declaration? A group of Christians in Mount Pleasant believed they needed to call that congregation back to the old paths, and they raised this issue there and then as they were being encouraged to such boldness by the religious awakening all around them in Wales. They met strong opposition by others in the church, and as a result, they were ejected from the congregation as disturbers of the peace. Therefore, they left and moved across the valley to Hengoed, half a mile away, and erected Tabernacle, which Mam and I began to attend forty-five years later, while Dad went to Maesycwmmer's

Tabor Congregationalist Church, which also had had its origin in the revival year of 1904.

But things had happened in Tabernacle during those forty-five years before our arrival, and its early testimony had been diluted. Thirty years earlier a Plymouth Brethren elder from Cardiff had befriended a couple of the leaders in the church and had begun to teach them J. N. Darby's Plymouth Brethren doctrines, that there was no special gift of God to be a pastor-preacher but each church was to be ruled by elders. Every Sunday morning there was to be the breaking of bread, and any of the Christian men in the church could speak to the congregation as they were led, giving out hymns, readings, and exhortations. Sunday night was the evangelistic gospel service. The churches were being confronted by a dispensationalist view of the Scriptures: the Christian no longer being under the law of God as a rule of his life; the imminent return of Christ and the secret rapture of all believers; the thousand years that the world would be evangelized by Jewish converts, a temple necessarily being rebuilt in Jerusalem; and then Armageddon, a great tribulation, followed by another return of Jesus Christ and the great judgment and eternal separation.

A group of families left Tabernacle accepting these teachings, and a Gospel Hall was built on a hill between Ystrad Mynach and Hengoed. In Tabernacle a conservative group remained, but they were drawn by this experience more firmly into the Baptist Union of Great Britain and Northern Ireland and toward the South Wales Baptist College in Cardiff from where they got their Sunday preachers. So, imperceptibly the Tabernacle returned to the religious state that Mount Pleasant had got into at the end of the nineteenth century. Declining and undiscerning, it shrank steadily in size, and Tabernacle finally closed by the end of the twentieth century. Most of the Baptist churches in the Rhymney Valley and throughout Wales went the same way.

That was the pattern for all the other denominations. The Downgrade had triumphed. However, of all places, it was Mount Pleasant that bucked the trend and went in the reverse direction. It called the humble and godly preacher Malcolm Jones, who gave his life to preaching and pastoring that congregation for forty years. After he retired, David George became the pastor, and that church continues to be living and vital in its witness today with a famously helpful Easter Convention weekend and preachers from all over the world addressing a full, attentive church. Secession was not the exclusive answer to ecclesiastical decline. It is possible to reform a congregation if you can control the pulpit and have jurisdiction over the money it might spend on denominational activities.

Conversion

When Mam and I arrived in Tabernacle in 1951, they soon were to call a student whose mother was one of the "children of the revival," a conservative prayerful Christian whose longing was that her son teach those gospel truths. During the first years that he led the church, he reflected his mother and preached to the congregation for a decision. In March 1954, as I heard his gospel message one Sunday night, I was given a heart assurance that Jesus Christ was the Lamb of God who had taken away my sins. It was an event of recognition. I agreed with the claim that in the beginning God created the heavens and the earth. It was not mere chance and luck that made the world and us. I agreed that the Creator is not silent, that He speaks to men and women through Moses and the prophets and especially through His Son, Jesus Christ. He is indeed the Savior of all who put their trust in Him. I believed that I was one of those sinners that Jesus had come into the world to save.

Each Sunday night the congregation was given a simple challenge in the after-service to stand, while all who desired to confess Jesus Christ as their Lord and Savior were asked to remain seated. It was saying to everybody there that they needed to be saved and that salvation could be theirs if they entrusted themselves to Jesus Christ. A single sentence was stated to the congregation. The congregation stood, and I had stood for years with the rest of them, but that night I came out. I remained seated there alone, while the others all rose to their feet. I was acknowledging my repentance toward God and my faith in our Lord Jesus Christ. The minister came up the aisle, shook my hand, and said, "God bless you." Not more than six weeks later I was baptized, and I became a church member taking the Communion bread and wine at the first opportunity, which was on the first Sunday of the month. It was thus an ordinary conversion. In what is now more than sixty-five years since that evening, there has not been a single day in which I doubted that I was a Christian, chosen by God, saved by the life and death of the Son of God, and made alive to this reality by the Spirit of God, even when I occasionally behaved in word, deed, and omission in an utterly sub-Christian way. At those times I knew I was behaving badly like that as a newly born child of God—shame on me.

There is much to be said for such a simple invitation sentence that at that time Hengoed's Tabernacle Baptist Church used. Yet, it brings unhelpful pressure to bear on the minister to have to accept all who have remained sitting or have stood up or walked to the front or have raised their hand, especially because all the church has seen it and been made to feel very happy. Occasionally a group of boys or teenagers will all make a corporate physical response. A pew of them might all remain seated. Some would be thoughtfully exercised young people, seriously counting the cost of such a decision, while their companions can make the response just wanting to do what the others did. A minister rejecting some of those who sat down as not really ready yet to be made church members brings reproach from their families and division in the church. This so-called altar call is also unhelpful in that it equates a physical act with an inner spiritual change. Listeners are touched and can even be stampeded into making a decision but know nothing of the Holy Spirit convicting of sin and of the living God whom they should petition for mercy. The period of inviting can be extended and extended, with the congregation being rebuked for not responding. They can even hear that God's hands are tied, that He can do no more, that it is entirely up to them whether they let Him into their lives or keep the door closed against Him. What erroneous conceit! When the emotions of the hour have faded, their religion can also fade. The decision to physically sit or raise a hand or walk to the "mourners' bench" has been motivated by a vague desire for improvement and rededication rather than by a conviction of sin and a knowledge that the Savior has come to deliver from ignorance, helplessness, and guilt.

So, I have never used an invitation to sit down while all the rest stand or to come to the front, but I do believe in challenging people to repent of their sins and to believe in Christ that moment as He is being freely offered to them in the gospel, not to be always waiting for a better preacher and better sermon and better emotions. I plead with them all to turn and entrust themselves to Him, as though God were beseeching the listeners through me. I tell people,

> He loves you so much He has brought you here tonight to hear of this Savior who is His only Son. And God is showing His love to you by giving me this message to tell you truly about the Father, Son, and Holy Spirit and what will happen to you if you entrust yourselves to this Christ whom, if you receive Him, can become your supreme Teacher, who can say nothing wrong, your Sovereign Protector, and the Lamb of God who will take away your sins and take you to glory. Come to Him now! Do not delay.

Others also professed faith in Christ at Tabernacle during those years, and among them were those who have gone on well in the faith. The minister whose preaching touched me completed his studies, picked up many ideas at the Cardiff Baptist College, pastored another Baptist chapel for a short time, and then became an Anglo-Catholic in the Anglican church in Wales. While the older evangelical members were still alive and in the majority, Tabernacle in Hengoed survived, and some fine men pastored there.

Once on a Sunday night after a particularly powerful sermon, before the congregation sang the final hymn, one of the old school, the aged and frail Mrs. Brooks, got out of her seat, and walked to the front, faced the congregation, and said, "Now tonight you have heard the gospel. You know that you need a Savior and that you must repent and believe in the Lord Jesus Christ. Come to the Savior now; He gently calleth thee." But that generation, "children of the revival," who believed in the absolute necessity of conversion, passed away, the majority became a decreasing minority, and the pulpit was no longer seen as one in which a totally true Bible was preached.

Across the valley was Malcolm Jones expounding the historic Christian faith. There could only be one pulpit and one congregation that could survive that juxtaposition, because it is Christ alone who builds His church. It is possible to grieve and quench His Spirit, and without His presence we can achieve nothing. Tabor Congregationalist Church in Maesycwmmer is today in ruins, and Tabernacle's building was knocked down in the early years of the twenty-first century, and houses were erected where once it stood. The only outward evidence today that a house of prayer and singing and preaching—and salvation for one teenager—was once standing there is the name of the two houses. They are called Tabernacle Mews. However, Mount Pleasant stands.

Lewis School, Pengam

The second advantage that living in Hengoed supplied was that it put me into the catchment area for a prestigious grammar school. The Lewis School, Pengam, opened in 1729 with the motto *Ni Ddychwel Ddoe*, meaning "Yesterday Never Returns." So Merthyr was never to return, and I had to get on with my life as this new chapter began. If there had been a station house in Nelson, then I would not have been permitted to attend the Lewis School. Children from that town went to a different secondary school. My Merthyr years were the past, and so I had to take the opportunity of a second chance at grammar school and feebly learn from the mistakes of my first year in Merthyr. I traveled daily the two miles from Hengoed to Pengam by train and later by the regular buses, though we lived too near to the Lewis School to have a free bus pass.

There was a uniform smartness about Lewis boys. They all wore black blazers, gray trousers, caps, and school ties. The grounds and playing fields were attached to the school. We had to choose (as second-year boys) what two languages we were to study over the next four years. The choice was, out of French, Welsh, and Latin, which one to drop. Most boys chose French and Latin—French perhaps because of their planned annual visits to Monte Carlo and the Riviera? In their dreams! Latin because entrance to Oxford or Cambridge required at that time a School Certificate in Latin. Neither destination was on my agenda. Just six of us chose Welsh, and that brought us into the classes of the sweetest teacher in the school, S. I. Jones, the pacifist son of a Welsh Congregationalist minister.

Then there were the compulsory new subjects for all of us, physics, chemistry, and biology. There was a good spirit in our class, and three very smart boys who were always leading it went on to have glittering careers. Our form teacher was a fine man, a Baptist and Welsh-speaking, but also he knew my minister uncle, Stanley Lloyd. He showed his affection for me. He attended the old Welsh-language Baptist church in Cefn Hengoed, and one Monday he happened to talk to me and told me about the sermon he had heard the previous day. W. J. Gruffydd of Cardiff University had been preaching to them on the conversion of Saul of Tarsus on the Damascus road, and the preacher had gone through the changes that had taken place in the persecutor's life after he became Christ's disciple. It had obviously impacted him if he chose one day later to share it with a fifteen-year-old boy.

The consequences of his knowledge of me and my family were that he expected more from me, and I disappointed him. His end-of-year comments about me on my school report were rather unflattering—but accurate enough—I suppose. As an only child I had a lot of rough edges to smooth off. I wish I could say that they have all been removed.

The trick in dealing with those annual reports before our parents saw them (so we were told with a nudge and a wink) was to open the envelope after the postman pushed it through the door and doctor the report. When the maths score was 10 percent and the maths teacher had added the remark, "The mark speaks for itself," the pupil was to add another zero to his mark before his parents saw the report, making the score 100 percent. Well, that's the tall tale that was told us anyway.

The day at Lewis School started with the morning school assembly, 9:05 to 9:30. It was an act of worship, and the only boys not present were the Roman Catholics, the Jehovah's Witnesses, and two sons of a local doctor who was an atheist. These thirty boys sat in a supervised classroom. In the assembly the head boy made an occasional announcement, typically Monday morning, of the rugby score of the school team and its usual victory on the previous Saturday, which brought a cheering response. The staff standing on the stage wore gowns; the headmaster entered and announced the chanted psalm, whose tunes were written by old boys of the school and printed in our own psalm book. The reading was done by a different prefect each day from a high brass eagle lectern. The headmaster made the announcements and read a prayer, and we sang the final hymn. Then we disappeared to our seven classes for the day. All the teachers had nicknames: Mighty Atom, Baldy, Killer, Froggy, Ianto, Gryff, Baby Face, Katey, and Ma Simms. The two latter were the only women teachers, and they both taught biology. The male staff ate their lunch at some noisy tables in the corner of the dining room, but the headmaster ate alone in another room.

A despicable feature was a small conduct book that each of us was given and had to carry around with us. Information and instructions and homework details were written in it, but the back page was a conduct page where bad conduct was punished with a *C* conduct mark, the reason for the penalty, and the signature of the master or the prefect. When you had three conduct marks, that necessitated your spending an hour in detention after school on a Thursday evening. You spent that hour in writing out arithmetic sums. You were given a three-digit number, which you multiplied by the same number, such as 861 x 861, and then you went to the next number, 862 x 862, and multiplied that number, and so on. The master on duty had a book with all the correct sums and would check that you were not simply writing down numbers. He would ask you for your final sum, and if it was wrong, the final sum of the next multiplication or the next. You had better get it right, too, or there might be a further detention.

I had been an avid reader of comics through junior school. There were five, *Wizard, Hotspur, Adventure, Skipper*, and *Rover*, produced by D. C. Thomson, and somehow I managed to read four of them each week, I cannot remember how. They were story papers and at the height of their popularity. The last of these, the *Rover*, ceased its publication in 1973. The stories covered a wide range of genres, with the most famous being Wilson the superathlete. There were also mystery stories, westerns, Second World War aeronautical battles, and school stories, the latter of English private boarding schools for boys, like Marlborough, Harrow, Eton, Westminster, Winchester, and Shrewsbury. Devouring these stories week by week must have influenced me and given me an ethos to imitate, one of a ridiculous sense of superiority from being in Lewis School and then of being over all the boys in lower forms, whom I, shamefully, talked down to. I was uninterested in them and their fine achievements. I punished them when I was a prefect, as I myself had been by my peers. It was the pathetic imitation of the private school fagging—that is, senior boys have junior boys to serve them, clean their shoes, and such, as their "fags." One reads about it in *Tom Brown's Schooldays*. I am embarrassed to think of the vain spirit in me.

Some teachers were brilliant at actual teaching. I think of a mathematics teacher in my School Certificate year who caused my averages to zoom. Simultaneous equations suddenly became lucid. The same was true with chemistry and with Bryn Jones teaching A-level economics, but particularly M. I. Morgan, the history teacher for the last years of Advanced Level preuniversity preparation. How he worked for us, and we took it all for granted. He prepared his classes for us, and we wrote our weekly essays for him. It was a trade-off. We history boys were sponges, and he opened up the British Civil War to us.

But we never saw our teachers again at any place, on any level, to talk about what had happened in those seven long years in grammar school and how we were getting on since that time. There were no structures that brought us together. We were ships passing one another in the night, disappearing from sight forever. Fifty years have

My final year at Lewis School, Pengam, aged 18

gone by, and there is one boy from those years at Lewis School that I have seen once, but no teachers at all. Most of them lived beyond the catchment area of the school, and for our part we were off, "going far."

On Friday nights after school had finished, a meeting of the Scientific, Literary, and Debating Society (SLADS) was held from 4:00 p.m. until 5:30. The French master remained behind each Friday and supervised the meeting. We had meetings and speakers and discussions under all the headings of the society. It was terrific, and I began public speaking there, though I had all the nervousness of my father in my first years.

There were the boys who were unique. There were, of course, the sportsmen like John Dawes, the future captain of the British Lions, who once came to hear me preach in Trinity Calvinist Methodist Church, Treorchy. There was J. C. Jones, an excellent sprinter who ran the 220 yards for Wales in the Commonwealth Games of 1958 in 21.9 seconds. I later ran the relay race in the Glamorgan School Sports in Maindy Stadium in Cardiff with him, John Dawes, and John O'Shea (both of whom later played rugby for Wales), and we broke the Welsh schools' record. Then other boys were unique because of their musical prowess not just with the violin, clarinet, and piano, but I remember one day a group of boys came into the empty hall and opened the grand piano, and one of them sat down and played magnificent boogie-woogie. Another boy played the school pipe organ.

Some of the boys had other distinctions. One rode upright and straight-shouldered to school each day on a polished Raleigh bicycle. Two others played chess together every break time on a handheld board. One boy was an artist. Another was a carpenter and built a shining chest of drawers. One boy's first language was Welsh, and he lived on a nearby farm. One drove a car to school and parked it just outside the school gates. One was an actor. And I was…"religious."

Teenage Years

I was a naïve and gullible boy. One embarrassing indication of this is revealed by my response to Roger Bannister's running the first four-minute mile. I had heard so much of this great goal, and that night, May 6, 1954 (a month after my baptism), I listened to the result of the mile race on the radio news, that at Oxford University's Iffley Road track Roger Bannister had run the mile in 3.59.4, but I was disappointed. Why? Because he had failed to run a four-minute mile. You see, I thought the goal was to run a mile in exactly four minutes. I was not a child and yet….

Brian Dicks and I had both professed our faith in Christ and were baptized in April 1954. In 1955, on Good Friday, Billy Graham preached on television live from a crusade meeting he was having in Glasgow at the Kelvin Hall. We had no TV set, and I went along the road to the house of my friend Willy to watch it on their little black-and-white set. It was six more months before our home obtained a set. Billy's preaching was powerful, and when I got back to school after the Easter break for the final summer term, Brian and I discovered that two boys in our school year had professed conversion through watching and listening to the American evangelist. Soon it came to me that we had to start a weekly meeting, a Christian Union, and we went to one of the young mathematics teachers who was a Baptist to get his support and to liaise with the headmaster to get his permission. It was readily given, and we started meetings.

We had little discernment and knowledge. The form buzzed with debate about Christianity when those two boys were converted, but the only boy who knew what he believed and why was the Jehovah's Witness, and I did not know how to answer him nor knew where I could get information to do so. We had Bible studies, but we were the blind leading the blind.

A boy named Neil Kinnock, who was three or four years younger than me, came to the meetings. He followed me to Cardiff University and then in 1970 became the member of Parliament for the very safe Labour seat in Bedwellty and later Islwyn. He was the leader of the Labour Party and leader of the Opposition from 1983 until 1992. His main opponent was Mrs. Thatcher, who led the Tory party, and so there was press interest in him. Interviews with him appeared in some papers, and in one he was asked if he were religious. He replied that he admired Christians and respected Jesus Christ but he "could not make that leap into the dark."

So, I wrote to him and reminded him of the days in Lewis School and the Bible studies and told him that becoming a Christian was anything but a leap into the dark. It was a thoughtful examination and understanding of Jesus Christ and His claims, His teaching and works, and especially His resurrection. It was coming to the one who said, "I am the light of the world," rather than jumping into darkness. I told him that next time he drove to North Wales to visit the parents of his wife, Glenys, that they were welcome to call in and have a cup of tea with us in Aberystwyth. I got a reply from his secretary telling me he enjoys hearing from his old friends.

Brian and I kept the dwindling group of Christians going until we finished school. We invited any local clergy to speak to us. I remember two in particular. The 1950s was the time of the rise of the World Council of Churches and the ecumenical movement. A local Baptist minister came and spoke to us and was enthusiastic about ecumenism. "Would you Baptists be prepared to give up your baptism for the sake of one united church?" he asked. Then he inquired, "How many of you are Baptists?" I raised my hand and looked around. Every single boy had raised his hand. The Rhymney Valley and west Gwent was Baptist territory.

Later a boy named Clive came to me and suggested, "You ought to get our new minister in Tredegar. His name is Malcolm Evans." So we invited this Congregationalist, and he came to an after-school meeting and explained the gospel with lucidity. There was a question time at the end, and I asked Malcolm, "Why did God allow all this to happen, to create Adam with the possibility of defying God and sinning, so bringing sin and death into the world, and then having to send His Son to become incarnate and die on the cross? Why?" I can still see Malcolm in his three-piece suit standing there and in his deep voice replying, "I have thought about that for a long time, and my conclusion is that it was all to God's greater glory." It was an answer that I found totally satisfying then, and as the years have gone by and I have thought of all that is implied in that answer, I still am satisfied. I have reminded Malcolm of that meeting during our long friendship.

I became a Christian at the right time in my life. I increasingly loved popular music, unlike my parents. I tuned in to Radio Luxemburg as I did my homework. At first it was the voice of Frank Sinatra that touched me, then reissues of Glenn Miller's band. Then the birth of rock 'n' roll moved me. Little Richard recorded "Tutti Frutti" in 1955, and I was introduced to the immediacy and energy of that American world. Feeling and spontaneity were all important there. First was the music of Buddy Holly and the Crickets and Bill Haley (all so ordinary looking with horn-rimmed glasses and even quiffs), and then came the more dashing Everly Brothers, Elvis Presley, and Cliff Richard. They were handsome, understandable, and accessible to me, though we did not have a record player. This music could be heard, enjoyed, whistled, and sung without much money. I was being affected by an age revolution and a class revolution, though I did not know it, and I fear I was influenced too much, but more through one bad companion than through any of that music. Thank God I had Him as my Father and Jesus Christ as my teacher. I also had an inquisitive mind, and the pop world though very wide was also shallow. I discovered jazz, and so as groups from America came to Cardiff, I heard the leading jazz musicians of the world, like Stan Kenton, Lionel Hampton, Johnny Dankworth, Duke Ellington, Count Basie, the MJQ, Dave Brubeck, Dizzy Gillespie, Ella Fitzgerald, and Oscar Peterson, and was able to talk with a number of them. Dave Brubeck's wife was named Iola, like my wife-to-be. It was to be another four years before I discovered classical music. But none of this curiosity with what the world was listening to and thinking disturbed my trust in Christ as the Son of God and that my life was to be spent serving Him.

Finally, the seven years in Lewis School came to an end. JDF went to Balliol, while Brian went off to the University College of Wales, Aberystwyth University. I was perplexed about my career, finally telling people that I was thinking of becoming a religious instruction (RI) teacher (though perhaps in my heart of hearts I could see the challenge of the Christian ministry ahead). Until then, when I was asked about my future career, I had told people I was going into "personnel management." When I later told the headmaster that RI teaching was my plan, he astonished me by saying, "Then you can come back and teach here. We need an RI teacher."

There was no biblical studies department in Aberystwyth or Swansea, and so I went down the valley to what is now known as Cardiff University (then known as the University College of South Wales and Monmouthshire). Dad had had his last promotion to stationmaster in the stations around Barry, and that is where we moved, finally purchasing our own house at 28 Court Road. For three more years I was to live at home with Dad and Mam until I was in my twenty-third year. Yet I had the privilege during those years of exploring the valleys and towns and people of South Wales—what a terrific education.

CHAPTER 5

University in Cardiff

In 1958 I entered the last months of my teens, and the unconscious search for Christian fellowship was being rewarded. A friend in school told me that when I got to university in Cardiff I would find two separate religious organizations, the Inter-Varsity Fellowship (IVF) and the Students' Christian Movement (SCU). That initially seemed rather sad and unnecessary.

J. I. Packer's *Fundamentalism and the Word of God*

My friend further told me he had two books to loan me that would explain the reason for having two separate organizations. He gave me an SCM Press publication by Gabriel Hebert entitled *Fundamentalism and the Church of God* and then the response to it published by the Inter-Varsity Press entitled *Fundamentalism and the Word of God*, written by J. I. Packer. There in school I read them in that order, first Hebert explaining that ultimate authority lay in the church determining what Christians should believe. That seemed to make sense. Then Packer's response showing that the church was created by the Word of God. The apostle Peter, filled with the Spirit on the day of Pentecost, was given the word to preach by Jesus Christ his Lord, and he declared it with the result that three thousand men repented and believed that gospel word. They were baptized and continued steadfastly in the doctrines of the apostles and in their fellowship of teaching and trusting; then they prayed together and broke bread. It all began with the word that the Son of God had brought that was taught exactly as He had given it to His servants. This was one of the first Christian books I had read—certainly the first about theology and doctrine. It was not long before the Christian Union at Cardiff invited J. I. Packer to come over the Bristol Channel and speak at one of its meetings, and so in 1959 I heard him in the flesh.

Dr. Martyn Lloyd-Jones

I was starting to move in evangelical Christian circles. In the summer I went to a camp in Llanmadoc on the Gower Peninsula and also to a beach mission of the Children's Special Service Mission south of Dublin in Greystones. It was at the Llanmadoc camp one evening, as I was hanging around the student officers, that I overheard them talking with quiet smiles about someone they called "the Doctor." There was unadulterated respect for this figure, who apparently was a preacher from London whose name was Lloyd-Jones. That deferential response among students was unusual and unexpected, that there could be awe for a living preacher. Seeds were being planted, and then a month later some fruit came from it, for in the Saturday edition of the daily paper for Wales, the *Western Mail*, in the religious section where Sunday meetings were generally announced, a notice broadcasted the induction service of Dr. Eifion Evans that very week in September. It was at the Memorial Hall in Cowbridge Road, Cardiff, and Dr. Martyn Lloyd-Jones was to preach.

I took the train into Cardiff from Barry and walked along Cowbridge Road, passing the Elim City Temple and arriving at one of the Forward Movement buildings erected seventy years earlier by the Calvinistic Methodists with the specific purpose of reaching the working classes in Wales with the gospel. There were a few other such buildings in Cardiff, one at Saltmead and another (that was one of the largest congregations in Wales) at the Heath in Whitchurch Road. None of them possessed any independent identity any longer as "Forward Movement" causes. They had been merged into the Presbyterian denomination. During the 1920s the Calvinistic Methodists had chosen to take on the nomenclature "The Presbyterian Church of Wales."

I entered a large building holding seven hundred or so people, where soon every seat had been taken. Many of the women wore hats, and the men were in suits. It was a delightfully sober atmosphere, nothing giddy or manipulative about it at all. It was our minds that were being engaged. A bus had brought a crowd from Sandfields Forward Movement Church in Port Talbot (where it was customarily referred to as "the Forward"). We sang the hymns of Toplady and Watts and Wesley. Dr. Lloyd-Jones announced his text, telling us that he "wished to draw our attention to" this verse in Scripture, 2 Corinthians 5:20, "Now then, we are ambassadors for Christ, as though God were pleading through us: we implore you on Christ's behalf, be reconciled to God." Eifion Evans had been preparing for a career as a pharmacist, and then God directed him in another way to become a preacher of the gospel as God's ambassador. Dr. Lloyd-Jones said that the preacher is to deliver the very message that Christ Himself would be delivering were He physically present in our church services. That is the function of an ambassador, to represent the monarch and to act in every way according to the position, subject to the direction of the monarch himself. So the preacher represents the King and acts as the King's legate and in the King's name.

This occasion was different from the meetings and preaching I had heard before, and it was important for me to discover the reason for this. Of what did this specialness consist, and why was it significant? I was occasionally to worship in Memorial Hall during the brief ministry of Eifion Evans there and appreciated hearing his vital preaching. So, I was getting what I believe was another divine prompt pushing me to the places where I might find the living God and His truth and my vocation. I went back to Barry and told the family about the meeting. My mother responded immediately. "I would hear Dr. Lloyd-Jones in the 1930s when he would take big meetings in Merthyr. I remember him telling us what the verses were saying, and then he said to us, 'See how nothing fundamentally has changed from the first century. Man is just the same, and the answer is still the same in the gospel.'" She had learned that from the Doctor, and it had stuck in a memory cell. How often he made the same point across the years.

Biblical Studies at University

I started university in Cardiff the next month, in October 1958, as I was reaching my twentieth birthday. There followed three fascinating but also oddly frustrating years. "Fascinating" as university was a destination dreamed of and imagined for a long time. What a step up from secondary school to university. Instead of being the oldest children in school, you became "freshers" (which is how first-year students are referred to in Wales, not "freshmen" as they are in the United States). At university your initial relieved discovery was that you had been well prepared by those final two years at school by the Advanced Level Certificate of Education. You also learned that the standard of instruction was not very different from what you had been writing down in your manuscript books at school but that at university there was just more and more of the stuff.

So university was fascinating, but my own time in Cardiff, along with a small minority of other students, was odd for this reason, that I was among those who lived at home. I took a twenty-minute train ride back and forth from Barry to Cardiff each day. I did not share my meals, evenings, and weekends with a gang of students in a hall of residence or in a fraternity or dormitory. I always went back to Dad and Mam. My involvement at university events was limited. I went once to the Friday night debate, the protected and magnified event of the week, where, via Hegel, thesis was to meet antithesis and a satisfying synthesis was to be attained just through person-to-person discussion. That was the theory, but the loud personalities at the debates did not attract me, and I did not find such evenings helpful. By the twenty-first century, those debates in almost every redbrick university in the land had declined drastically to attract a mere handful of students, if held at all, because today's students believe that no one has the truth. It does not exist to be found by Hegelian methodology. They live in a cosmos where truth, by any means, is unattainable. One would lose credibility to announce that one had it.

Even "rag week" was disappointing. I had long known of rag week, a weeklong period when various playful events were organized to raise money for charities. The students produced a kind of newspaper called *The Wail*, and they fanned out from Cardiff to the surrounding towns and up the valleys selling these papers. "Buy a whale, sir?" They stood outside our school gates in their beards, jeans, and duffle coats, coming fifteen miles to our Lewis School in the service of rag week. We were admiring and envious. The money raised supported a number of worthy charities. The students did amusing and mischievous stunts that were reported by the media. These gave greater publicity to the rag and sold more copies of *The Wail*. For example, a group of workmen were digging a hole in a road in Cardiff, and so the police were called and told that some students were dressed as workmen and were excavating the street. Then the workmen were approached and told that a group of students dressed as policemen were soon going to come claiming to be real policemen and would try to stop them digging up the street. Then the students hung around unobtrusively to watch the ensuing clash.

Nor were there any sports groups I was drawn to. I did, however, get to know the select group of fellow students who took the final two years honors course in biblical studies. And I would simply return from the college to my aerie in Barry every evening and weekend, a counterpoise to the artificial atmosphere of three thousand students all living together.

Of course, I admired the exhortations we Christians were given by visiting speakers to become the salt of that world in which we lived. That was good and true and needed. I nodded my head gravely but could do little about it except bear witness to the other seven students who were taking my degree course. The ideal lifestyle of the Christian student was portrayed in alluring colors: playing outside for the college rugby team, singing madrigals in the choir, getting a first-class honors' degree, doing research, editing the student newspaper, singing tenor in the annual musical, putting forward the Christian position in the Friday night debates, and standing for office in the Students Union to become the student president. But few of us had a single one of those talents or a taste for any of those activities. Just keeping up with assignments was demanding enough, along with finding Christian counsel and friendship and sharing the gospel with others—all that took so much time and was not done terribly well. But if a thing is worth doing, it is worth doing—even badly. University was not all that different from being in school, but everything was bigger and far less regimented.

I was in Cardiff on a much more important enterprise: to know God and to comprehensively enjoy Him, to grow in my relationship with my Creator, to understand the incarnate majesty of Jesus Christ, to see His glory in every blade of grass and drop of rain, to adore Him for the love that kept Him on the cross until my redemption was achieved. I was also looking to find people who would assist me and inspire me in our corporate quest. And I found them. That was not the goal and ethos of the University College of Wales at Cardiff. I understood that. The university did have much to offer, however, like M. I. Morgan teaching history to us. How profitable it was. I would commend anyone to take such courses. My daughters and grandchildren all profited from university life as well. It was simply that I longed to achieve something immensely and eternally profitable. That was my nonnegotiable priority. Then there was the sad reality that I was not academically capable of the course I had mistakenly taken.

I had chosen as my three first-year courses at university classical Greek, biblical studies, and philosophy. I was going to be a preacher; that was the notion in my heart of hearts. That is why I chose in my ignorance what I chose. What madness to select such new subjects! I received no advice and had no knowledge of what lay before me. I had never taken a classical language, having rejected Latin as a twelve-year-old when confronting a little fork in my journey. I had battled with the Welsh and French languages, gratefully dropping them for my last two years at Lewis School. I now was reimmersing myself in two ancient languages with different scripts, Sigma and Semitic. I then scraped through my first year at university when even philosophy turned out to be a year of being told about Plato's *Republic*.

Somehow the biblical studies department had pity on me, and I was accepted in the honors class for two more years of attendance at their lectures. Then there came the discouraging discovery that all we did for that time was to sit and take notes—for two whole years. We wrote no essays, did no exercises, wrote no papers. There was never any discussion or religious issues that were raised in class by us students. We simply copied down what we thought they were saying in an atmosphere as quiet as a chapel service. I cannot remember one question being asked in all the lectures over two years. No student raised his voice, not even me. They gave us no exams for that same long period of time, but then came the denouement—along with nine three-hour papers, day after day for two weeks, five of which were translation papers and some consisting of material we had been given two years earlier. In these papers we were asked to "translate and comment"—the only words in English on the examination papers—on the Greek and Hebrew passages before us as well as on the unpointed Hebrew of the Zadokite document (first published in 1910 from copies discovered in Cairo).

Get a life! I had gone to university as my natural and expected goal, clueless and naïve. No one sat me down and gave me a description of what lay ahead if I were to take one subject dominated by the Semitic languages department. There were no words of counsel such as "Stick to history," "I suggest you take archaeology," or "Why not take English in your first year?" I was not up to this course. I was out of my depth. Our four lecturers were all right, decent, hardworking, moral men but as uninspiring as blancmange. Three of them were Baptists, one having been a missionary in India for some years, so where were the anecdotes and memories shared, the theological issues, the humor? Almost totally absent. Was there one occasion in the years following university that I returned to those lecture notes once the final lecturer closed his folder and I had finished studying assiduously for my final exam? Not once. I was gone, out of that archaic and artificial world.

Most of what I have been describing has long changed. I have opened up for inspection a mere relic. For many years since the 1950s, the three-year course at university has now been divided into six semesters. There have been changes in structures and courses, different options are described and offered before you come to make a now informed choice. That department in Cardiff in the late 1950s was a pale pastiche of ancient Oxford and Cambridge attitudes but without their tutorials. We provided an opportunity in a small provincial university for some lecturers to have a platform, an audience, long vacations, and a salary.

The Christian Union

Knowing more of God at Cardiff University was great gain to me. Each day at 8:10 a.m. I caught a train from Barry Dock Train Station to Cardiff Queen Street, where at 8:35 the train promptly arrived. I walked across the quiet streets to Cathays Park and the university building. Then I climbed up a few flights of stairs to a floor where there was a honeycomb of small rooms. In one of these the Christian Union students met for prayer from 8:40 to 9:00 a.m., when lectures started. I attended almost every daily prayer meeting with about four other students throughout all the time I was there. That is how I began the day. We kneeled down and we prayed and we departed. Our main Christian meetings, with sixty students, were held on Saturday nights and in the Memorial Hall where I had a month earlier heard Dr. Lloyd-Jones. We always had a speaker, and I learned much both from the Christian speakers I heard and the Christian students there.

Books

Christian books published by the Inter-Varsity Press were available for sale on those Saturday nights. The book that meant so much to me was Martyn Lloyd-Jones's *Studies in the Sermon on the Mount.* It remains one of the most splendid books I have ever read. It made me want to live a righteous life. It showed me the beauty of such a life, and it made me want to preach like the Doctor did. "This is true preaching; every sermon should be like these sixty expositions," I thought.

Many other books on the Saturday night book table impacted me in different ways, such as Leon Morris on the atonement, totally vindicating the propitiatory aspect of the death of the Son of God. I was introduced to B. B. Warfield on that book table. There were a couple of books on the Gospels written by Ned Stonehouse, the New Testament professor at Westminster Theological Seminary (WTS) in Philadelphia, as well as *An Introduction to the Old Testament*, written by Edward J. Young, who was the Old Testament professor at WTS. There was also a volume called *Principles of Conduct* written by John Murray, the systematic theology professor at WTS. I thought, "That must be quite some theological seminary to have such learned and holy men tackling these enormous themes such as the biblical infallibility of the Old Testament, Christian ethics, and the synoptic question concerning the relation of Mark's gospel to the other gospels."

Books were central in assisting my understanding of historic Christianity. I realized that I had begun to move among readers. One of my fellow students, Pam, was the future wife of Andrew Davies, the son of I. B. Davies, the mighty Presbyterian preacher who filled the Neath Mission Hall in the 1950s with over twelve hundred people. I. B. became a subscriber to a new magazine called the *Banner of Truth*, and when he had read it, he passed it on to Andrew, who passed it on to Pam, and finally, she gave it to me. It was number 17, and after reading it I became a subscriber.

I preached for the first time in Elizabeth Street Presbyterian Church in Dowlais and stayed for the day with a remarkably mature Christian woman, Bessie Jones, a widow who kept a corner shop. She had been converted under the ministry of I. B. Davies. She was the first woman I met who read books—in fact, she was reading Lloyd-Jones' *Studies in the Sermon on the Mount*—and was the first person who talked to me about becoming a preacher: "If you were my son, I would give you no peace until you were settled in your decision that your calling was to be a preacher."

I remember in 1959 when the Banner of Truth published John Owen's *The Death of Death in the Death of Christ*, with its dynamic foreword by J. I. Packer, how it introduced me and the evangelical worlds of Great Britain and the United States to the unfamiliar biblical doctrine of the limited purpose of the atonement. It asked and answered the question, For whom did Jesus Christ die to save? When the angel announced that His name was to be Jesus, why was He given this name? Because He was intending to save His people from their sin. When Paul tells the church in Ephesus what the purpose of the dying sacrifice of Christ is, he asserts, "Christ also loved the church and gave Himself for her, that He might sanctify and cleanse her with the washing of water by the word, that He might present her to Himself a glorious church, not having spot or wrinkle or any such thing, but that she should be holy and without blemish" (Eph. 5:25–27). That was the accomplishment of the dying love of Jesus Christ for all whom He saved.

In John's gospel, several references are made about the Good Shepherd who was giving His life, and it was for His sheep, not the goats. Who does Christ pray for? He tells us in His great prayer in John 17 that He intercedes for all that the Father has given to Him, specifically saying that He does not pray for the whole world. It is a limited intercession. It is inconceivable that a full propitiation could be made for sinners so that the wrath of God toward them was appeased and placated because it has fallen without restraint upon the Son of God, but that then, once again, God should demand for a second time another judgment should fall on those same sins and on those same sinners in hell.

So, the *Death of Death* appeared with Packer taking no survivors in his introduction, and how we students in 1959 in the midmorning coffee break would take our Eccles cakes and cups of tea and sit and argue about limited atonement with the students from the Baptist College, whether that doctrine was a mere philosophical necessity logically imposed by Calvinism on theology, or if it was something unrequired and opposed in the Scripture. If that is the case, who will receive it? Why should we? Or was it plainly taught in the Bible that the Son of God was "once for favored sinners slain"?[1] I was persuaded that it was so, that in the Old Testament there was only a particular redemption. Though there were all the temples and sacrifices in Babylon and Egypt and Persia and Rome, the only particular atonement that atoned was by the spotless lambs on the altar in Jerusalem. And even in Israel there was no atonement unless the lamb was taken and sacrificed exactly as God required with a heart that cried to God for mercy. The mere form alone could not redeem, and God did not ask for form obedience. Eternal redemption from the lordship and penalty of sin is limited to those who put their hand on the head of the sacrifice, reflecting a heart dependent on the innocent shedding His blood for the guilty.

I heard Dr. Packer speak in 1959 in Cardiff but did not talk to him until four years later. I was engaged to Iola in 1963, and her father loaned us his car. They lived in the heart of Snowdonia, and one day Iola and I took the car and determined to visit the ancient Baptist chapel, Salem, in Pentre Gwynfryn in an isolated lonely valley. There the most famous painting of a Welsh scene of the early twentieth century is set. It is of a lady in a Welsh costume settling into her pew in that delightful little eighteenth-century chapel. A watercolor of this scene was painted by Vosper in 1908, and copies were given away with bars of Sunlight soap wrappings. Thousands were obtained, and it hangs still in many Welsh homes. One original is on permanent display near Liverpool in a gallery in Port Sunlight, not far from Liverpool, while the other is in Aberystwyth at the National Library of Wales, bought for £60,000 in 2019.

The road there is single track, and every hundred yards is a little lay-by allowing cars approaching you to pass. This had happened a couple of times, then we drew into a lay-by again to allow a limo to pass us. It did so, inexpertly scraping the side of my father-in-law's car. The driver stopped and got out, and I got out, and immediately recognized the driver. "Dr. Packer!" I said to him, feeling like Stanley discovering Livingstone in the heart of Africa.

1. Charles Wesley, "Lo! He Comes with Clouds Descending," 1758.

"Do I know you?" he asked.

"I heard you speak at the CU in Cardiff University a few years ago. I am presently a student at Westminster Seminary."

"Good to meet you, brother. Sorry about scraping your car. I passed my driving test just six weeks ago."

"Oh, that's perfectly all right, Dr. Packer," I said, and we smiled and shook hands, and Iola and I went on to Salem. I wondered whether I would ever have the opportunity of introducing him in a meeting and could relate how we had first bumped into one another. Mercifully, that never happened. It might have put him off what he had to say, though he was so quick-witted, he would have found some retort that would have had us all in stitches—and me, the embarrassed one. Strangely enough, we are both the only children of railway clerks.

We got back to Iola's home that afternoon and with some gentle abrasive removed Packer's light gray paint from the side of my father-in-law's car so it was as good as new. Packer preached for me once in the early 1970s. I asked him to preach a well-known sermon of his on the archer that shot an arrow "at venture" that had killed Ahab as he stood in his chariot, piercing the joint where two pieces of armor met. It is a fine message.

Elwyn Davies

The leader of the Inter-Varsity Fellowship in Wales was Elwyn Davies, whom I soon met in Cardiff in 1958. I was twenty, and he was thirteen years older. He wore a double-breasted overcoat with a belt. He looked warm and old-fashioned, but in those black-and-white photos of everybody at that time, we all look positively Dickensian, students in their sports coats and ties with Crusader badges in their lapels, untrendy. Each term he visited Cardiff University and filled his diary with appointments to hear and counsel mainly male students (while Mary Clee of Swansea talked to the women). He was a wonderful listener and the best chairman of discussions. He was also to write a reference for me as part of my application to Westminster Seminary, Philadelphia, three years later, and was the single greatest influence in my life as a student. Many of my contemporaries in the universities of Wales would say the same. As a student in Bangor in 1947, he was converted, and the change in life was such that within weeks the girl he later married was converted. He spoke at the preterminal conferences of the Christian unions, and they did much good creating a standard of spirituality for the next semesters. He drew out from students their spiritual needs and beliefs. He certainly ministered to them.

Elwyn Davies had become a preacher in Blaenau Ffestiniog in 1950, and under his ministry there, the parents of Iola (who would become my wife in 1964) came to trust in the finished work of Christ, as well as Iola and her sister Rhiain. Elwyn preached on 1 Corinthians 13 at our wedding, and we shared a room together in the home of Hannah Griffiths the night before the wedding day. He was reading Hendriksen's commentary on the gospel of John in bed. I don't think I read anything.

I owed much to the Cardiff Christian Union. We had monthly evangelistic meetings, from the first freshers' welcome "squash" right through to the final term. A preacher whom I much admired was John Thomas, the late minister in the Sandfields church in Port Talbot. I asked him to come and take three meetings for us, Monday, Tuesday, and Wednesday at 5 p.m.:

1. The Deity of Christ: Can You Believe It?
2. The Death of Christ: Can You Plead It?
3. The Discipleship of Christ: Can You Receive It?

He told me on that Tuesday that he had grieved over the inadequate presentation he had made on Monday of the first address. I guess he thought it was too cerebral and academic. The next two were nothing like that. He was a sweetly humble and sensitive man, and yet what a speaker in the open air. He had preached in every street in Port Talbot. Then he told me that on the previous Sunday morning, he had struggled with his preaching, feeling that he had let down the congregation. Then an old lady had shaken his hand as she was leaving the church and said to him, "Thank you, Mr. Thomas.

You are a born preacher." Those words had meant so much to him. I was quite surprised that a cliché like "you are a born preacher" was being treasured by such a prince of preachers, but once I had been a pastor for a few years, I understood exactly his response.

We had a retreat for a few days at the end of the Christmas vacation of my first year at Cardiff, and about thirty-five of us went to a conference center on the Gower Peninsula. The inspirational speaker was Elwyn Davies. We sat in a big circle while he explained to us the doctrine of justification by faith in three messages. I had been justified by the grace of God, through the work of Jesus Christ, since I had put my faith in Him over four years before this meeting. But I did not understand what that meant. The plain teaching of the Bible was a mystery to me, and the preachers in the Baptist churches were not explaining it to their congregations. That weekend I saw something revolutionary.

Elwyn's text was "Christ Jesus, who became for us wisdom from God—and righteousness and sanctification and redemption" (1 Cor. 1:30), especially opening up the fact of God making Jesus Christ *our righteousness* so that the righteousness of every Christian is in heaven at the right hand of God, and that God imputes that spotless righteousness of the God-man to everyone who repents and believes. Elwyn explained the imputation of our sin to Christ via the well-known, simple-but-effective illustration, with the help of a black pocket Bible. He said, putting the book on his open hand, "Imagine that this book is your sin, all the sins of omission and commission, of emotion, thought, word, and deed. God has taken all that guilt, and He has laid it on the Lamb of God, who has taken it away. That is what He is doing in Calvary." And he removed the black book from one hand and put it on the other—all our trespasses laid on the sinless Christ. So I was assured of being delivered from the guilt and dominion of sin.

Ah, but there is more! God has constituted a righteousness that is a human righteousness found in the righteous life, heart, soul, body, and spirit of the man Christ Jesus, the true and proper man, the last Adam who lived east of Eden, not in paradise but here in our groaning world, tempted as we are in every way yet without sin. But this righteousness was also the righteousness of the eternal Son of God, a righteousness as holy as God Himself, as filled with love as the Father is full of love, infinite, eternal, unchangeable righteousness. Here is a measureless righteousness that can cover the whole cosmos, every atom, every raindrop. The whole new heavens and earth will be characterized by that righteousness, and it is certainly sufficient to be imputed to every single sinner who believes in the Savior alone for salvation. It is a dynamic righteousness, coming to all and upon all who believe.

So, the Son of God became the Lamb of God without spot and yet made in the likeness of sinful flesh, and He took away the sin of the world because the guilt and condemnation of our sin has been imputed to Him. But, also, the righteousness of the man Christ Jesus is imputed by God to us as we are joined to Him by faith—even if that faith is as thin as a spider's thread. We are then justified—that is, declared righteous in Him. Coming from God to us and in our world, the Lord Jesus is made our righteousness as we entrust ourselves to Him. Being justified by faith, we have peace with God through our Lord Jesus Christ.

Justification through faith in Christ was never more clearly and powerfully presented to me, and I embraced it with joy. That is what I ascertained from Elwyn that weekend near Swansea, on the Gower Peninsula, learning what Luther had had to learn five hundred years ago, a truth that had been misunderstood and never taught by the Roman Church so that many immense errors had crept in to compensate for its absence.

A year later Elwyn, in the same venue, to a larger group of students, taught us a more challenging subject concerning our chief end in life, that because from Christ and through Christ and to Christ was to be everything we had and did, then our purpose in life was to glorify and enjoy God in all we were, forever and ever. It was a magnificent picture of the life of the mere disciple of the Lord Jesus, whether they were a housewife and mother or a father and husband or a schoolboy, a garbage or refuse collector, someone locked away in prison, an OAP [old age pensioner]—whoever it might be—earthed in all the mundane duties of daily living, facing the tasks of every hour, but as a follower of the Lamb doing whatever his hand touched for God's glory. So drudgery can become divine. Those times hearing Elwyn Davies were golden hours.

Discovering more of the fullness of the status and deliverance and hope that God had accomplished for us was from that moment the ongoing experience of the rest of my life. There were continuing new discoveries of what God had done for me through Christ. I had been blessed with every spiritual blessing in Christ, and as the years went by, I learned what these blessings were. I was complete in Christ, and I understood more of what my completeness consisted. Books I bought, such as John Murray's *Redemption Accomplished and Applied*, indeed helped me. But the speakers in the student meetings were foundational. For example, I heard another beloved preacher, Gareth Davies, expounding the blessing of the sonship of the Christian through the adopting grace of Christ. I had received Christ back in 1954, and so I had been given the right to be called the son of God, but it was years later that I realized the privileges of my new sonship: access at any time to a heavenly Father; His provision of all my needs from the one who urged me to ask for my daily bread; a Father's protection of His beloved child—"A Sovereign Protector I have, unseen yet for ever at hand"; obtaining an inheritance as a son and heir of God, a joint heir with His eternal Son, Jesus Christ. Thus, my indebtedness to these student-organized meetings was great. I had learned far more than many of my fellow first-year students when we arrived together at Westminster Seminary in 1961. I had been exposed to excellent experiential preaching the past three years in Wales, which was a ministry in short supply in Philadelphia, a city whose population was the same size as the Principality of Wales.

I was so glad of the friends I made in those IVF circles: Neville Rees, Tony Horne, Eryl Davies, Pete Morgan, Peter Jones (who married Ed Clowney's daughter), Owen Milton, Hywel Jones, Keith Lewis, Andrew Davies, Phil Williams, Geraint Fielder, David Brooks,

Cecil Jenkins, Sulwyn Jones, Pam Judson, Iola Williams, and Shirley Williams. What helpful Christians they were.

During the biblical studies course, we were occasionally given essays to read by our lecturers. One day we were told to go to some bound copies of the *Expository Times* in the college library and read a certain article. I found the journal and then the issue in which the article was found, but on that page was an advertisement for WTS Philadelphia with the address. I was in the way of knowing God better and serving Him, and so He led me. That was the overall direction of my life, however much I limped and fell. God was tenderly leading me. I wrote to the seminary, and within a week I had an encouraging letter from the registrar, Paul Woolley, the professor of church history. We corresponded, and they were generous and encouraging. I was going to the USA to Westminster.

Or was I?

My Fall

Writing one's autobiography can be a dangerously ego-reinforcing exercise. My secret falls are between me and God. Many times I wonder about the people I have hurt, how they are doing now, and have deep regrets all over again. But there are other costly falls of mine that are already known, and I cannot pass over them. I am a Christian not because I am a good person but because I have a good God who is merciful and forgiving and works all things—even my falls—together for my good.

In May 1961 came the weeks of the finals, the ultimate degree examinations, nine in all, each one three hours in length. Each of the first four exams consisted of five essays you could choose out of ten possible choices of subjects. The first exam was on Old Testament history, the next was New Testament history, then Old Testament literature, and finally New Testament literature. You can bluff your way through essays, but the next five three-hour papers were all language papers, Hebrew and Greek, translating and commenting on the passages.

The first morning of the translation section, I gazed at the six Hebrew passages before me and panicked. I had little idea what they were writing about, even from which of the books of the Old Testament we had studied. Blind panic. I looked across at a fellow student, and I could see what he had written, and I copied down a sentence or two of his. I cheated. Then I pulled myself together and got on thinking and translating the rest of the exam as best I could and did the same the next day in Hebrew and the next two days in Greek and then the unpointed Hebrew exam. I completed the exams and was awarded a BA 2(ii) class degree.

But I had cheated, and that thought would not go away. Coals of fire were burning, and eventually on my own, not having discussed it with anyone, I wrote to the professor and confessed to him exactly what I had done. He wrote back and informed me that he had to inform the university. I was then requested to meet with some of the staff, and two senior men interrogated me, not unkindly. I was pretty low. Had I done this sort of thing before? They asked. Yes, once, and I had told the professor that I had. Why for such a trivial slip, a sentence or two, had I written to acknowledge my misdeed? I told them I had done what I had done because I am going to be a preacher, a herald for God, and I am going to ask people to make a costly change in their lives, confess their sins to God, and repent. How can I ask people to do something I was not prepared to do myself?

My graduation from Cardiff University in 1963

The huge issue before me was the possibility of sailing to the United States and studying at Westminster Seminary for the next three years. They required some official notification from the university that I had completed my course. Going to Philadelphia was the longing of my life, but I could not go there while the fact of having cheated was on my conscience and unresolved. God made me prepared to give up America, John Murray, E. J. Young, Stonehouse, Van Til, Clowney, Kline, and then to look around Wales for a job and face whatever the unknown future might hold. It was a life-changing option. William Cowper wrote the hymn "O for a closer walk with God," and in one stanza he prays,

> The dearest idol I have known,
> Whate'er that idol be,
> Help me to tear it from thy throne
> And worship only thee.

That was my prayer then. I explained the American request to those two lecturers whom I had put in such a difficult situation, and I left the matter with them and with God. Richard Baxter says in "Ye Holy Angels Bright": "Take what God gives, and praise Him still,/ Through good or ill, whoever lives." It was the very greatest test of my life, but it was not the first and not the last fall to be experienced when I became compromised by my own folly. It was such a test that other Christians, maybe all of us, have also had to face at one hour in our lives, and God was merciful, and with this test made a way of escape that I was able to bear it.

The decision the university came to was to inform Westminster that I had completed the three years at the university and then to advise me that I had to re-sit the whole nine exams again in the next year or two. It was a balanced response. So, two years later, in the summer of 1963, I sat my second-year divinity exams in Philadelphia, and then flew home and the following week or two went through the nine papers for my BA. Some of the courses were the same, while others of the books I had to translate from Hebrew and Greek and exegete were all totally new to me, without any assistance being given me from my lecturers. But I wrote something in those exams, without any cheating, and that is how I got a third-class honors BA degree. I have never heard anyone asking any graduate what class of a degree he or she got. Nowadays there certainly seems to be an abundance of first-class honors. Good for them!

Ed Clowney, the president of Westminster Seminary once said, “Sometimes Christians speak of each decision of their lives as though they were launching a moon-shot where a single miscalculation would send the capsule into a trackless void. Even space scientists do better than that, correcting the flight of the space-probes by radioed signals. God does much better. He knows that we are often incapable of distinguishing trivial decisions from momentous ones, and that we are foolish and imperceptive. He knows—and keeps us in His hand.”

During my long ministry in Wales and my commitment to confessional Christianity and church reformation, it was often said of me by my opponents, “He went to America.” The suggestion was being made that if I had stayed in Wales and gone to a theological college there, then I would not have been the “ultra-nonconformist and seceder” that I was portrayed as becoming. The facts are different. I had grasped the historical Christian faith before I left Wales. I was prepared to sacrifice a great deal for it. I returned from the United States in 1964 as I had gone there thirty-three months earlier, my basic convictions about Christianity I had learned in Wales still intact. I had heard liberal religion taught at a Welsh university for three years and had debated it with other students. Westminster Theological Seminary provided me with an all-around grasp of the Christian faith, for which I will always be grateful. The study of the Bible in America did not begin with German theologians at the end of the nineteenth century—as one would have gathered from lectures at a Welsh university. The issue of what I believed was not one of geography and an alien culture. The issue facing Wales and the world is one of truth. Is the system of faith as outlined in the great historic confessions of faith a faithful expression of true Christianity? Is modernism another religion? Should a Christian sacrifice everything, even his life, for the truth?

CHAPTER 6

Seminary Days, Philadelphia (1961–1964)

I had to take a boat to America because I had so much stuff to take with me. I was an utterly naïve Welsh boy, an only child who had lived at home for almost twenty-three years, and I was about to cross the Atlantic for the first time. Can you believe I took thirty or forty of my books with me, as though they would not be available in America, and three years later I brought them all back, with many others, inside strong US Mail sacks?

Cargo Boat to Norfolk, Virginia

I found the cheapest way to travel to America was by cargo boat. I bought a single fare trip for £60 sailing from Liverpool docks on a German boat called the *Carl Fritzen*. My parents came with me from Barry on the train and then the bus from the Liverpool station to the docks. We found the ship and took my trunk aboard. It was an old metal trunk, faded brown in color. My father wanted to spruce it up, and so he painted it black, but the temperature when we landed in America was so hot the paint was melting, and those who transported it were not happy. I walked with my parents back to the bus and waved goodbye. They were both in tears, but all I had was a massive sense of relief, freedom, and anticipation.

Three other passengers were on the cargo boat—a Buddhist from the Philippines and a Seventh-day Adventist missionary's wife and her private-school-educated son who was not religious at all. We ate three times a day with the captain and the chief engineer at their table—fine men, fluent English speakers. We had a lot of soup and sausages on the ten-day journey. In the middle of the Atlantic, this empty cargo boat hit a big storm. The crew told me to wedge my lifejacket under the side of the mattress of my bunk so that I was lying in a V-shaped wedge against the bunk's wall; consequently, as the *Carl Fritzen* tossed and rolled, I was not thrown out of bed. I am contented enough at sea. I have never gotten seasick on my rare voyages to Ireland, the continent, or the Channel Islands.

The boat's owners sent a radio message to the captain to tell him to sail to Newport, Virginia, in Chesapeake Bay; so it was there on Labor Day, Monday, September 4, that I first saw America. From an old-fashioned valve radio in the dining room, before there was any sight of land, I could pick up American broadcasting with its advertisements and music and disc jockeys, which was quite new in the United Kingdom in 1961. Then we sailed up Chesapeake Bay, and for hours I leaned on the ship's rail and gazed out on the shore at the barbecues taking place in the homes on the water's edge and the water skiing and the speedboats. I had to pinch myself that this was not a dream or a movie. I was actually in America. We picked up the pilot who told me he was a Baptist.

"A Southern Baptist?" I asked him. He shrugged.

"I guess so," he replied.

In the late 1950s there had been an American Embassy in Queen Street, Cardiff, above the "gentleman's outfitter" Austin Reed, and all my documents were dealt with by them. They required me to get a chest X-ray and take it to the United States with me. I handed that over to the immigration officials in Newport. They were easygoing men, and soon I waved goodbye to my fellow passengers and I was in. When John Murray arrived in the 1920s on Ellis Island, New York, to start his studies at Princeton, he was refused entry lacking the right documents. He had to stay for hours on the island until someone from the seminary traveled there and delivered him.

New York

I got a taxi and took the sticky black trunk to an agency to ship it to Philadelphia, where it safely arrived. (It is probably still in the basement of Machen Hall with the mice.) And then the taxi took me to the Greyhound bus station, where I boarded a bus to New York. We left that evening and arrived in New York at six o'clock on Tuesday morning. I walked around the quiet city and asked my way to Grand Central Station. The city was the cleanest I have ever seen it, and the station itself was and remains enormously impressive.

I had actually met two Americans on that beach mission in Greystones, Ireland, three years earlier, when I first heard of Dr. Martyn Lloyd-Jones. They were Eddie Meyer III and his wife, Linda. I knew no others. I had written to them infrequently over the years, and then I wrote to them asking if I could stay with them a week before the beginning of my first semester at the seminary. Americans take the duty and privilege of hospitality seriously, while I alas tended to take what I received for granted. Eddie was a lawyer in New York, a Yale graduate, the leader of the InterVarsity group there, influenced by a mission John Stott had taken to that Ivy League school in the late 1950s. The Meyers lived in Hastings-on-Hudson not far south of Nyack, or West Point. So, I bought a ticket and boarded a commuter train with a very smart conductor who had a de Gaulle hat and a starched white short-sleeved shirt. He knew most of the passengers, and the funniest repartee transpired as he checked all our tickets. I called the Meyers from the station, and they came and picked me up and were delightful hosts for the next eight days.

They introduced me to their circle. One friend was selling his home on the next street. He was moving just five minutes away, and that was important to him as he wanted to sell his home to a black American couple and did not want to run away from the consequences of such a sale. He stood by that decision as a moral choice. He knew that other people on the street would be upset with him for doing this, thinking it would depreciate the values of their homes, and of course, a number of them did not want to live in the same street as "people of color." I much approved of his action, wondering what neighbors would think back in Barry, Wales, if a West Indian family moved in next door to them. The race issue was very big in America in the 1960s, just as it is today, and this was my introduction to it.

The next week I took the train down to New York City most days and explored. I did the touristy things—I went to the top of the Empire State Building and took the lift to the top story of the Guggenheim Museum and walked down the circular ramp, round and round, inspecting the modern paintings. One night we went to Broadway and watched a Gilbert and Sullivan production of the *Pirates of Penzance*. But the climax of those days in New York was an evening at Yankee Stadium. The Yankees were at the height of their fame. What a team that night, including Yogi Berra, Mickey Mantle, and Roger Maris. I witnessed Maris hit home run number fifty-two on his way to breaking Babe Ruth's record, and Mantle also hit a homer in that game. On my way into the stadium, someone gave me a copy of Mark's gospel with a photograph of that superb defensive shortstop and second baseman, Bobby Richardson Jr., stapled to the front, with his testimony on the back of the photograph. He would organize church services for the Yankees when they were traveling. Mickey Mantle described him as a "clean-living, practicing Christian," and he officiated at Mantle's funeral. In 1970 President Nixon invited him to preach at the White House. In the 1980s he was the baseball coach at Liberty University in Lynchburg, Virginia.

Westminster Theological Seminary

After those fun days I was itching to get to Westminster Seminary. I caught a train to Philadelphia, an hour or so away, and then another train from center-city Philly to Glenside where the seminary was located. The journey there through the terraced streets of the city as the decades have gone by increasingly reveals something like a journey through a war zone, with acres of derelict and abandoned buildings. On one journey a large rock punched a hole in a carriage window a few yards from where I was sitting. Glenside was at least sixteen miles out of the city, a pleasant little town, unlike the views from the train, with open-air market stalls exhibiting beautiful pumpkins for sale.

I finally walked up the seminary drive. I had arrived. A few students greeted me, and we stood on the wide veranda and talked about music with A. Donald Macleod and Ben Short. I remember that they told me of a composer called Mahler. It was like hearing students talking together of a preacher called Lloyd-Jones, making me think, "I must look into this."

Today, this is how the seminary briefly charts its origins and tells its own story, and I believe that it is truthful and accurate in all its claims:

> The great theologians of Princeton Seminary championed Reformed Christian scholarship during the early 20th century. Internationally renowned, the faculty included the insightful biblical interpreter Geerhardus Vos, the steadfast defender of biblical inerrancy B.B. Warfield, and the esteemed New Testament scholar J. Gresham Machen.
>
> In the 1920s, the mainline Presbyterian church struggled with liberalism. J. Gresham Machen set the terms of the debate with his book *Christianity and Liberalism*. He argued that liberalism teaches not a lesser form of Christianity, but an entirely different religion.
>
> Princeton compromised by reorganizing its board to include members tolerant of liberalism. Princeton's new leadership slowly transformed the seminary from an institution that trained biblically faithful ministers to a mirror that reflected the shifting trends in the mainline Presbyterian church.
>
> Machen left the prestige of Princeton to stand for the truth of the Bible. He knew that theological compromise would harm the spiritual power of the church. His fight for Christianity cost him a great deal. Not only did Machen lose his position at Princeton, but his church also declared him guilty of insubordination and stripped him of his credentials as a minister.
>
> In 1929, Machen founded a new school, Westminster, with senior faculty members from Princeton and bright young scholars to carry on Princeton's noble tradition. Machen's

> prized faculty (John Murray and Cornelius Van Til, among others) shared his sacrificial heart and vision for robust theological education. They followed Machen to Westminster in order to build a new stronghold for Reformed theology and train the next era of passionate Christian pastors and theologians.
>
> Machen's faculty and their successors equipped generations of incisive scholars and bold preachers throughout the 20th century. Their scholarship and commitment to the Word of God established Westminster as one of the most highly regarded Reformed institutions in the world.[1]

I regret that there was no course at Westminster on Machen himself and his theology. Most of the faculty at that time had been taught by him and adored him; however, there were no talks on Machen. I had to purchase all the biographies on him I could get. In recent years I have acquired a volume that tells of his time working as a Red Cross worker in the First World War on the front with the fruit of carnage all around. The book contains the letters he wrote home most weeks to his mother describing what he was experiencing. It must have been far worse than what he told Mother.

Westminster Seminary was built around a little mansion that was named after Machen when he died in 1937, Machen Hall. Classrooms, a library, and a football field were nearby. It was small—not impressive at all—and modest but loved. The grounds had some wonderful trees. That October, an early snow fell that lasted a day or so, and it brought down the large, crimson blossom petals of an exotic tree. They lay on the snow like great drops of blood.

John Murray had lived for years on the top floor of Machen Hall, but the increase of students in 1961 meant that he had given up his rooms. He moved into lodgings in Glenside, and as a result five students could live in those two rooms. I was one of the five, and I slept on his mattress in his former bed for a time; his hip bone was not in

1. "The Heroic Stand of Our Founder," Westminster Theological Seminary, accessed February 20, 2021, https://www.wts.edu/history.

Machen Hall, Westminster Seminary. In the room through those french windows, I ate in the dining club with my fellow students for three years.

the same position as mine. It is demanding enough for two students to live together; it is impossible for three to share one bedroom, such also being the study room and the place to listen to music, while all the time remaining in harmony. We did not. Fortunately, it was just for one year.

About thirty-five of us students had three meals a day in the dining club beneath a fine oil painting of J. Gresham Machen. A number of Korean students attended the seminary and ate at one table at the French windows overlooking the walled garden. Students took turns reading and praying at the end of the evening meal, then we closed in unaccompanied song. While Mr. Murray was there, it was metrical psalms exclusively that were sung, but in October the first edition of the *Trinity Hymnal* appeared, and the dining club was given forty copies. I learned many fine new hymns and tunes.

The students were such a cross-section of Christians. Almost all were academically excellent, a few like John Frame exceedingly so. He would have gained a first in any university in Great Britain.

The Faculty at Westminster Seminary in the early thirties.
Four of these men taught me.

The student body at Westminster Theological Seminary September 1961.

(We two were bachelor buddies together on campus for three years.) Others struggled with the academic demands of the course. Not a few I privately judged rightly (though sometimes wrongly) to have no call to become preachers of the gospel.

The opening exercises took place for the new seminary year in mid-September 1961. The devotions were taken by a Reformed church pastor from a town nearby in New Jersey. It was my introduction to Dr. John Richard de Witt. We were later to become assistant editors of the *Banner of Truth* magazine. I looked with interest at the elderly faculty whom I would get to know well and admire much. I searched in vain for R. B. Kuiper, but he had been professor of practical theology there from 1933 to 1952—I had missed him by nine years. I was sorry never to have had him teaching me with his vast pastoral experience, remembrances, anecdotes, illustrations, and his popular ability to present the Reformed faith. He was an earlier Dutch version of R. C. Sproul. One could never claim that there was an abundance of that sort of personality among the Westminster Seminary faculty members. He would have been good fun to have had as a teacher. Once at a graduation he turned to his friend Cornelius Van Til and asked him a question. "Why do you suppose, Kees, that I never write out my name in full, not even on the graduation certificates of the seminary? Did A. Z. Conrad [author and pastor of Park Street, Boston] ever write out his name in full? 'Arcturus Zodiac Conrad'? My name would sound as bad as that: 'Rienck Bouke Kuiper.' And why do you suppose, Kees, that my parents gave me such a peculiar name? Well, I'll tell you. I was named after an aunt of mine. I was supposed to inherit her money but never did. And here I was stuck with this name all my life."

Then, to the faculty of the seminary in 1961 we must turn.

John Skilton

First-year lectures started at 8:20 every morning, usually with New Testament Greek using Machen's own book for Greek learners, which remains a superb guide to Greek. It was still being used in Princeton in 1961. I was in the central stream of learners as one of those who had done some years of Greek already. I think it was only John Frame whose Greek was sufficiently accomplished that he did not need any classes. The issue Westminster Seminary raised for us was concerning accented Greek. Every word in New Testament Greek has an accent, but teaching this and asking students to memorize these accents is ignored in every seminary and university in the United Kingdom and in America wherever *koine* Greek is taught—except at Westminster! So I, who had had three years of Greek, had to learn it again, this time with the accents.

It was no chore, however, for our teacher was Dr. John Skilton, one of the godliest and happiest men I've ever known. He was simply wonderful in his ability to teach men Greek. Skilton taught as he had been taught by Machen himself. The grammar book set exercises of translation at the end of each lesson. We went to the Greek classroom upstairs in Machen Hall, a room with blackboards (that were dark green) on three of the four walls, and each of us got up choosing his own board. We were then assigned by Dr. Skilton a different one of the exercises we had completed the previous evening and wrote out our Greek sentence on the board. After we returned to our seats, board by board was examined and judged by one another, pointing out the mistakes we spotted in accents and in spelling, if there were any. The lesson then continued; the next step in developing our grasp of the Greek language was taught, and the next set of exercises was allocated to us. The bachelor John Skilton left a fragrant memory behind him. I remember his preaching once in Calvary Orthodox Presbyterian Church (OPC) Glenside on the need of a spirit of thanksgiving, that great mercies earnestly and importunately sought, and then received, call for a proportionate appreciation being rendered to God. The praise we return for answered prayer should always be at least commensurate with the earnestness of our intercession. Doxology should comprehensively reflect the glimpses we have received of the Lord's goodness.

John Murray

One September lunchtime at the dining club, an older man with one eye joined us at our table. I thought he was the janitor, but someone whispered to me that it was John Murray. I was a little disappointed, expecting that the author of *Redemption Accomplished and Applied* would appear as majestic as his prose and his concept of God. I had imagined him to look something like Charlton Heston. I was so worldly in my thinking, wasn't I? This attitude was a common failing of young seminarians. We were but novices. We did not realize we had been sold images of greatness by the media nor how much that was influencing us. The apostle Paul was described by his opponents like this: "'His letters,' they say, 'are weighty and powerful, but his bodily presence is weak, and his speech contemptible'" (2 Cor. 10:10). I was judging a man of God as basely as the opponents of Paul had judged him.

My roommate Tommy Carlson went for a few days to Virginia and visited Union Theological Seminary, where he was interested most of all in sitting in on a lecture of the fifty-four-year-old John Bright, the Cyrus H. McCormick Professor of Hebrew and Old Testament Interpretation. In 1959 his *History of Israel* had been published and was mightily impressive and readable to me in my undergraduate biblical studies course—compared to all the earlier dry academic histories. Bright's history was not definitive for evangelicals but a considerable step forward.

So, Tommy had spent a day looking around Union and had heard Bright lecture. I was envious. "How was he?" I asked him.

"Terrific—like a film star," he replied, and then trying to communicate with me at my level he added, "Like Meredith Kline!" You could never make a comparison with language like that concerning John Murray. It would be demeaning to hint at it. But if you attended any of Mr. Murray's lectures, you would, I hope, say, "Terrific!"

To prove my point, let me give you a sample taken from my treasured notetaking of his lectures, the memento of blessed hours in his classes. These are my notes on one part of John Murray's lecture on man's inability to do the will of God:

> 1. It is often objected that this assessment of human nature is incompatible with the obligations that revolve upon men to repent and believe. "So," they plead, "there must be at least some modicum of ability which will at least provide for them a true interest in the grace of God." In answer to that objection, we say that the laws of God are a transcript of His own perfection, and so there cannot be any adaptation or adjustment of demand to our sinful condition. Any such supposition would impinge upon our view of God's immutability.
>
> Again, if the demands of God presuppose that ability, they must presuppose *total* ability. What purpose would be served in a vestige of ability if the demand is for total conformity to God's image. Obligation is total; a vestige of ability is psychological nonsense. Pelagius was magnificently consistent: "Obligation presupposes ability and so complete ability."
>
> 2. It is frequently objected that it is incompatible with the demand for the use of the means of grace. "Why preach the gospel if man is unable by nature to respond?" The fact is that it is necessary that men who are dead in trespasses and sins be told of their condition and be confronted with the demands of their God and their own helplessness in the face of these demands. Conviction in us should correspond with this reality. It is through the proclamation of the Word of God that this conviction of human helplessness be brought to bear upon men. If men are sealed off from encounters with the demands of God's law and His gospel, then they are sealed from the very

> means by which their convictions can be brought into accord with the truth.
>
> The means of grace are, after all, the channels of grace—that is, the channels through which the gospel comes into our helplessness and becomes operative to our salvation. If men are to be excluded from hearing the only means whereby they learn that there is a remedy for their helplessness, then that cannot possibly serve the ends of the gospel. The means of grace are the means whereby God relieves the helplessness of men and women.
>
> Some may dismiss this truth saying, "This doctrine is a counsel for despair and therefore inimical to the interests of evangelism," but the basic consideration is this: Is this doctrine true? Are men dead in trespasses and sins? How could it be against the interest of evangelism if the truth of their own helplessness is hidden from them? The only gospel that exists is the good news that assumes and addresses man's total helplessness. It is therefore that truth that lays the basis for the proclamation of the gospel of grace. Nothing is more inimical to the interests of evangelism than some vestige of hope or trust in one's own resources. Sinners can be told that there is a point when the sovereign life-giving grace of God is dispensed. That is a day of power, and then men are made willing.
>
> Finally, experience will demonstrate that feeling one's own utter helplessness is the very condition of appreciating the gospel of grace. It is when men are convinced of their total inability that they despair of themselves. When they despair of themselves, they are prepared to appreciate the promises of God's grace. Then "the lame man leaps as a hart, and the tongue of the dumb sings." Men and women are failing to face up to the gravity and reality of their ruin, and that is the reason they raise these objections to the scriptural analysis of their lostness.

When spending time with him, you were entranced to have had his real interest, and yet you were so careful in what you said to him. After lunch at dining club, he would go for a walk along the road that went around Machen Hall. Students would call it the "Murray Mile," though it was not a quarter of a mile. You could walk with him. He would often put his arm through yours and ask about your parents and family. He was most affectionate and could be more like your brother than your professor. I once bumped into him on a Monday morning in one of the seminary corridors. "How are you, Mr. Thomas? How are your parents? You are a Welshman, aren't you? We learned a new tune to one of the psalms yesterday. It was lovely. It went like this..." And in his quavering voice, he sang it to me. I never sang a new tune to a fellow student. I might sing one later to my wife and daughters; they were family.

John Murray was a loving man, yet he was holy, and so you were careful. I remember when he had retired and I visited him in the home in which he was born, Badbea in Sutherland, and asked him if he was coveting anything back in Philadelphia. As soon as I had clumsily asked him in those words that question, I felt guilty because was I not asking him if he were sinning? But he answered easily, "I *would* covet the library and its books."

He could ask you a question and put you on the spot. He asked me why I thought Jesus had told Mary not to touch Him but had asked Thomas to handle Him and realize that He was not a ghost. I think the answer lies in the relation that Mary had with our Lord, that there were elements in it of a tactile affection, that He was perceptible to be loved and touched. That was not the relationship that henceforth she would have with Him, though it would be far more real and loving. It was not going to be accompanied by a touch, whereas Thomas was confused as to the nature of the appearances of Christ that he had heard of, that his fellow apostles had been confused in their low emotional state and had merely seen a ghostlike apparition and not a physical resurrection. Our Lord pastorally deals with Him in a different way from dealing with Mary and thus assures Thomas that He had been bodily raised from the dead.

John Murray was a member of Knox Orthodox Presbyterian Church, a little congregation that met above a fire station. After the morning service there was Sunday school, and he taught a class of half a dozen adults, taking them through Romans. What a humble man he was! If you were unwise enough after that Bible study to ask him if he had marked your semester papers, then he would quietly say that he did not speak of such things on the Lord's Day.

No questions were asked during his lectures. He had, say, twenty-two lectures in the semester course. He needed each one to get through it all. But he never hurried off after his lectures were over. He would be there to entertain your queries. I once asked him what the teaching of the Bible was concerning every Christian being ready to testify to his faith in Christ. He thanked me for the question, telling me that he enjoyed getting questions like that and would answer the question in a few days. Later in the week after a lecture, he gave me a piece of paper on which was written in his black fountain-pen ink ten verses. He had taken that trouble to answer my very "studentish" question. If you asked him for his interpretation of a verse in a Bible, he would ask whether you had been given a test in the interpretation of that verse or whether you had been given the task of preaching a sermon on that verse. He was not prepared to do your work for you.

One black-and-white TV sat in a small room at the seminary, and we crowded in to see Major Glenn sent into space from Cape Canaveral on May 20, 1962, and again on November 23, 1963, when John Kennedy was assassinated. Students did not watch many other programs, though one or two enjoyed *The Dick Van Dyke Show* with its innocent humor. Four students were in the room one night when Professor Murray came in, stood and watched for a minute, and then said, "Sometimes you feel like putting your fist through the screen!"

John Murray traveled from the most northern county in Scotland, Sutherland, to Aberystwyth, over four hundred miles, on two occasions to preach for me. We had such a delightful weekend with him. We had just had our second daughter, and he had had his first son. I was away preaching early Saturday evening, and so there was a lot of baby talk between him and my wife, Iola. She spoke to him about a baby's hand and how it would grip your finger. "It's a miracle, isn't it?" she commented. Cautiously he said to her, "Yes—but not in the technical sense of the word." She made him a meal of cauliflower cheese, and in the sauce she had cooked little pieces of bacon.

He loved it. "Do you often have this?" he asked, and refused bread and butter as he just wanted to enjoy the cauliflower. From that time onward we always referred to that meal as John Murray's favorite.

Mr. Murray and I went for a little walk around Aberystwyth, and we passed the ironmonger shop where some shepherds' crooks were displayed in a stand on the pavement. He took one up and gestured with it to me how one caught and captured a sheep. Further on in that walk, a small boy came toward us on the sidewalk dribbling a large soccer ball [UK: football]. As he sought to pass by us, the professor stuck his foot out and tapped the ball away from him and dribbled with it down the pavement, finally stopping, looking back at the dumbstruck boy, giving a big smile, and then kicked the ball back to him. "I loved to play soccer as a boy," he told me breathlessly.

One year I thought of sending him a New Year's gift as he did not make anything special of Christmas. So I went to the tobacco shop in Aberystwyth and bought the best Cuban cigar for him. The one-time long-term bachelor at Westminster enjoyed an occasional cigar. It was enclosed in an aluminum tube, and I posted it to the home in which he had been born: Badbea in Bonar Bridge, in which home he later died. I heard nothing from him for a month, and then I received a letter with his characteristic black fountain-pen handwriting. It was quite curt, a brief thanks and then an explanation that if I sent him another cigar would I please write the fact on the envelope. The Independent Republican Army in Ulster were sending bombs through the post, and consequently, the post office was suspicious of the cigar I had sent him. The bomb disposal crew was called from the army to examine this package, and it had been weeks before Mr. Murray received it.

John Murray's lectures were unmissable. He began with quiet prayer, bowing before God and asking for His blessing on the hour before us, and then his lectures were given with passion and zeal. I would mutter occasionally an *amen* to what he said. In my first year I had no lectures at all from John Murray. The seminary was looking for his successor and had asked Ed Palmer to teach, and so he helpfully taught us first-year students on the doctrine of Scripture. John

Murray never taught a course on infant baptism. He had written a book on it, and we were tested in a one-hour exam on the contents of the book. The next year John Murray resumed teaching that course, and so I audited it and still have and still consult my notes on those lectures on the doctrine of revelation and the attributes of God. But I was the only student to do so. Think of it! I did this with all the courses he taught, which were mere options. That is why I had crossed the Atlantic. I took them for my own personal help, such as courses on covenant theology, the Westminster Confession of Faith, Romans chapters 13 and 14, sanctification. Not a single other student did that except those who were taking the course for examination purposes. Incredible! I would have loved to have taken his courses on Christian ethics and on New Testament biblical theology, but he did not give them while I was at Westminster. Maybe one day his notes on those lectures will be published. Iain Murray has written a beautiful life of John Murray.[2]

Cornelius Van Til

Dr. Cornelius Van Til, the professor of apologetics, was one of the most famous teachers at Westminster. I once was talking with someone who had been a fellow student at Westminster, in fact, the senior student in my first year, Palmer Robinson, the first student from the southern Presbyterian churches to cross the Mason-Dixon line and study in the north. (I was later to become his best man in his second marriage.) I had made what seemed to me to be an obvious point: "A seminary needs four professors, Old Testament, New Testament, church history, and systematic

2. *The Life of John Murray*, rev. ed. (1984; repr., Edinburgh: Banner of Truth Trust, 2007).

theology." Palmer thought for the briefest moment, then added, "And apologetics."

When Machen was gathering the faculty for Westminster Seminary, he wanted Van Til to be the apologetics professor. Van Til had done some teaching in Princeton but had finished a year earlier, and his sole desire was to pastor a Dutch congregation in the Michigan countryside. Machen sent Stonehouse to talk to Van Til and bring him back to Westminster. But the journey was quite unsuccessful. Van Til had no desire at all to teach in a seminary. He wanted to preach to his fellow Dutchmen. Stonehouse failed completely and returned empty-handed. So, Machen himself had to go. He explained the situation to Van Til and did so with great effect, not only bringing Van Til to join the team but making the life of Westminster Seminary enjoyable and exciting so that Van Til quickly grew to love being a seminary professor.

I had actually not heard of Van Til in Wales, although a lecture of his on his apologetic system that he had given in London in the 1950s was published by the Inter-Varsity Fellowship. I had not noticed it. Van Til had come to prominence with his early book *The New Modernism*, which was his initial criticism of Karl Barth's neo-orthodox theology. This theology was immensely popular in all the denominations in the United Kingdom and was called by its supporters "the theology of the Word." It allowed its followers to follow all the theories of higher criticism—for example, that the five books of Moses were compiled from various schools: one that followed Jehovah, another that followed Elohim, the Deuteronomists who wrote the fifth book of Moses, and then the priestly writings, so they were known as "JEDP" sources, and that these sources were all joined together, after the return from the Babylonian exile, as we have them today as the Pentateuch. Another widespread liberal view was that the prophecy of Isaiah was written over a few centuries by three different men. Or again, the theories that there was no literal Jonah, the ax head did not float, the shadow did not go back, the whole world was not drowned in the great flood, there was no ark with all the animals, the Red Sea did not open, and so on.

We had been given, they said, a flawed word that makes claims that these men believed and taught to be erroneous. Everyone had to choose what they wanted to keep and what they wanted to discard. We were not given the criteria or the code that informed us with any authority at all what were actually the very words of God that were there within the Word of God. Everyone chose what these were with his own insights, and there was to be no condemnation of another's ideas. An antisupernaturalism characterized neo-orthodoxy. It claimed to be the theology of the word but failed to produce any evangelists or even preachers with an awakening ministry that could build up churches. When you were "zapped" by a certain verse, then that "became" the word of God to you. But there wasn't a whole lot of zapping going on.

Cornelius Van Til challenged Barthianism in his first book and then again in a much longer book that appeared in 1962, *Christianity and Barthianism.* After two years in Philadelphia, I returned to Wales for the summer and noticed that Dr. Lloyd-Jones was preaching in the Rhondda Valley, and I went to hear him. His text was Hebrews 2:3, "How shall we escape if we neglect so great a salvation?" It was inspiring. A great salvation because of the nature of the Savior, because of what He saved us from and because of what He had saved us to. I had been two years without hearing any preaching like that. I was reassured. I waited to speak to him and thanked him. "I am a student at Westminster Seminary," I told him. He showed great interest. "Do you know the one whom I like most at Westminster Seminary? Van Til." When I returned to the seminary in September, I met Dr. Van Til in the corridor, and I told him of my hearing the Doctor's sermon. "Oh, I think he is the greatest, and whenever I am in London for a weekend, I worship there." I told Van Til that "of the professors at Westminster, he appreciates you the most." Within weeks he had sent a copy of his new book, *Christianity and Barthianism*, to Dr. Lloyd-Jones and asked him to review it for the *Westminster Theological Journal*, which Dr. Lloyd-Jones did in a very positive way.

With a couple of carloads of students, we visited Princeton Theological Seminary in 1962 at the 150th anniversary of its founding in

1812. Karl Barth himself was giving three lectures. Dr. Van Til and John Murray sat in the congregation, and Van Til went on to Barth afterward and introduced himself. “Ah, you are my enemy!” said Barth. Van Til blushed, shaking his head, and resisted that designation. Princeton has one of the vastest libraries in the world with a special collection, the Karl Barth Research Collection in the Center for Barth Studies. The seminary manages an endowment of $1.13 billion, making it the third-wealthiest institution of higher learning in wealthy New Jersey. How many conservative evangelical Christians left legacies to the seminary in the last two hundred years? But how many people had given in order that Barthian neo-orthodoxy should be promoted? How many gave that the doctrines summarized in the Westminster Confession of Faith should be defended and advanced? Many more, especially in the early decades of the seminary.

Van Til was loved by the alumni and supporters of the seminary, and by the members of the Orthodox Presbyterian Church—for his piety, his sermons preached at numerous graduations, his visiting the local hospital and talking with patients from bed to bed, his Sunday afternoon correspondence with old Christian friends, and his open-air preaching, especially in Wall Street, New York.

Van Til lectured twice a week to the first-year students in the most popular of all the first-year lectures. We all had purchased the spiral-bound studies that were the backbone summary of the lectures, studies that he would not for some reason refer to as “books.” But they were never read to us in class. He lectured without a note and, with his piece of chalk, covered the blackboard and soon came to his famous two circles. The world's view of religion included God, represented by one large circle, and mankind and creation, represented by a small circle within the big circle. In other words, for the world of unbelief, there is no ontological distinction between its god and itself. All was one. Then there was the two-circle position of God (and one large circle again was drawn) and His creation (and a small circle was drawn *beneath* it). Thus Van Til sought to establish as the foundation of apologetics the Creator-creature distinction. That was enormously helpful to me.

How we teased him, and he would laugh with us. If a student went to sleep in his lectures (and I never personally witnessed that event), then he was likely to be awakened with a well-aimed piece of chalk thrown at him by Van Til. A man who did suffer that actual indignity returned to the next class wearing a motorcycle helmet. When I chaired the Christmas banquet, the gift I presented to Van Til on behalf of the student body was a Y-shaped slingshot. This story was told at one of those events: "People say to me that Einstein is the greatest brain in America because there are only three people in the United States who can understand the theory of relativity. But I say, 'No, no. Van Til is the greatest brain in America because no one can understand him!'" It was not an original observation but still amusing.

Edward Joseph Young

The most well-known name of the staff at Westminster Seminary, at least for me, but surely also in the United Kingdom in the 1950s, was Edward J. Young, the Old Testament professor and prodigious author. Princeton Seminary had had a fine history of Semitic scholars going back to Joseph Addison Alexander, later followed by Robert Dick Wilson and O. T. Allis. I once was invited to dinner at the home of Professor and Mrs. Paul Woolley with the eighty-two-year-old O. T. Allis and his wife and two daughters. I bided my time until there was a lull in the conversation, and then I asked Dr. Allis my prepared question, "You were taught by B. B. Warfield and were a colleague with him at Princeton Seminary. What was he like as a man?" His eyes twinkled, and he replied, "Very interesting!" And that was all! I got no more from him. He was an old man, while I was young and inquisitive. I wanted incidents and observations to put some flesh and blood on one of the great early twentieth-century figures.

The mantle of those holy Old Testament scholars fell on Edward J. Young at Westminster, and he did not fail to take it up, maintaining and enriching the trust they had displayed in the full truthfulness of the Scriptures of the Old Testament. His only son, Davis, a lecturer at Calvin University, has written a full biography of his father entitled *For Me to Live is Christ.*[3] I believe that no one in Europe read it as avidly and with such pleasure or received as much as what I was to receive from this biography. Edward Joseph Young was generally called Joe by his colleagues at Westminster. He was from California, born in 1907, and graduated from the prestigious Stanford University, going on to study at Westminster Theological Seminary in 1935, having two years of Gresham Machen's teaching. His wife, Lillian, was a very beautiful woman, and their courtship as described by their son in his biography of his father is fascinating. His late daughter, Jean, was an old friend of mine, almost two years older than me; she was married to Professor Richard Gaffin.

Edward J. Young fully grasped the issue that was facing the Presbyterian Church (USA) concerning the baleful influences of liberalism, and eventually he left that denomination in 1936 and became a minister and churchman in the OPC until his death in 1968. As the Australian Old Testament scholar Allan Harman wrote, "Edward J. Young held unswervingly to a high view of Scripture," was "deeply read in the literature of his chosen field," and "dedicated his outstanding gifts to the service of Christ's church and kingdom."[4] His high commitment to Scripture and the Westminster Confession of Faith was exemplary.

Incidentally, he played the cello. I heard him play it at one seminary staff-and-student evening along with various contributions from others. He played "Sheep May Safely Graze" by J. S. Bach. He had played the cello somewhat as a young man, and then, at thirty-

---

3. Davis Young, *For Me to Live Is Christ: The Life of Edward J. Young* (Willow Grove, PA: Committee of the Historian of the OPC, 2017).

4. Allan Harman, "Edward Joseph Young," in *Bible Interpreters of the 20th Century: A Selection of Evangelical Voices,* ed. Walter A. Elwell and J. D. Weaver (Grand Rapids: Baker, 1999), 200.

seven years of age, he took cello lessons, spending from thirty minutes to a whole hour each day practicing. He attained a high degree of accomplishment playing the six unaccompanied cello suites of J. S. Bach, Brahm's Double Concerto for violin and cello, Haydn's First Cello Concerto, and even Dvorak's Cello Concerto in B Minor. He was a member of the local Old York Symphony Orchestra.

Dr. Young's first major work was his *An Introduction to the Old Testament*, published in 1949 in the United States by Eerdmans. That was picked up by the Tyndale Press in London and published in Great Britain, and we Christian students taking courses in theology and biblical studies had our own copies as there was little else we knew to help us resist being steamrolled by our higher criticism teachers. Generally, we were not aware of the existence of O. T. Allis's major work, *The Five Books of Moses,* which comprehensively examines and destroys the documentary hypothesis of the JEDP school of authorship of the Pentateuch, as the Liverpool based Dr. Kenneth Kitchen has also done so helpfully in more recent times.

It was most perplexing when Edward J. Young's successors in the Old Testament department at Westminster Seminary, Tremper Longman III and Ray Dillard, brought out *An Introduction to the Old Testament* in 1994, which appeared to accept such liberal hypotheses as aspects of the documentary theory. Edmund Clowney once said to me that he had asked Ray Dillard why he always referred to the author of Deuteronomy as "the Deuteronomist" and never as Moses. "Because that is how all the scholars refer to him," replied the late Raymond Dillard. Some of the men in the next generation at Westminster were for a time moving in another direction from the founders, quite thoughtlessly. For a period, the seminary seemed to be losing its way. But while Dr. Young was on his watch, unbelief did not enter the seminary via the Old Testament department, as has happened in most of the other seminaries in America and Europe.

Edward J. Young's output was prodigious. Following *An Introduction to the Old Testament* in 1949 came *The Prophecy of Daniel* that same year, and three years later *My Servants the Prophets*, of which again I knew nothing until arriving in the United States. The theme of the cultic prophets was enormously important to Aubrey Johnson, the professor of Old Testament in Cardiff, and Dr. Young was fully aware of what he had written, and he deals fairly with Johnson's observations. In 1953 came *The Authority of the Old Testament*, and in 1957 *Thy Word is Truth*, which the Banner of Truth reprinted in London. Then there followed his magisterial accomplishment, his three-volume commentary on the book of Isaiah (1965–1972). The *Evangelical Quarterly* commented on these three volumes, "The special value of the book lies in the fullness and depth of the exposition and the erudition of the footnotes. These alone justify its purchase by the layman, the minister, and the student."[5] Then in the next years there followed a number of briefer studies, *In the Beginning: Genesis 1–3 and the Authority of Scripture, Isaiah 53, The Way Everlasting: A Study in Psalm 139,* and *The God-Breathed Scripture*. His plan had been to proceed in writing two full commentaries, one on Genesis and another on Daniel. I once was commiserating with Professor Murray in our mutual sadness that Young had died at only sixty-one years of age. "I would have coveted a commentary of his on Genesis," I remarked to Mr. Murray. "Oh, I would have coveted his commentary on Daniel," he replied. Professor F. F. Bruce wrote a most respectful obituary for him in *Faith and Thought*.

Edward J. Young had struck up a friendship through correspondence with the English Baptist scholar H. H. Rowley, who happened to be my external examiner in Cardiff and the father-in-law of the head of our department Aubrey Johnson. Rowley was eighteen years older than Young, and from 1948 they corresponded for over twenty years. Young sent Rowley each issue of *the Westminster Theological Journal* until the end of his life, for which Rowley always thanked him. Young also informed him of important new books that had appeared in America. Rowley had been a missionary to China for several years, and in 1949, Edward J. Young sent some food parcels from America to H. H. Rowley and his wife there. The Englishman

5. H. L. Ellison, "Studies in Isaiah," *The Evangelical Quarterly 27*, no. 3 (July–September 1955): 179–181.

felt a little embarrassed in receiving Young's care packages, though most grateful, writing, "Don't take our grumbles too seriously. It is part of our national habit to grumble—and there is indeed plenty to grumble about." In 1967, Professor and Mrs. Young visited Professor and Mrs. Rowley at their home near Stroud and had extended conversations. Two years later, Rowley died.

Rowley's interesting response to Young's *Introduction to the Old Testament* was "Professor Young is a scholar who is widely acquainted with views he does not share, and his work is a *vade mecum* of views that he accepts and rejects; few will not learn from it or fail to find it valuable for consultation." In May 1958 there was the dedication of the new premises of the London Bible College at which E. J. Young gave four lectures, later published as *The Study of Old Testament Theology Today*. The service of dedication had as its climactic aspect a sermon by Dr. Martyn Lloyd-Jones, to which Dr. Young gave rapt attention. During that same visit to London, he gave the Tyndale Lecture on "Daniel's Vision of the Son of Man." As a conservative scholar, it was essential that he had the closest knowledge of the latest writings of Old Testament scholars. That study is not necessary for most of us ministers, but it is very helpful for us to have access to someone who can explain what is being taught. Don Carson does the same with New Testament writings.

Edward J. Young set the standard for evangelical Old Testament interpretation. One of the most vital challenges the Christian church has always to face is the attitude that the infallible Christ, the Son of God, took to the Scriptures. For us He can say nothing wrong, and Jesus said that God's Word was truth and that it could not be broken. In order to resist devilish temptation, He quoted the Old Testament book of Deuteronomy, saying, "It is written." The infallible Christ gives me an infallible Scripture. But today there are still those who claim to hold to historic Christianity and the lordship of the incarnate God, and yet they view the first eleven chapters of the book of Genesis as "poetic" truth. They do not believe in a historic Adam, in a supernatural creation of Eve after Adam, from Adam, for Adam, and they reject a historic fall which came from the defiance of the first man and at which point death first entered the human race. For Edward J. Young these truths were nonnegotiable.

I would not say that Edward J. Young was an inspirational lecturer. Many hands were raised in every lecture of his, especially in his course on the exegesis of the first eleven chapters of Genesis, and he would pause, listen, and answer patiently every one. Consequently, there were not many pages of notes taken in the whole course.

At fifty-three years of age, Young invented a new approach to teaching the Hebrew language. We were the second year of students to be exposed to it. He had compiled and written a spiral-bound textbook of sixty or so lessons that were based on the Hebrew of Exodus 3:1 and following, "Now Moses was tending the flock of Jethro his father-in-law...." He transliterated the Hebrew verse by verse, lesson by lesson, into an English script, and we all progressively chanted it, as we were introduced letter by letter to the Hebrew language.

Contemporary Israel has had considerable success in teaching the nation modern Hebrew by the *ulpan* method. *Ulpan* is a Hebrew word for "instruction" or "teaching." Most big cities in Israel have several *ulpan* programs. Dr. Young sought to implement that approach at Westminster. It was a radical innovation. He was emphasizing the oral acquisition of "this strange and beautiful language," as he called it. By this means he sought to engage us students as quickly as possible with Hebrew so that we felt comfortable using it. He was an enthusiast and encouraged us not to be afraid of the Semitic script. The enormous advantage today of learning Hebrew in the land of Israel via *ulpan* is that the classes are set within a vital social structure, in a nation where everyone speaks Hebrew. You can sing together in Hebrew and you shop in Hebrew—and best of all, the children speak Hebrew, and you can talk to them with your own childlike, mistake-laden Hebrew, and instead of giggling at your mistakes, they reply to you. You can read baby stories to them in children's books. None of that is there in the rest of the world to enhance one's learning of biblical Hebrew. But how one applauded the initiative and desire of Dr. Young to get Hebrew under our skins! He did not consider our exposure to Hebrew to be some irksome task to be delegated to a graduate student or a new assistant lecturer. He personally took on this challenge. These classes were a fascinating and challenging experience. It is still my belief, confirmed through my own sad experience, that the most difficult part of any divinity or theology course is learning Hebrew. How successful Young's new approach was to teaching biblical Hebrew in the United States is questionable. It has not yet had many followers in the small group of teachers of ancient Hebrew.

Meredith Kline

The finest lecturer at Westminster in my estimation was the forty-year-old Meredith Kline. He was the best I had ever had anywhere. He gave you material that was stretching and stimulating. He was approachable in class, but you had to have a sensible question. He was an inspirational teacher. One of his former students, Lee Irons, came out of a dispensationalist background, and he writes,

> Sitting in his class I felt as if the Bible made sense for the very first time. The key was his chalkboard diagrams. (Yes, we used chalkboards not whiteboards back then.) It was as if he couldn't think without simultaneously drawing and/or scribbling something on the chalkboard. As the class progressed, the board was so filled with a scramble of common grace lines, theocratic boxes, and eschatological intrusion arrows, that he had to erase a little square at a time to make room for new flashes of chalky brilliance. I can still remember the pounding sound of his blackboard poetry. By the end of each class, he was covered with dust, his chalk-holding hand leprous with the radiance of the epiphanic glory of God.[6]

6. Lee Irons, "My Tribute to Meredith G. Kline (1922–2007)," The Upper Register, accessed February 20, 2021, http://www.upper-register.com/papers/kline_tribute.html.

Kline was a delightful family man, and his wife, Grace, was both an artist and a shy Londoner from the UK. They enjoyed visiting art galleries. His children loved the Lord, and one son followed his father into teaching Old Testament biblical theology and being a librarian at Gordon. In family devotions his sons thought it was perfectly natural for Dad in his prayers to say something like "such chiasms occur in the sanctions of Hittite suzerainty treaties."

We students were captivated by his ideas, like our tendency to go for new translations, new hymns, new musical accompaniments, and new ideas that promise younger, growing congregations. While Edward J. Young was the Puritan pilgrim who walked carefully on, Kline was the irresistible eagle soaring across the scenario of the history of redemption. When in my last year Dr. Morton Smith gave a lecture series on worship, our class was, alas, contemptuous because we had imbibed Meredith Kline's approach to the Old Testament, and Dr. Smith was constrained to give us a rebuke as future church leaders and so needed to be models of gentleness and respect. He spoke well.

Of course, we students were captivated by Kline's ideas, but then a friend said soberly, "He is dangerously innovative." He was certainly creative. For example, I was fascinated when I first heard his suggestion that the two tablets of stone on which the Ten Commandments were written were duplicates, one belonging to the sovereign who laid out the requirements of the covenant, and the other belonging to the vassal people who agreed to be committed to obey them, and of course, both were kept in the holy of holies inside the ark of the covenant. I still like that suggestion!

John Frame and I sat near one another in Kline's lectures for three years, and John's assessment of Kline is typical of the response of many Westminster graduates, that he was the most impressive biblical theologian of Frame's lifetime, that his work was orthodox, often original, with always a rich analysis of Scripture. But Kline wasn't so preachable compared to Edward Joseph Young. It is the question we pastors often ask: Does it preach? I did find that Kline's commentary on Zechariah gave some assistance to me, and I sought to blend it with the Puritanism of T. V. Moore's excellent commentary. I wish that Kline had commented on the whole book, not just the "easy" chapters of the visions. I struggled making the last half of the book relevant and understandable to Welsh Christians in the twenty-first century.

I am not at all suggesting that Kline was cerebral, a merely academic biblical theologian. Then he would not have captivated me. My heart and mind were earthed in the experiential emphases of Calvinistic Methodism. Lee Irons recounts, "One time my friend Bill Baldwin and I were talking with our professor about some postmillennial theonomists who derided our preoccupation with heaven as 'pie in the sky.' Meredith got this radiant look on his face, looked heavenward with his hands in front of his mouth grabbing for some unseen substance dropping from the sky and said, 'Give me more of that pie!'"[7] That is Calvinistic Methodism!

Lee's wife, Misty, experienced a painful miscarriage when he was a seminary student. In their sorrow they were looking for answers, so they talked to the sympathizing seminary professors and asked whether their baby would be in heaven. They all said, "Yes, of course," and offered various theological explanations. But Meredith's answer was for them the best and the simplest. When Lee asked him why he was so sure that their baby would be in heaven, Kline said, "Because God is a good heavenly Father. Not even a sparrow falls to the ground without our Father's knowledge."[8]

That was it! No complex covenant theology here. Just simple, childlike trust in the heavenly Father, as Jesus taught. Dr. Kline combined all his profound understanding of theology with a joyful confidence in God's grace. One time Lee expressed to Kline that he was fretting about the state of the church with all the confusion going around about justification. Kline said, "God will take care of his own truth."[9]

7. Irons, "My Tribute to Meredith G. Kline."
8. Irons, "My Tribute to Meredith G. Kline."
9. Irons, "My Tribute to Meredith G. Kline."

Kline was born in 1922 in New England and studied at Gordon College outside Boston. Then he came to Westminster Seminary where he helped raise some money for his expenses by teaching swimming in the YMCA. At the seminary he was taught by Edward J. Young, whom he held in the very highest esteem. He said that Joe Young breathed "a spirit of humble adoration of the Holy One of Israel." They were both ministers in the Orthodox Presbyterian Church, and Kline often spent a week in the summer ministering in the Boardwalk Chapel in Wildwood, New Jersey, where Dr. Young also spoke for a week. While Young played the cello, Kline played the violin and had done so in the Boston Youth Symphony. He was very artistic and would even sketch colleagues during long committee meetings, but he never learned to type. All his books were written long hand. He got his PhD in Assyriology and Egyptology from Dropsie College and then taught for almost thirty years at Westminster, going on to be professor of Old Testament studies at Gordon-Conwell Theological Seminary for a further twenty-eight years (1965–1993). I remember my sense of disappointment when I heard that he had left Westminster. Gordon-Conwell was not a confessional seminary like Westminster. Dr Kline was the first basic translator of the books of Job and the Psalms for the New International Version of the Bible.

Kline's role model was Geerhardus Vos and his *Biblical Theology*. Of course, all the men who studied at Princeton before the discipline and excommunication of Machen were impressed, out of all the staff teaching there (and they were fabulous scholars and holy men), by Vos. His grandson Mel Vos was a fellow student of mine at Westminster; he became a pastor in the Reformed Presbyterian church and then was killed so prematurely in an automobile accident.

Kline is remembered especially for his framework interpretation of Genesis 1. This is most accessible in his commentary on Genesis in *The New Bible Commentary Revised* published by the Inter-Varsity Press in 1970. Kline taught that the triad of the first three days in creation delineated kingdom-spheres and the second triad of the final three recapitulates the series as it appoints kings over these realms. Day one dealt with the separation of light from the darkness, while the parallel day four introduces the creatures God made to rule over the day and over the night—the sun and the moon. Day five describes the creation of the fish of the sea and the birds of the air, and these living creatures dominate the realms surveyed in the second day—the waters and the firmament. While day six contains two works: land creatures rule over the earth's produce and man, the godlike king, takes dominion over dry land and its creatures that were made on day three.

In November 1962, Edward J. Young wrote in the November issue of the *Westminster Theological Journal* his first major challenge to Dr. Kline's framework view of Genesis 1. He judged that "the framework view treated the content of Genesis 1 too lightly and seemed like an attempt to rescue the Bible from appearing to be in conflict with the date of modern science."[10] Kline refuted both the twenty-four-hour interpretation of the days of Genesis 1 and the day-age view of them. The days were for him heavenly days, not earthly twenty-four-hour days. Young wrote at length dismantling the notion of parallelism between days one, two, and three with days four, five, and six. He disputed the view that Genesis 1 maintained a topical rather than a chronological emphasis. He said the days of Genesis 1 were "periods of time that can properly be called days."

Kline expected Young to be chairman of Westminster's Old Testament program for years to come, and then Kline was offered the chairmanship of the Old Testament program at Gordon. There he would be free to teach the courses that he preferred. Gordon also offered a more substantial salary. But the main attraction was the fact that Meredith Kline was a Massachusetts native. He missed New England. His oldest son, Meredith M., relates that his father let out a loud cheer whenever the family crossed the state line returning to Massachusetts.

He and his wife used to leave the cold East Coast and go out to California for the winter academic quarter every year. It was a

10. Young, *For Me to Live Is Christ*, 271.

grand tribute to his commitment to Westminster Seminary on the West Coast and to teaching covenant theology to the students. This he continued to do well into his seventies, when most men would be glad to be free of teaching and would begin to take their ease in retirement. Not so with Meredith. He and his wife believed he had something valuable to contribute to the students at Westminster Escondido.

Kline was certainly a gospel man. The debate and division concerning the doctrine of justification was caused by the spread of a radically different understanding by the so-called New Perspective on the apostle Paul. It came home to Westminster with the confused teaching of Norman Shepherd in the systematics department, which ended in his dismissal. Meredith Kline was very clear concerning his view of the place of works in a sinner's justification. He taught that heaven must be earned, but it has been accomplished by the last Adam's obedience and merit; He is the one who has earned heaven for His people. Lee Irons relays,

> This understanding of the gospel is precious because it provides the assurance that in Christ we are "beyond probation," since the right to heaven has been won by him and cannot be revoked. Christian obedience is merely the evidence of the genuineness of our faith, but not in any way becoming the condition or means of receiving the right to heaven. There was a polemical context to Kline's teaching on justification, but that came from his love for Christ. He wanted to make clear that there was a direct connection between the meritorious work of Christ as the last Adam and the believer's entrance into heaven. There is nothing in between. Not the believer's Spirit-wrought sanctification or our perseverance in good works.
>
> Meredith wanted to say that Christ's obedience unto death is the immediate cause and ground of our receiving the eternal inheritance. He wanted the sheep to have this full assurance by looking not to themselves or their own imperfect obedience, but to Christ and Christ alone as the all-sufficient guarantor of the new covenant. It was clear that as he taught this, that this understanding of the gospel was not merely some doctrine but

> that he had a personal relationship with Christ, and that Christ was the anchor of his soul lodged within the veil on the other side of glory, thus guaranteeing that he too would be brought safely there in due time.[11]

The biggest critics of Federal Vision theology owe a great deal to Kline's understanding of the Old Testament and justification. Dr. Kline died in 2007 aged eighty-four.

Ned B. Stonehouse

I have often conjoined Ned Stonehouse, the New Testament professor, with Paul Woolley, the church history professor, for several reasons. John Muether has pointed out that in the year 1902, within the space of three days, Paul Woolley (March 16) and Ned B. Stonehouse (March 19) were born. The two of them would meet as students at Princeton Theological Seminary and would join J. Gresham Machen in the founding of Westminster Seminary in 1929. They became part of the original faculty and served there in Philadelphia for thirty years. They were both among the thirty-four constituting members of the OPC in 1936. They gave a historical consciousness to that denomination, through Stonehouse's biography of Machen and his helpful editing of some of Machen's writings, and through Woolley being made the denomination's first historian in 1974.

But I also join them together as they both possessed a certain modesty, a retiring manner, Westminster Confession men but not preachers, both admirably suited for seminary life, given to reading and to editing the *Westminster Theological Journal*, men of total integrity, and fellow members of the same congregation, Calvary OPC, a little modest building in Glenside just across the road from the seminary. When John Murray would preach there, Ned Stonehouse would take the first part of the service and Murray the second

11. Irons, "My Tribute to Meredith G. Kline."

part. Murray and Stonehouse: we smart-alecky students would dub them Moody and Sankey.

Dr. Stonehouse did not teach any first-year courses. The only time I would hear him during my first two semesters was in the morning chapel services when all the faculty were on a rota of speakers. His parents came from the Netherlands and changed their surname on entry into the United States from Stenenhuis to Stonehouse. He had received his bachelor of arts degree from Calvin College when he was twenty-two, and he then proceeded to Princeton Theological Seminary, gaining his master of theology degree in 1927. He loved Geerhardus Vos's teaching and would tell us students that every minister of the gospel ought to read Vos's little book of one hundred pages, *The Kingdom of God and the Church*, once a year.

After studying in Princeton under Machen and Vos, Stonehouse then returned to his Dutch roots and got his PhD from the Free University of Amsterdam in 1929. That was the year he joined with Machen in the founding of Westminster Seminary. The new faculty comprised a balance of men from an American Presbyterian background like Machen, Paul Woolley, Edward J. Young, Edmund P. Clowney, and John Skilton with others from a foreign background, Cornelius Van Til, Ned Stonehouse, R. B. Kuiper, and John Murray. The latter's name was more common than those Dutch names, but his Presbyterianism was of the Free Presbyterian Church of Scotland and differed in obvious ways from the American tradition, out of which came the OPC. Yet the OPC and the seminary did not simply find a place for these men; it drew them in with affection and respect as their valuable helpers in preserving Westminster confessional Presbyterianism. But the OPC's critics were never tired of referring to the "foreign leadership" of the theological college and the denomination. As a foreigner myself in Philadelphia, I appreciated the European dimension and could see the Reformed faith in America without the blinders of national pride or patriotic civil religion.

At the start of my second year, I moved to one of the campus gatehouses and shared a room with the student president, the Canadian Alistair Donald Macleod. His father came from Stornoway and had been a missionary in China with the China Inland Mission, marrying an American missionary. He had spent five long years during the war in a Japanese prisoner of war camp. I was to be Donald's best man within a few years. At the beginning of my second year, I also got a job as a desk clerk in the Benson Manor not far away, working six nights a week, 1:00 a.m. to 9:00 a.m. during one year and midnight to 8:00 a.m. the second year. It was easy, very quiet; I could work and also sleep. I needed to run a car, and I was weary at twenty-four years of age of the continuous life of a student. I was glad of a job and a pay check [UK: pay packet]. I was able to purchase a pink 1955 Chevrolet.

So it was then in the fall of 1962 that I began the important second-year course of a number of lectures each week given by Ned Stonehouse on the Gospels. It was a multiperspectival course on the synoptics, examining them through the lens of Vos and Ridderbos. This latter he had grown to greatly admire, and whenever Ridderbos came to give a lecture at Westminster, he stayed with Stonehouse and they conversed in Dutch. Donald Macleod had loved the course, and he considered Ned Stonehouse the best lecturer at the seminary. He began to lecture to us for a month, on and off, as he was experiencing bad health.

Then on Sunday, November 18, 1962, after attending the morning service at Calvary Glenside OPC, he died at home. At his funeral service John Murray preached powerfully on Hebrews 9:27, "It is appointed for men to die once, but after this the judgment." It was a mighty sermon that I could take and adapt myself and preach at many funerals. So, I was to experience very little of Dr. Stonehouse.

One incident at his funeral sticks in my memory. His daughter-in-law (the wife of his only child, Chip) was expecting a baby and had gone into the hospital. As we awaited the commencement of the funeral service, a message came from the hospital and quickly whispered from one to another that a healthy child had been born and "mother and child were doing well." The news spread. The family shed a few tears.

But to end on an amusing note. One evening during a seminary break, before retiring to bed in an empty Machen Hall, John Murray went for a stroll around the deserted campus. A police car keeping an eye on the neighborhood spotted this figure and drove in to question the man. On closer inspection they discovered he was wearing "bummy" clothes, as they put it—the garments a bum wears. He had no identification on his person. So they arrested Mr. Murray and took him to the police station. There Mr. Murray called Ned Stonehouse, who went immediately and put in a word for him, and Mr. Murray was free again.

Paul Woolley

Paul Woolley was the professor of church history at Westminster from its inception in 1929 until his retirement in 1977. But he had many other vocations at the seminary. He served as the secretary of the faculty for over thirty years, and at various times he was registrar, dean of students, and chairman of the faculty. He was a remarkable administrator. He contributed over fifty articles to *The Presbyterian Guardian*. He edited the *Westminster Theological Journal* for many years; though never composing a single article, he contributed ninety-five book reviews—more than anyone else.

He was also a happy man. He was the first professor with whom I ever had any communication. He was a kind of acting registrar as the "dean of admission," and so when I wrote my first letter to Westminster wondering about the possibility of becoming a student, the reply to my query arrived in less than ten days from Paul Woolley, and such were all his letters: prompt, courteous, and warm. It was said that he never failed to reply to a letter the very day that he received it. We had worn academic gowns to all our lectures in the University at Cardiff, and so I asked in one letter if that was a requirement in Philadelphia. Mr. Woolley told me he did not know of a single institution anywhere in America that required its students to wear gowns. Hooray!

Mr. Woolley became an expert in the US railroad system after advising students from Montana or Utah or North Dakota how to travel across the country to Glenside, Pennsylvania. He knew the timetables of the major railroads as well as such convenient information as local train and bus schedules. But his knowledge bank was immense as he sat behind the table at the front of the class giving fascinating details of the life of Pelagius or summarizing the *Summa Theologica* of Thomas Aquinas or Finney's campaigns in western New York state. Ed Clowney once said, "Only his dignity and his crisp stewardship of time prevented nearly everyone from asking him nearly everything to the neglect of the impressive reference collection that he had built up in the library."[12]

Paul Woolley's father, E. Y. Woolley, was the acting pastor of Moody Memorial Church in Chicago from 1911 to 1915, and in 1926 Paul Woolley was ordained in that assembly. He had been considering going as a missionary to China, but issues within the Presbyterian Church prevented that. Machen said to him, "No doubt it is a great disappointment to you that you cannot go into your chosen field at once; but sometimes such dispensations of Providence lead a man only into greater service."

With this Moody background, it is not surprising that he was the only premillennialist faculty member in Philadelphia. He was once rebuked by the premillennialist Dr. Donald Barnhouse of Tenth Presbyterian Church in Philadelphia that after coming from such a background he should identify himself with a nondispensationalist organization like Westminster Seminary. The Tenth Presbyterian Church youth group once did a series of three meetings on various millennial views, and it invited Paul Woolley to speak on the subject of premillennialism, but he declined. It was a long time since he had studied that subject, he informed me.

12. W. Stanford Reid, ed., dedication to Paul Woolley in *John Calvin: His Influence in the Western World* (Grand Rapids: Zondervan, 1982), 9.

But there were other ways in which Mr. Woolley was quietly different from the other faculty members. He was a Democrat, while virtually all of them were Republicans. He was also a member of the American Civil Liberties Union (ACLU), which was founded in 1920 when he was eighteen years old. The ACLU works in courts, legislatures, and communities to defend individual rights and liberties. He never spoke of it, and it was becoming steadily more left-wing in its pronouncements.

Paul Woolley was a delightfully interesting and unique person. He could cast a dissenting vote in faculty meetings, sometimes on incidental matters. But he was never awkward and would give a reason for how he spoke.

As a lecturer Professsor Woolley was wonderfully comprehensive, each of us being given a three- or four-page outline of that semester's entire course where the subject or theme for each individual lecture was given, and we were requested subsequently to go to a section in the library where the original works of the person being studied were kept on the shelves. We could not borrow them. They were not to be removed from the library but to be read there in the day or two following the lecture. He expected not only information from his examination papers but interpretation. Clowney specifies one examination question that Professor Woolley set: "Assuming that the work of the church is the preaching of the Gospel and the nurturing of its members in Christian living, what has been contributed to this task by each of these emphases—orthodoxy, rationalism, pietism, modernism? Discuss each contribution and illustrate with copious examples." Or again, another question challenged students to "provide a critique of the World Council of Churches by proposing changes or replacements as you think necessary."[13] Woolley was more like a Princeton professor than were any of his Westminster colleagues.

Ed Clowney felt Woolley's greatest gift was his ability of combining warm understanding and appreciation for the men and

13. Reid, *John Calvin: His Influence*, 9.

movements in the history of Christ's church with undeviating commitment to biblical standards in evaluating them. He conjoined that to a generous spirit so that a student in financial duress could be told by him that there was no way that more money from the seminary funds could be given to him, but then, taking out his own wallet, Mr. Woolley would give generously to help the man. A fair number of students could imitate Woolley's distinctive, back-of-the-throat accent, but imitating his godliness was more challenging.

One student he particularly influenced was Harold Ockenga, who became the minister of Park Street Church in Boston. He was influential in starting the Gordon-Conwell Seminary in Massachusetts and Fuller Seminary in California. To that latter seminary Professor Woolley was invited to move to become the head of the church history department, but he declined the invitation, not that he had anything against Fuller but that it was particularly an "evangelical" seminary and Woolley believed that that was too limiting a theological position for the confession of biblical doctrines that teachers of the Bible needed to make.

A critical issue lay before the evangelical church that Woolley noticed and which irritated him—the itch for rapid congregational growth. That virus was almost a national plague in the United States. Professor Paul Woolley resolutely opposed it, saying,

> The question is really a very simple one. Does the Orthodox Presbyterian Church want to have a growing revival of the preaching, teaching and application of the Bible and Reformed Faith in these United States in the year 1944? Or does the Orthodox Presbyterian Church want to have so many members and much money and read about itself often in the newspapers? It can have one. It cannot have both.... Large churches are generally much more closely oriented to money and power than Jesus was. It raises the question of whether an increase in the size of a church is always a blessing. The people who are running things

> become tremendously interested in their authority and in those means by which they can realize their dreams.[14]

Yet he never embraced a remnant mentality that encouraged a church to relish its small size. He was simply saying that the true sign of a healthy church would elude simple quantitative measurement. He was also fearful of a small church's cultivating exotic theological specialities.

In 1927 Paul Woolley was traveling in Germany and met Helene von der Pahlen. They were soon married and had two sons. The story circulating Westminster was that she was a Russian princess, but Ed Clowney has written more guardedly that her "historical reminiscences stretched back to Russian court life under the Czar."[15]

Edmund P. Clowney

One of the most delightful faculty members at Westminster Seminary was Ed Clowney, the professor of practical theology and then the president. I will bookend my friendship with him with two incidents. In my last semester at Westminster, I still had no assurance that I was going to be a preacher. Isn't it one of the most outrageous claims that a man can make that he believes this: *The Creator of the cosmos has summoned me to stand in His name and proclaim His Word to everyone who will hear and to open the door of heaven's glory to those who receive His Son, and warn those who reject His Word that they will be condemned forever*? It is little wonder that the longer a man has known God, studied His Word, heard the finest preachers, realized the challenge of the pulpit ministry, and become aware of

---

14. Quoted in John Muether, "The Significance of Paul Woolley Today," in *Confident of Better Things: Essays Commemorating Seventy-Five Years of the Orthodox Presbyterian Church*, ed. John R. Muether and Danny E. Olinger (Willow Grove, Pa.: Committee for the Historian of the OPC, 2011), 7–8.

15. Muether, "Significance of Paul Woolley," 11.

the power of ego and greed and lust in his own heart that he will hesitate before issuing a public statement that this is going to be his lifelong vocation.

So, four months before my graduation and return to Wales in early 1964, I went to see Ed Clowney, who was soon to become the first president of the seminary. Westminster had seen how Princeton's appointment of a moderate to be its president had destroyed Princeton as a bastion of confessional Christianity, how the appointment of liberal trustees and lecturers diluted its consecration to the historic faith. Therefore, the Westminster faculty met for years every Saturday morning to discuss the affairs of the seminary from trivia to major decisions. But every ten years or so there had to be an academic accreditation visit of a group of examiners to assess the seminary and its right and privilege to continue awarding degrees. One such accreditation took place in my final year, and though the conclusion was positive with a high esteem of the academic standards of the seminary, the accreditors judged that its administrative structures were inadequate and should be improved, especially in the light of its steady growth. They recommended that a president be appointed. Two years later, Ed Clowney became the first president. He was brilliant. In a typical year, Westminster Seminary had students from eighty denominations and forty countries.

The massive gifts that singled out Ed among the other members of the faculty were exemplary piety, empathy, holiness, and the gift of encouragement. Of course, as a professor of practical theology he was outstanding in his ability to kindly evaluate students' sermons. It was his pastoring of fellow faculty and students and the trust he engendered in all who loved the seminary that made him an obvious choice for his future office. You would want Ed Clowney on your team, to be a member of your congregation, to be one of your staff, to have as your father or grandfather.

Accordingly, I went to his office one morning and sought his advice about my future, whether I should consider becoming a preacher. I was obeying his exhortation that "private soul-searching is not enough to determine your call to the ministry. The judgment of the people of God must be sought; long before the time when it must be given formally, it should be sought informally." His response was to tell me that if I had been intending to remain in the United States that he would do all he could to encourage me to become a pastor in the Orthodox Presbyterian Church. We prayed together, and thenceforth the matter was solved. I was going to be a preacher. Ed said, "If you yearn to serve Christ in the gospel ministry, then that desire is surely a calling to prayer for the Spirit. Likely it is also a foretaste and earnest of greater gifts to come."

The other bookend was almost forty years later. I was teaching a class at Westminster Seminary Escondido and spent some time with Ed, who was then a professor there. He took me one afternoon to the San Diego Zoo. We rode together in an elevated vehicle around a vast savannah where many deer, zebras, and giraffes were grazing. As a pensioner he did not have to pay for this visit and could bring a friend. What a happy time. "Come and see me tomorrow morning," he said. His query then was this: "What are your present concerns? I have prayed for you every day since you graduated, but it gets a little demoralizing praying only, 'O God, bless Geoff Thomas.' What are your current needs? What should I pray for?" I was pretty impressed by that affection and faithfulness. I wish I'd had some wise original requests to make to assist his focused praying for me, but my needs then and always were and are for my growth in grace and the blessing of God in saving and sanctifying those to whom I preached week by week.

Ed was wonderfully encouraging to have in your congregation. When I preached on the redemption of Christ at the fiftieth anniversary of Westminster, he said to me, "I hope they will never forget what they heard tonight."

Ed Clowney was no "foreigner" on the faculty because he was born in Philadelphia in 1917 and knew about Machen as a teenager. He went from a Christian home to Wheaton College, where he heard of Machen's death and where he graduated in 1939. Then he went to Westminster Seminary where he studied for three years. He received his master's degree from Yale in 1944 and served in a number of

Orthodox Presbyterian churches until Westminster invited him to become assistant professor of practical theology in 1952. I met up with him as full professor nine years later.

To hear him, week by week, kindly evaluating a student in preaching classes was an education. The student who preached and listened to criticism one week was then the first to get up and evaluate his successor's sermon the following week, followed by any comments from the rest of us. The hour ended with Ed Clowney's gentle evaluation, which was always very helpful. Students were more critical than the professor. We were never humiliated, and the weak lambs in the flock were helped. I can remember spending one morning in the 1970s with Ed in London. He told me that on the previous day he had been preaching in Westminster Chapel and there in the congregation listening to him, he spotted Dr. Martyn Lloyd-Jones. "I felt like a student in the preaching class," he told me.

I had read his book *Preaching and Biblical Theology*, published by the Inter-Varsity Press in the United Kingdom, before I had set sail for America. I suppose it was helpful in the most general way. I did not know much about biblical theology then. His commentary on 1 Peter is fine, as are *Preaching Christ in All of Scripture* and *How Jesus Transforms the Ten Commandments.* However, his one course at the seminary on the church I did not find so helpful. I wanted practical counsel about such things as church government, Presbyterianism versus congregationalism, admission into membership, doctrinal requirements for church members, and age requirements for a credible profession of faith and membership. I wanted to know about the administration of church ordinances, especially the Lord's Supper, about church discipline, officers' meetings, church members' meetings, the offering, the prayer meeting, youth meetings, local and national church associations, and recognition of one another's churches and discipline. I wanted tips about dangers to avoid and practices to maintain and so on. There was just very little of that sort of thing. Rather, we had the material that is now in his book *The Church: Contours of Christian Theology*, which is a biblical-theological study of the people of God in the Old and New Testaments.

So, what of his stress on biblical theology and preaching? Sermons that expound and apply the Word of God are essential and show an awareness with the progress of redemptive history. Yet we know the dangers in a tight commitment to expository preaching—for example, the possibility of the dullness of it as it becomes merely a glorified Bible study; its potential irrelevance and monotony; the possibility of overload by going through a whole section, even the chapter of an epistle with a wide variety of contents, verse by verse; and the possible indigestion caused by bringing all the food preparation into the serving of the meal. The danger of the absence of applicatory and discriminatory preaching and the failure of distinguishing between believer and unbeliever in the congregation are very real. There can be other absences such as the failure to stress the divine imperative to holy living, the failure to draw moral lessons from biblical characters, the sameness of the "sound" of the preaching week by week, the insistence of the big picture, and the Word as a bludgeon, while there is the absence of reference to the importance of mere prepositions and the scalpel of the Word.

Some of Ed Clowney's sermons were very memorable, especially those based on the Gospels, like his sermon on the prodigal son. His sermon on David's three heroes bringing water to him from Bethlehem's well is a good example of historic redemptive preaching that avoids a good number of the potential pitfalls of this kind of preaching. I was thankful to have had that injection into my life but was glad that it came after the men I had met in Wales who were Welsh Calvinistic Methodists and stressed an awakening and experiential ministry. I don't think that the men I most admire in the United States, who give addresses at the big conferences of T4G and Ligonier and the Shepherds' Conference and Banner of Truth, are men who have become the grand preachers they are because they have elevated the biblical-theological to becoming the silver bullet to an awakening ministry. But they all have come to find biblical theology very helpful for structure and flavor, and for stressing the Lord Christ.

Clair Davis, the professor of church history who followed Paul Woolley at Westminster, paid a little tribute to Ed Clowney, writing,

> Jay Adams was right; he was the most brilliant of all of us. He used that brain to show us Jesus everywhere in the Word, and to expose all the phony ones out there. He shaped a Westminster of love and respect and mutual blessing, not that easy in a seminary. He laughed with us the laughter of Abraham and Sarah when they heard Isaac was coming, first with their sceptical laughter, then their laughter of blessing, as Ed led us in maturing together in gospel joy. Being a church historian wasn't always good for me, tempting me to be cynical about God's people. But Ed wasn't that way, though he knew a lot more about unbelief and scandal than I did. He rejoiced in Jesus and in his people and brought me far along that way. Thank you, Jesus, for him![16]

We hope that the family might find a biographer who could give us a life of Ed Clowney. Boxes of his literary remains are in a state of air-conditioned preservation in the basement of Westminster's library, including the invaluable, lengthy private journal he kept during the last years of his life. We long to know as much as is possible about such a Christ-centered man.

Arthur W. Kuschke Jr.

There is a certain piety, a life of humble, cheerful godliness, that I associate with the United States. It seems more abundant there, the emphasis on hospitality, family and personal devotions, prayer, evangelistic and missionary concern, and warm affection. It is present in my own country and congregation, and I thank God for that, but I have met it all over the United States and benefited much from such a fragrance of heaven on earth. Alan D.

16. Clair Davis, "A Wee Tribute to Ed Clowney," https://banneroftruth.org/us/resources/articles/2014/wee-tribute-ed-clowney/

Strange teaches in the Mid-America Reformed Seminary in Dyer, Indiana, and is a pastor in an OPC congregation in New Lennox, Illinois. He has paid a happy tribute to the late librarian at Westminster Seminary, his friend Arthur Kuschke.[17]

Strange begins by referring to a Presbyterian wag who suggested one could get an idea of eternity by imagining John Skilton and Arthur Kuschke arriving at a narrow passageway at the same time and one saying to the other, "Apres vous, Claude," to meet the response, "Non! Apres vous, Cecile!" and each one saying this to the other over and over again, insisting that the other go first, continuing on forever, neither of them willing to go before the other. It is a humorous and a true picture of the humility and dignity of each of those delightful men.

Arthur is described by Strange as a dignified man, cultured, well-mannered, and a true gentleman who genuinely considered others better than himself and delighted in the vocation of serving his Lord, the church, the seminary, and his family. He was a particular encouragement to me as he had been to so many others. He is the only member of staff at the seminary to turn up in Aberystwyth on a Sunday morning, so that my first sight of him was from the pulpit, sitting in a pew in Alfred Place Baptist Church.

He was born and raised in Wilkes-Barre, Pennsylvania. There was Welsh blood in the family as many Welsh people had emigrated to that area to work in the coal mines. In his lectures on hymnody, Kuschke had a special category consisting of Welsh tunes and hymnwriters. If I had known he was to be there that morning in Aberystwyth, I would have had more time to effectually plead with him not to hurry off after the service: "Please come to the manse for lunch—please!" And I would have chosen magnificent hymn tunes like *Blaenwern, Trewen, Cwm Rhondda*, and *Pantyfedwen* to accompany our praise.

17. Alan D. Strange, "In Memoriam: The Rev. Arthur W. Kuschke, Jr.," *Ordained Servant* 22 (2013), https://opc.org/OS/Ordained_Servant_2013.pdf.

Once I retired from Aberystwyth, I went around many churches, sat in the congregations, and longed to hear the gospel being preached, not in word only but in power and in the Holy Spirit and in much assurance. I once preached in Glenside OPC, and most of the faculty were in the congregation with their wives and children, but it was Kuschke who came with the utmost seriousness to talk to me afterward, to thank me and say that he lived to hear free-grace preaching.

Arthur had studied in Wheaton, graduating in 1936, the year the OPC was formed, and he proceeded to study under Machen for a few months before Machen's death in January 1937. In 1940 he got an MTh degree and was ordained, and he served in the Philadelphia presbytery all his life. In 1946 he became the librarian at Westminster and remained in that post until 1979, the longest-serving librarian in the seminary's history. The library was built up and is quite magnificent today. In 1963 the new library was opened. Of course, it was John Murray who was asked to cut the sod at its dedication. We all stood around and watched keenly. We had never seen anyone cutting the sod before. He did it as if he had always been doing this kind of thing. He dug the spade in deeply, drew it out, and at a ninety-degree angle dug it in again, drew it out, then drove it in again. As he did this for the fourth time, he lifted out a mighty sod of earth and turf, to our tumultuous applause.

About a year later the library was ready to receive its books, and Arthur had planned the whole layout of the new library and had organized the means of the transfer. A line of willing volunteer students with forty blue-mesh baskets carried the books from the old library to the new to designated numbered and lettered shelves. It worked like clockwork, and soon a wonderful library was full of books while the old, bereft wooden carriage house was empty. It was there that in one long summer, a very long table was covered in open commentaries on Romans and John Murray was moving about in consulting them, finally completing his magisterial commentary on the epistle. That building was soon to become extra lecture rooms, but there was the smiling and relieved Arthur Kuschke (it had not rained), mission accomplished, in his fireproof, air-conditioned domain.

Retirement did not mean golf and gathering shells on Florida beaches. Arthur continued to be "valiant for truth," longing that the seminary and denomination that he loved would continue to be institutions bearing the clearest testimonies to the gospel that once had been revealed to us, as summarized in the great confessions of faith. So he was drawn into the main controversies that were raised in those institutions—the Gordon Clark matter, the Peniel case, the Shepherd controversy, the Jon Pedersen case, the John Kinnaird case, and more. Where there is zeal for the true gospel and the challenge to its utterly gracious character, then there are going to be some divisions.

Arthur Kuschke was the chairman for many years of the Committee on Candidates and Credentials in the Presbytery of Philadelphia. At the origins of the OPC, there were mainly examination of men who were leaving the Presbyterian Church (USA) over that denomination's liberalism. Then as the decades went by, men from various denominations and diverse backgrounds sought a pulpit in its midst. Arthur was keen that such men grasped the Reformed faith and knew what its confession stood for, which meant spending time with them personally and advising them in their studies and in further preparation.

He loved walking, was a nature enthusiast, took particular interest in the trees and bushes on the seminary grounds, liked to stroll along the Wissahickon Creek, knew the varieties of trees and the birds, even by their song. Summer vacations were spent in Maine. He loved reading, of course, and was a member of no less than five local libraries. He loved to read the books of John Murray, Cornelius Van Til, and Dr. Martyn Lloyd-Jones. He was also a philatelist. He had a special interest in music, and I remember showing him some vinyl I had bought of an early opera that he also knew and liked. He had his own extensive collection. He was very involved in the choosing of the hymns and the planning of the structure of the *Trinity Hymnal's* first edition.

On Sunday afternoons were the "apple parties" with his children, as described by Mrs. Kuschke: "Here catechism instruction took place, interspersed with a snack of cheese, crackers, and a slice of apple offered (carefully) on the tip of a paring knife to each as he had his turn." In the first grade the children were each given a Bible at Christmas. Mrs. Kuschke recorded, "It was a special joy to see our children make their profession of faith, to be thankful to the Lord for their fine Christian spouses, to welcome grandchildren and see them make professions of faith within the OPC."[18]

Alan D. Strange summarizes his affectionate tribute to his friend Arthur W. Kuschke Jr. thus:

> If asked about his hope, however, he would undoubtedly have answered in something of the fashion of J. Gresham Machen: "So thankful for the active obedience of Christ; no hope without it." Arthur Kuschke, to any who knew him, was a man who sought to magnify Christ and to give all glory to God. He was a man who knew that he was a miserable sinner, having no hope of eternal life apart from the grace of God in Christ. Christ, and Christ alone, was all his hope and stay. *Soli Deo Gloria.*[19]

Robert Knudsen

Robert Knudsen was from California. He could remember as a boy of seven putting his trust, by Spirit-worked grace, in the Lord Jesus Christ as his Savior and Lord. When he was a teenager, God's providence led him to meet an eminent OPC minister, Robert Churchill, and in 1944, while America was still at war, he became a student at Westminster after graduating from the University of California. He impressed the Westminster faculty with his intellectual gifts, and Van Til encouraged him to pursue further studies. He went from Philadelphia to study in Union Seminary under Reinhold Neibuhr and Paul Tillich.

18. Strange, "In Memoriam: The Rev. Arthur W. Kuschke, Jr."
19. Strange, "In Memoriam: The Rev. Arthur W. Kuschke, Jr."

Van Til encouraged Bob to study in the Netherlands in 1949. He became fluent in Dutch and married a Dutch woman, Ali Molder, with whom he had four sons. He also did graduate studies in Basel under Barth. He returned to Westminster and obtained his PhD in 1958. During his years in Amsterdam, he had acquired a love for Herman Dooyeweerd, a professor of law and jurisprudence at the Vrije Universiteit and a principal founder of Reformational philosophy, and his *New Critique of Theoretical Thought.*

After obtaining his PhD, Knudsen was invited to teach at Westminster in 1958. His compulsory course was called "Evidences." We are told that students said, "If you want the basic principles, go to Van Til. If you want application, go to Knudsen."

Professor Knudsen was a splendid family man. They lost one of their sons, Timothy, to cancer. Bill Edgar says, "Rather than becoming embittered, Bob and Ali have been extremely sensitive to the suffering of others." Some of his praying then at faculty meetings was incredibly moving. Many at Westminster could remember him saying, "Now if I were running the universe, I would have done it differently, but thank God I am not." He had abundant personal trust that the Lord's ways are better than our own ways. The family attended Trinity Church in Hatboro. He often played the piano in the assembly; in fact, the very Sunday night he was taken ill, he had been accompanying the singing at church. I once heard him play a piece by Chopin in a student-and-faculty fellowship evening. He was often heard to say that he wished people could be more Romantic, that Chopin and other composers of that time were neglected. He was a deeply feeling person. Bill Edgar judges that he was perhaps the last great Romantic hero at Westminster. He also had a special burden for the poor and minority groups in Philadelphia.

Professor Knudsen took his teaching at Westminster seriously, and he exhorted the younger staff in the department to be wise and hardworking. He was their friend, resource, counselor, and example. Bill Edgar remembers how he would pay occasional visits to him in his little office in the library basement and give him some fatherly wisdom that he thought was needed. "Then he always called me

'William,' like a parent being stern with their children, but not all that stern at all. I was eager to know what was on his mind, whether getting the right balance between family and work or how he worked things out with his wife, becoming quite wistful in the process, saying once, 'I am amazed that one woman could love me and want to be with me for so many years.'"

He wrote a book of essays called *Roots and Branches: The Quest for Meaning and Truth in Modern Thought*. In the volume is his inaugural lecture, "The Transcendental Perspective of Westminster's Apologetics." It is, according to Professor Bill Edgar, "something of a masterpiece, an apt summary of the genius of presuppositional apologetics." Professor Edgar describes him as "an extraordinary gentleman-scholar," concluding his preface to the book thus: "We have here an astonishing vintage! Let us consume with gratitude and humility!"[20]

Norman Shepherd

Norman Shepherd returned from his years studying in the Netherlands while I was in my second year, and every subsequent contact I had with him was delightful. He taught us a most helpful course on the canon of Scripture. During that time the InterVarsity groups from the Philadelphia and Pennsylvania universities were invited to a Saturday conference at Westminster to attend some lectures by Van Til and Young and ask questions. Norman was on a panel, and then sat among the students over coffee and answered their questions. One man was obviously a student of theology, and he argued that the authority for what we believed lay in the church, not in Scripture. He did not know that he

20. William Edgar, introduction to Robert D. Knudsen, *Roots and Branches: The Quest for Meaning and Truth in Modern Thought*, ed. Donald Knudsen (St. Catharines, Ont.: Paideia Press, 2009).

was debating this with Norman, who'd had to go over this ground very thoroughly in the relation of the church making pronouncements concerning the New Testament canon. I sat back and listened with inward delight as Norman gently and clearly answered every point the man raised.

Another course, New Testament Biblical Theology, or NTBT as it was always called, was taught by Norman as he set out before us an understanding of the great New Testament words and phrases like the *kingdom of God*, the *Son of Man*, the *Son of God*, and the *Messiah*. Again, it was most helpful. I heard him preach once, as he occupied the pulpit regularly at the exclusively psalm-singing Knox Orthodox Presbyterian Church, with John Murray in the congregation.

Later an issue was raised concerning his views of justification: Are we justified by a faith that obeys the law of God? What is the relationship of our works to our being declared righteous? It became an international debate. Feeling the temperature rising and the possibility of major division in a theological atmosphere already poisoned by the teaching of the New Perspective on the apostle Paul, I would long that Norman could have backed off at the beginning and asserted his total satisfaction with the chapter on justification in the Westminster Confession of Faith, letting the issue die and never returning to that theme again, as it regards the very heart of biblical Christianity.

Dick Gaffin and Norman Shepherd at that tense time of conflict once flew to Nairobi. Dick was speaking in the Reformed Ecumenical Synod in South Africa on the Holy Spirit, and they visited Thika to call on Keith Underhill, a graduate of Westminster Seminary who was a member of our congregation in Aberystwyth. When they had settled down, Keith raised the issue. "What is this controversy all about, Norman? What do you believe about works and justification?" So, Norman Shepherd explained to him and Dick his understanding of the subject. It seemed so very orthodox; in fact, when he finished speaking, Dick said, "Norman, if you said that to the faculty and board at Westminster, they would be totally satisfied with your convictions." But there were always some qualifications Norman referred to that raised questions and frowns. It was a grievous dispute, and was it necessary? In God's providence, it certainly resulted in a firm assertion in numerous conversations and books written by those of Reformed orthodox persuasion of the imputation of the righteousness of Christ as the only foundation of a believing sinner's hope.

Jay Adams

In 1963 I would occasionally see this big-bearded figure in a sports coat turning up on the campus where he was teaching a course on pulpit speech. I privately dismissed him as a lumberjack whom we would never hear of again. It was thirty-four-year-old Jay Adams. When he was in school as a fifteen-year-old, a friend gave him a copy of the New Testament, which God used, as Jay read, to save him. He attended the prestigious Johns Hopkins University and then went to the Reformed Episcopal Seminary and then Temple University in Philadelphia. He got his PhD at the University of Missouri. He pastored congregations in New Jersey and Pennsylvania. He made his own translation of the New Testament, and for men entering the ministry, his main exhortation was always that they have a sound theology and become serious exegetes of Scripture.

In 1965 he gained confidence and insight through some acquaintance with the counseling convictions of Orval Hobbart Mowrer of the University of Illinois with his emphasis on behavior therapy. "Individuals must accept responsibility for their own deviant behavior," Mowrer insisted. "For healing and life transformation, you must acknowledge your own failures to meet the problems that are common to all." Jay examined and reformed this tangible secular methodology by the claims of biblical revelation so as to develop a radical approach to Christian counseling. He took seriously such Scriptures as 2 Peter 1:3, "His divine power has given to us all things that pertain to life and godliness, through the knowledge of Him who called us by glory and virtue." So, in 1970, now on the staff at Westminster and soon to become professor of practical theology, his best-selling book, *Competent to Counsel*, exploded on the scene. This book was to be followed by one hundred other books and one or two regularly appearing journals that were all worth owning.

Jay Adams reminded his readers of Romans 15:14, "Concerning you, my brethren, that you also are full of goodness, filled with all knowledge, able also to admonish one another." The word *admonish* there is a translation of the Greek word *noutheteo*, and Jay used it to define his approach to counseling. "Nouthetic" counseling involves three *c*'s—concern, confrontation, and change. Though it is common for the broader professedly evangelical world to criticize nouthetic counseling for lacking in compassion and being simplistic, I have found Jay Adams to be most helpful and have read most of his writings. I believe that his main thesis is dead right.

And We "Vegetables"

It is the most famous joke about the late British prime minister, Mrs. Margaret Thatcher that goes like this: Mrs. Thatcher took her cabinet colleagues out to dinner. The waitress came to her first and asked what she would be eating that night. She told the waitress that she would have the steak. Then the waitress said, "And the vegetables?" "Oh, they'll have the steak too," Mrs. Thatcher is reported as replying. Of course, this incident never happened, but it challenges the authority with which Mrs. Thatcher led the government for over eleven years. The joke is making her out to be an autocrat.

Now, I must add this postscript to my appreciation of this extraordinary galaxy of faculty members—the "steak"—that established Westminster Seminary and nurtured its first thirty years. One mighty result of the example they set for theological training was the birth and growth of at least ten confessional seminaries springing up across the United States in the next fifty years, all modeling themselves on the original Princeton and later Westminster. The faculty created a credible and attainable example of a seminary that was contemporary and scholarly but maintained the historic Christian faith. These seminaries all hold J. Gresham Machen in the highest honor. In 2023 we will be celebrating the centenary of his book *Christianity and Liberalism*, and thousands of students are being prepared for the ministry in all those seminaries today who hold to his same convictions.

"And the vegetables?" What about my fellow students? Seminaries are a lot like conferences. The messages or lectures are the bonus, while the people who teach, to whom you have personal access, and particularly the men with whom you study and eat and pray and talk and argue and correspond with for the rest of your life are the abiding momentum of your consecration and service. They in their faithfulness continue to say to you, "Keep the faith. Go on! and go on! Don't break our hearts by falling away," and we repeat those last words of Cornelius Van Til to ourselves as we would bid him goodbye after a delightful conversation. He would say, "We shall soon meet at Jesus's feet."

There were the nonfaculty: first, a little group of graduate students who were occasionally on campus to catch up with their tutors, as they were now pastoring and completing their PhDs. There was George Knight III, the author of that splendid commentary on the Pastoral Epistles and his work on the "faithful sayings" in those letters of Paul, lecturing in Florida. There was the tall Henry Krabbendam, the professor in Covenant College for many years, the evangelist, the visitor to Uganda, and one of the chief teachers of biblical evangelism today, who got his PhD in 1969 at the same Westminster commencement as Richard Gaffin. Dick had studied in Marberg, Germany, as Machen had done, and worshiped there in the same Baptist church where Machen spent his Lord's Day mornings. Dick taught in Westminster for about thirty years, while married to his late wife, Jean, the daughter of E. J. Young. Dick is loved by faculty and students alike for his piety, soundness, and lively lecturing. Some vegetables!

Then there were us undergraduates. Larry Mills is a Presbyterian Church in America (PCA) pastor and officer in Belhaven College in Jackson. He and his wife were particularly kind to me throughout my time there. Will Metzger was and remains an impressive godly

Geoff Thomas and Walter Chantry, once students together at the seminary, at the occasion of Geoff receiving an honorary DD from Westminster around the year 2012.

man and the author of a fine book on evangelism, *Tell the Truth*. He worked all his life for the InterVarsity Christian Fellowship with students at the University of Delaware. Thomas Nicholas was also in the class of 1964, and he returned soon to Westminster to teach Hebrew. Then there was a special friend, Walt Chantry, one year above me, pastor for years in a Baptist church in Carlisle, Pennsylvania. I hold him, his wife, Joie, and his three children in the highest respect. Owen Palmer Robertson was the student president from 1961 to 1962 who welcomed us new men with that beautiful unreconstructed Mississippi accent. What an output of books he has written on the Old Testament, a true son of E. J. Young, and what a blessing his labors have been in Africa at the Christian universities that he has led and where he has taught. My roommate in my final year was a Kikuyu student from Kenya, the late Leonard Kaguru Guchu. George Marsden is four months younger than me, and we were also students together, though he was a year ahead of me. What an array of profitable books he has written! Also in my year were two outstanding men, Bob den Dulk, who became the first president of the Westminster Seminary that opened in Escondido, California, in 1979. What a privilege to be with him and Nelly. And there was John Frame, the prodigious writer. I have found the three volumes of his selected shorter writings the most helpfully informative, though I have read his autobiography and his systematics. I suppose if we make generalizations, I would contrast us as my being a British Puritan in my background, while John was American Presbyterian. I do much admire the lucidity of his writings and the energy and consecration of his mind to serve his Savior. Then there was Ben Short, my first-year roommate and a pastor for years in the United Reformed Church in Canada.

After my time at the seminary, I was to encourage two Aberystwyth graduates, Austin Walker and Keith Underhill, to study at Westminster, and the consequences for their families and churches have been immense, especially in Kenya—but more on them later. So, there you have the vegetables! Aren't those some of the most delicious vegetables you have ever tasted in your whole life?

The evening before graduation, we couple of dozen men, buddies for three years, and a dozen of the faculty, all met for a meal together. There was no bifurcation of teachers and taught. We met as fellow pilgrims, intermixed with one another and scattered around the dining room, and then our dear professors gave us a word of exhortation one by one about the future. John Murray asked us to consider thinking of some subject and specializing in it over the next years, reading as widely and deeply as we could, for there might be an issue facing the church in twenty years' time that our study could directly address and we be of help.

At the graduation, the weather was fair. The service was held in the garden at the back of Machen Hall, full of family and friends. I wished someone from my family could have been present, but a couple of sweet friends from church were there. The highlight, as always, was Dr. Van Til's sermon to us.

Finally, there was the pervasive sense of sadness that it was all over. America. Westminster Seminary. Finished. I had gone there and completed the course, had that molding experience, and now my student days in my twenty-sixth year were at last all over. I should have made much better use of this priceless privilege, not just so satisfied to have got by. I would never see some of those men again. Before me was Wales, earning my living, marriage to Iola, finding a church, becoming a father, and growing up. My sufficiency for all of that was of God.

CHAPTER 7

Coming Home to Wales and Marriage, 1964

I had spent three good years in America, but the day after my graduation, I sailed home. Many non-American students remain in the States, and it is a land of opportunity for the gospel, but some are called to bid it farewell. I returned home for lots of reasons. Love for Mam and Dad. Love for Iola, whom I married six weeks later, she who could certainly live happily nowhere else in the cosmos but in the nation of Wales. But I, too, was constitutionally conservative. I loved the land in which I had spent those long, formative twenty-three years of my life, loving those Christians who had touched my life for good and the pastors whose ministry had shown me what was true preaching.

What Is Wales?

It is not difficult to have a bird's-eye view of Wales, a land of approximately two hundred miles north to south and varying from sixty to over one hundred miles from east to west. Snowdon, the highest mountain in England and Wales, is 3,560 feet high. Standing on the top, you are surrounded by the mountains of Gwynedd, and the peninsula of Llŷn stretches out to Ireland in the west, while England is sixty miles east.

A school friend of mine once flew on a clear day from Cardiff, the capital of Wales, to Dublin, the capital of the Irish Republic. He wrote, "It was a perfect day to pick out the landmarks, and I was hopping from one side of the plane to the other like a little boy.

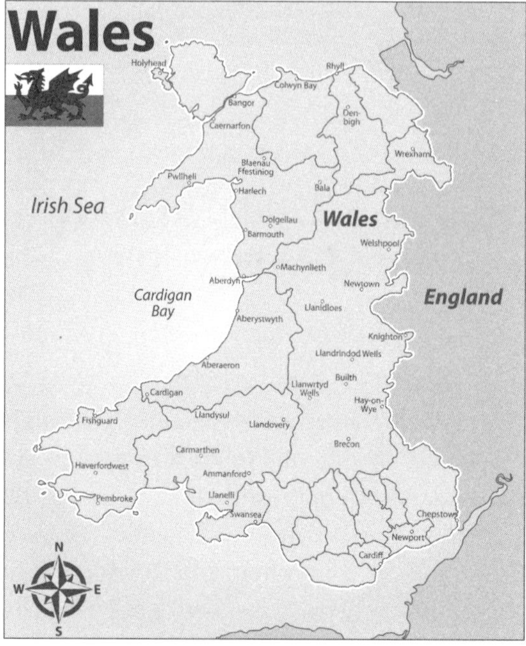

Map of Wales

Pontypridd market, Cadair Arthur, Llyn y Fan—and then, under Tro Gwew, I could see Pantcilwrach, where my parents were staying, and in a field I could pick out my mother. Yet at the same time I could see the whole of Wales from Eryri in the north to the coast of Pembrokeshire in the south, looking just like the map. That moment had always symbolized Wales to me—large enough to fill the horizon but small enough to recognize every human being as an individual."

A country as small as this is just large enough to get to know in a lifetime. The hordes of vacationers who flood in every summer testify to the shrewdness of our neighbors in recognizing a beautiful land when they see one, a more compact Scotland but lacking its abundance of lochs, which seem to double the height of the reflected mountains. For those fortunate to live here, one lifetime is just enough to travel every *A* road and most of the *B* roads, climb every mountain over two thousand feet, bounce flat pebbles along the surface of every lake, swim in every bay, catch a glimpse of all the native fauna, and photograph every waterfall, with plenty of time to see that Victorian invention designed to draw the tourists once the railways were built, the "Seven Wonders of Wales"—Snowdon's mount, Wrexham's steeple, Gresford's bells, Llangollen's bridge, Winefride's well, Rhaeadr's waterfall, and Overton's graveyard—especially if you live in the northeast corner.

There is no need to be in a hurry to know all the towns of Wales, enjoying in each one tea and Welsh cakes before riding on the Transporter Bridge at Newport, going up the Cliff Railway in Aberystwyth, taking a boat trip to Caldey Island, going down deep into the Big Pit in Blaenavon, Torfaen, or into the slate mine in Blaenau Ffestiniog, visiting Bodnant Garden in the spring, or the great castles of North Wales, Harlech, Caernarfon, Conwy, and Beaumaris.

My conviction was that every part of Wales was small enough to know and care about, and being away from it for three years made me increasingly concerned about its life and future. I could never feel like that about an adopted land, however great my debt for the education it had given me or the welcome I'd had from its people and the privilege of sitting in its godly, loving households.

You can also know roughly the state of the gospel throughout the entire principality: the Bible belt from Haverfordwest to Caerwent, then the Bible button, Cardiff, the religious consumer's dream. The valleys suffer from the aridity of materialism, and people today have access to bigger churches elsewhere, so congregations are static and vulnerable to disputes. There is the empty countryside in the middle of Wales, where few preachers will stay for long—that is the villages near Cardigan Bay and the Irish Sea in the west and then along the border with England in the east in Breconshire, Radnorshire, and Montgomeryshire. There you will meet declining, elderly congregations as you do in the Highlands of Scotland or in the west country of Somerset, Devon, and Cornwall.

Yet Wales is a place where you quickly learn of the encouragements, the explosion of activities in the summer months on beautiful beaches and in camps and conferences. New faces are inquiring about

Christianity. What a change for the better has taken place in North Wales in the last fifty years. I know that next year, as every year, I will make fresh discoveries of awakening ministries of men I had never heard of, and I will meet growing Christians. Those have been the regular milestones I have come across on my long journey. In past years, if there was one remarkable outpouring on a single Welsh congregation, Brazil and Finland would catch wind of it within a month. Planeloads of people would soon be visiting the church. But we do not see that today. It has not been God's way. What we do see is thousands of anonymous followers of Christ, instructing their children in the Scriptures, worshiping in Bible-believing congregations, reading Christian magazines, attending conferences and camps,

Our three daughters dressed in traditional Welsh costume one day in the year and going to school.

visiting Christian websites, praying for one another, grieving over the self-destruction of educational institutions, the drug culture, the collapse of marriage, and the irrelevance of so many pulpits, and yet finding assurance that over Wales the Lord Jesus Christ is reigning and building His church.

And one day might they not see a new Wales in a new heavens and earth, where the earth they love, from its mountains to its blades of grass and drops of rain, will be replete with the righteousness of Christ? That hope energizes us to work today, always abounding in kingdom activities. This is never in vain in the Lord (1 Cor. 15:58).

Blaenau Ffestiniog

It is time I revealed my wife of fifty-two years without whom I would never have stayed in Aberystwyth for fifty years of ministry, without whose patient support and love I could not have continued as a preacher. This Baptist church had had a succession of pastors, none staying long after the first preacher 150 years ago who remained for twenty years. When people discussed my staying in Aber for a lifetime, some would nod their heads and say, "It's because of Iola." But I never had a serious call to go anywhere else, and Iola and the children loved living in Aberystwyth. I never set out to stay in this little town.

Iola was born in the middle of the Second World War in North Wales in a town called Blaenau Ffestiniog near Snowdonia National Park, sixty miles north of Aberystwyth. It was then a remarkable community, founded on one industry, that of slate mining (though the mines were called "quarries"). It was a town of work for men—men who labored in teams, drilling into the slate in underground caverns, inserting dynamite, exploding the charge, and then bringing huge boulders of slate to the surface. There they set to and dressed those stones, making roof slates of different names and sizes such as Empress 26x16, Princess 24x14, Duchess 24x12, Countess 20x10, and Wide Lady 16x10. The industry brought men together to support one another and trust one another because it was dangerous, manly work. The very toil brought camaraderie and mutual recognition to them, their families, and even the children of the town. But these people, because of an earlier grace, were also committed to the value of education and to nonconformist religion, radical thought, and the morality of the Bible. They'd talk freely and feelingly about these matters. Conversations and debate in their cabins over their sandwiches and flasks of tea were vital to them. Those were the days when radio was in its infancy, and there were no TVs. It had been a monoglot Welsh culture for over a millennium, though the school education, by government policy, was through the English language.

Iola's father, J. R. Williams, was one of those Blaenau men, of medium height, strong, with a beautiful, distinctive voice and stubby fingers. He had a delightful sense of humor, and was musical and religious, a conscientious objector, with two of his three brothers becoming Congregationalist ministers. When J. R. was fourteen years of age in 1920, he became a slate quarryman working in the Cwmorthin quarry high above Blaenau, getting up at six in the morning and walking up a mountain a mile or two in all kinds of weather to work—at fourteen! But in the 1930s he married Grace, and she was restless about his continuing as a quarryman with its accompanying dangers, and eventually they opened a jewelry and china shop called Granville, which they ran successfully until the end of their working lives.

But even more radical was a change in their beliefs when the Rev. J. Elwyn Davies (whom I had met as a student in 1958) became their pastor in Jerwsalem Welsh Independent Church, and for the first time in their lives they heard historic Christian teaching and the theology beloved by the great figures in Welsh church life. They became acquainted with the translator of the Scriptures, Bishop William Morgan, as well as Ann Griffiths and Williams Pantycelyn, both magnificent hymnists, and Thomas Charles and Martyn Lloyd-Jones.

They admired their new pastor, Elwyn, and got on with him culturally. They were disturbed in a good way by this new style of ministry, with his evangelical emphases, and one evening they invited Elwyn to come to their home and explain to them personally this message. Why was it necessary for God the Son to die on Golgotha? The daughters, Rhiain and Iola, were sent to bed early while downstairs they faintly heard distant murmurings as Elwyn spent an enriching couple of hours with them so that they grasped and believed the message of what the New Testament calls the "foolishness of the cross." We deserve eternal death because we are sinners, but Jesus Christ, the Lamb of God, because He loved us, took our guilt and gave His life in our place. So, becoming a Christian was in fact not determining to turn over a new leaf and becoming a moral person but, rather, receiving God's gift of forgiveness through entrusting ourselves individually, in our first definitive response, into the hands of Jesus as our Lord and Savior because of all He is and all He'd accomplished, then going on doing this every single day while living and while dying. "I am trusting Thee, Lord Jesus, trusting only Thee, trusting Thee for full salvation, great and free."[1] Would that many more had been given the desire and insight that John and Grace received during those brief years of Elwyn's preaching. The sisters Rhiain and Iola grasped this truth for themselves in their own ways.

Rhiain Williams

Rhiain's best friend was Nerys, and she told Rhiain one day that she had become a Christian. Rhiain was flabbergasted and decided there and then that she would not follow suit. She was as good as she wanted to be. But the following year, six teenagers were constrained to meet in a discipleship class. During those meetings it dawned on Rhiain that Jesus Christ was a real person still and that He had a personal relationship and relevance to people other than preachers. In his quiet earnest way, Elwyn made clear to her that she needed to repent and receive Christ as her personal Lord and Savior. He explained that there was no point in becoming a member of the church without really knowing and trusting the Lord Jesus. She later recalled, "Nevertheless in my heart I was quite defiant, but during one restless night a few months later, I came to a moment of truth in the darkness. I prayed that I might not be physically or spiritually

1. Frances Ridley Havergal, "I Am Trusting," 1874.

blind. Later the following day on my way home from school, I went to see Elwyn Davies at his home. Yes, of course he would see me. He serenely took time to explain the gospel and to pray with me. From that time I knew I was a Christian."[2]

Iola Williams

To Iola assurance came in the first Evangelical Movement of Wales camp held in the summer of 1954. You know that the message of the Bible, first of all, challenges men and women to consider whether it is true or that everything is a matter of luck, that this world, as we live in it and experience its grandeur and wonder, came about by mere chance. Are Beethoven and Rembrandt and Shakespeare and Christopher Wren and Albert Einstein and Jesus of Nazareth the result of chance? Is it mere luck that has brought about an Iola or you or me? Isn't there design and rationality and glory and consistency and divinity everywhere in the cosmos? Don't our consciences warn us and rebuke us when we are motivated and moved by ugly lust and anger and pride and greed? Of course they do. Then that is the voice of God addressing us so that we are without excuse. We know God from what we hear of Him in the great monitor of the conscience that He has placed within us but also in what we see around us and above us, from the ocean's depths and the leaping of the dolphins in the waters of Cardigan Bay to the heights of the cosmos, the firmament, the night sky, the sunset, and the murmuration of starlings. We know we are guilty and helpless creatures who must answer to our Creator, the God of light in whom there is not an atom of lust, pride, or greed. We know of Him especially through His Son, Jesus Christ. Our uninventable Lord is the ultimate proof of the existence of God.

What hope, then, was there for Iola? Men love darkness, and God is light. The message of Jesus to her was that God has loved this world and given up His only begotten Son to incarnation and proclamation and to the sacrifice of Calvary that whoever entrusts themselves to

2. John Emyr, *A Father in the Faith: J. Elwyn Davies (1925–2007)* (Bridgend: Bryntirion Press, 2012), 59.

Him can be pardoned and have everlasting life. So, very simply that thirteen-year-old Iola Williams of Meirionnydd heard and understood this message during those days at the camp—as she had been hearing it from Elwyn Davies in Jerwsalem Chapel each Sunday. She believed in Jesus Christ, and she never doubted from that time on. It was an ordinary conversion. Her growing grasp of the gospel was making God the most important reality in her life. Of course, back then she didn't have a sophisticated and an intellectual faith. It was the trust of a young teenager but no less real and enduring.

Some things took place in that first camp that made her unhappy. Several of the women officers came around the rooms at the end of the week in the late evening and pressured the girls to make a decision for Jesus, to repeat a formula, and so on. Iola and others knew that activity was not helpful or kind, that a line had been crossed, that people were trying to do what God alone is able to do. Real conversion is His grand prerogative, and in that honor none shall share. Salvation is through the activity of the Lord alone, and so we are hemmed in to Him and must deal with Him. "Thou must save and Thou alone."[3] Either He saves us, or we are lost. He is the one who illuminates our minds, convicts, gives life, opens our hearts, and makes us new creatures. So, happily, after that first camp such intrusive activities of man were henceforth rejected.

With this work of grace going on in this group of teenagers, the young people began to meet of their own accord on Friday evenings. Their pastor watched this with much delight:

> There was given to them a missionary zeal greater than was to be seen in any other aspect of the church. As a result, the small circle of children in the reception class grew into a strong troop of local children. They would meet up with one another, and they pastored each other. Before every meeting, whether a talk or a Bible study, they held their own prayer meeting with a majority of them taking part. All this came from heaven, ever the source of quickening life. It came about: and eventually it

3. August M. Toplady, "Rock of Ages," 1776.

> came to an end, but its fruit remains today in the consecrated and mission-minded lives of many of the church's children. It was no flash in the pan, nor was it the fruit of natural effort. A breeze from heaven passed by, and as one who had the privilege of being present, I now know after what I believed then, that in the pure unpolluted breath of those same divine breezes lies the hope of the continuation of the gospel's witness in our land.[4]

Iola spent her teenage years in Ysgol y Moelwyn in Blaenau. She played netball for the school, especially against their great rival, the Dr. Williams' boarding school in Dolgellau. She was head girl for two years, and she took the leading role in the school play, *Agamemnon* by Aeschylus. One of her School Certificate exams was actually in Greek. She took a scholarship exam for Cardiff University and won the scholarship. University students all wore gowns to lectures during those years, but Iola wore a special gown with a diamond-shaped patch on the sleeve to show she had won a scholarship.

Marriage

My first meeting with Iola was one morning at the end of September 1959 in a student prayer meeting at 8:40 in that little room high in the Cathays Park campus building where half a dozen of us students met each day before the first 9:00 a.m. lecture. This pretty new first-year university student [UK: fresher] was there in a plaid dress, and she was different because when we kneeled to pray, she prayed in Welsh. It was impressive.

Iola Williams was a natural leader, intelligent, affectionate, without guile, spiritually minded, and holy. She warmed every encounter by her presence. She could sign the doctrinal statement of the Christian Union (CU) in Cardiff with complete confidence, grasping well what it was saying. She became the female president of the CU. She had chosen at university to study biblical studies as I had—I was one year ahead of her, and we shared lectures for a year. That choice of

4. Emyr, *A Father in the Faith*, 131.

the main subject to study was a mistake for both of us. Neither of us enjoyed the course, and she would rather have studied Welsh.

Her one and only teaching post existed in Gowerton Grammar School for Girls, but she taught for just two years, for at the end of her first year of teaching, I returned from my three years in seminary in Philadelphia, and we were married in 1964. That thwarted the plans of the Inter-Varsity Fellowship to have appointed her as the next women's staff worker for Wales. In September 1965, Eleri was born, and in November I began my ministry in Aberystwyth. This is where we lived together for over fifty years.

Iola was not perfect. She didn't like tea and refused to drink it! She hated driving a car and gave it up as soon as she could. She could be outspoken in occasionally blurting out words about "the English" but without malice. I felt marginalized at breakfast time as my four women planned and prepared for their day ahead. They won. That kitchen was theirs in the mornings. But Iola was a delightful wife and mother. We were given three daughters: Eleri, Catrin, and Fflur. We never lost a minute's sleep over a single one of them. They all became professing new covenant Christians in their early teens, were then baptized, and joined the church. They went to university, met the finest Christian men, and married them. One son-in-law became a preacher, one an elder, and the third a deacon.

My three daughters are all part-time schoolteachers. Eleri is a pastor's wife in London and has been chairperson of the governors of the London Welsh School. She and her husband, Gary Brady, are the parents of five sons, all of whom profess faith in Jesus Christ. Catrin is married to Ian and teaches in Emmaus Christian School in Wiltshire, which their son, Osian, happily attends. Fflur Ellis teaches in a Welsh-language school in Cardiff, and she and Glyn have three children. I stand in awe of all of them. Despite their seeing my inconsistent behavior—almost an angel in the pulpit and almost a devil in the kitchen—the girls have come to love and serve Jesus Christ. God has given me nine grandchildren, the majority of whom have professed their trust in the Savior, some even engaged in full-time

Christian work. All nine of them have Welsh as their first language, and my great-grandchildren also attend Welsh-language schools.

A Blessed Life

So very much of this was due to the influence of Iola, her warm affection and happiness, her constant prayerfulness for family and congregation. She was a woman of prayer, more prayerful than myself, I say to my shame. She had a card list of topics so that she prayed for me, for her daughters, and the grandchildren every day as well as for friends, church members, preachers, and missionaries through the week. All the children, grandchildren, and great-grandchildren have been prayed-for children. She read the Bible in Welsh and then responded to what she had read by speaking to the God of the Scriptures in prayer, in all for about thirty to forty-five minutes every morning.

Iola loved God and never challenged His right to do for her and in her what He judged best, even in permitting her dementia to waste her away near the end of her life. She humbled herself before the God of all grace. Our daughter Catrin can remember Iola coming back from the front room into the kitchen where Catrin was lying down (home from school slightly unwell). She was reading and then, looking up, noticed a red mark on her mother's forehead, evidence that she had been resting her head on something and praying for some time in that posture. She prayed with the girls when she put them to bed, and they prayed too. She prayed on Tuesdays in the church's midweek meeting until she could not do so any longer. But today in a sweeter, nobler song, she sings His power to save.

Iola led the women's work in the church. Alfred Place had never had a pastor's wife like her. She taught the women of the church the Scripture and the way of salvation and prayed with them and for them. The women's work became a gospel work. She taught in Sunday school. She was given to hospitality and invited students to the manse for Sunday lunch (she was a grand cook), and she talked with them during the week when they came to her with their questions. She read constantly and widely—Christian books but also Agatha

Iola and Geoff, circa 2000

Christie. She loved to be in North Wales with her parents especially. "Are we going to America *again* this year?" she would expostulate to me—with a twinkle in her eye—protesting. "I don't know Anglesey!" But the children loved going to the United States, and she did also if the truth should be known, and she had dear American friends whose friendship she treasured, from whom she received much.

Iola was very cultured. She played the piano, and she sang sweetly and clearly. I could hear her voice at times when congregational hymns were being sung from my place in the pulpit. She enjoyed concerts in the Great Hall, and during the last couple of years, she would hum along and try to conduct the music from her seat, though I would grab her hands. She knitted terrific sweaters and cardigans. She did needlework and made bed coverings and embroidery, especially marking the births of the grandchildren by their names and dates and weights.

Iola's Decease

Like all ministers' wives, Iola didn't rain down complements on me after every sermon. Occasionally she would say, "That was good," and especially so in our last year together. "Da iawn," she would tell me (that is, "very good"). She would occasionally express some reservations or questions, but fortunately not very often. I am my own worst critic.

Iola's affliction of dementia struck her grievously. There were times when she would cradle her head in her hands and say, "Oh, my memory!" It was a great strain for us to see someone so vital and affectionate struck down with confusion for those final years. There was a rapid disintegration during her last six weeks.

Her death was bittersweet on October 19, 2016. I was with her through the nights in a single ward in Bronglais Hospital where she spent the last six weeks of her life. At five o'clock that last morning, she sighed and swallowed and passed away, going from a state of grace to a state of glory. I called the manse where our three daughters, Eleri, Catrin, and Fflur, were dozing. They quickly dressed and drove the five minutes to the hospital where in her presence we hugged one another and wept and prayed. I read 2 Timothy 4:7–8: "I have fought the good fight, I have finished the race, I have kept the faith. Finally, there is laid up for me the crown of righteousness, which the Lord, the righteous Judge, will give to me on that Day, and not to me only but also to all who have loved His appearing." My voice cracked a bit halfway through, but Catrin quietly exhorted me, "Go on!" I swallowed and went on. We were thankful that God took her to Himself, but heartbroken that we would see her in this life no longer. She meant so much to us.

In Iola's last week there would be moments on her bed in her deep sleep when she opened her eyes and seemed to be seeing something, and her face would light up in a smile. I am glad that happened; I would expect such things to happen to those who are in Christ Jesus, but I do acknowledge that they also happen to people without any religion. I find no evidence in them as a proof of the existence of her soul being in God's presence right now. It is not her experience of Christ that saved her; it was Christ. It was not her good life and prayers that saved her; it was Christ. It was not her joy that saved her, it was Christ. It was not even her faith that saved her. That was a mere instrument that made her put her trust in Jesus Christ for everything in living and in dying and in the glory beyond. Her presence at the feet of Christ while I am writing these words and while you are reading them is all because of who Christ is and what He did and does do still. He once promised that whoever believed in Him would not perish but have everlasting life. He is not a liar, not self-deluded, not a madman, not a megalomaniac. He Himself said, "The Father loves the Son, and has given all things into His hand. He who believes in the Son has everlasting life" (John 3:35–36). Iola was a mere believer in the Lord Christ and whose hopes of life everlasting were in the achievements and life and promises of Jesus Christ alone. She was a wonderful person, and it was a privilege to be married to her. We lived in the church's manse on the Buarth all our lives together.

A few days after the funeral, I drove off to Cardiff to spend the weekend with Fflur and her family. I got in the car and drove off; it then hit me out of the blue that Iola would never again sit in the passenger seat alongside me as she had done for the last fifty years. I howled my grief and wept as I drove. That intense sorrow returned an hour later as I drove over the Welsh hills, but then God's peace came to me. She was safe in the arms of Jesus.

I have had a lump in my throat as I write this, but I do realize that all the ground of her hope of going to heaven and being forgiven was in the achievements of our wonderful Prophet, Priest, and King, the Lord Jesus Christ, the Son of God. I commend her Savior to all of you as you read my warm words of appreciation of her. I am urging you to receive Him today, just as you are. Take Him now, just as in His providence He has led you to take this book and read these sentences of affection and thanksgiving.

My Call to Alfred Place

How was I called to Aberystwyth? We lived in Swansea for a year after we got married, and then the minister in the Baptist church in Aberystwyth accepted a call to Blackwood. Alfred Place was looking for a minister, and my cousin Bobi on the staff of the university passed on my name and address to one of the deacons, who in turn gave it to the church secretary, who booked me for a Sunday service. The students came in droves to support me. That affected the opinions of many in the congregation. I was asked back twice. The Bible-believing men and women in the congregation prayed earnestly that I would receive the call to become the minister, and in the vote I just got the 75 percent majority needed. I started in November 1965.

CHAPTER 8

Aberystwyth, a Small Town with Almost Everything

I spent half a century in Aberystwyth, and so there must be something attractive about it to keep all the Thomas family very contented over that length of time there. William Cobbett once said, "It is a great error to suppose that people are rendered stupid by remaining always in the same place."[1] Maybe you live far away from Wales in America in someplace with a name like Bouncing Branch, Wyoming! It sounds lovely—living there would be different from anything I have ever experienced, but I can readily imagine it. We admire the paintings of Norman Rockwell of small-town America. So, I can picture the big blue sky, prairies going off to a distant range of mountains, cattle, cornfields, forests, and tanned men who work on their ranches wearing jeans and either cowboy or baseball hats. In the town is a square with a drugstore, two or three churches, a little town hall, a bar, a real estate business, a doctor's office, a studio where paintings are on display, and on the way out of town, I am seeing in my mind's eye the local radio station, a few garages, some fast-food restaurants, an avenue of shops, and then the school. And for months every year it is hot.

But I would expect that most people of small-town Wyoming have seen few if any pictures of a small town in Wales nor know anything of its history. So I must tell you about where I have lived for five decades. It is not easy to make history and geography and linguistics

1. William Cobbett, *Rural Rides,* vol. 2 (New York: Cosimo, 2005), 31.

The little town of Aberystwyth

gripping so that you would want to go there yourself, wander the streets, walk the promenade, and breathe in the refreshing sea air. Though I also need to describe it in such a way that the people who were born and raised in Aberystwyth might think, "I didn't know that. That is interesting." It is an important place in Wales and has been described as its cultural capital. I claim that there is only one "Aber" in Wales, and by using that abbreviation most people in the principality are referring to this town of mine. There are hundreds of places in Wales that begin with those four letters—*A*, *B*, *E*, *R*—as the word means "the mouth of," where the river enters the sea, or a "confluence" where one river joins another. I went to school in Abermorlais, where the river Morlais ran into the river Taff. My father was stationmaster in Abercanaid. Only one guess to know the name of the brook in that hamlet that runs into the Taff. Even Scotland has an Aberdeen. But in Wales there is one outstanding "Aber," and that is Aberystwyth.

An Ancient Town Halfway between the North and South of Wales

Aberystwyth is a significant place, not for its name, of course, but principally for its location. In many countries in the world there is a north-south division, and so it is in a small nation like Wales. They are quite different communities, with no major road linking the two. It is impossible to go by train from South Wales to North Wales except via England. There are slight differences in the Welsh language between the two communities, especially in their different pronunciations and some unique words. The northern people are referred to in the south as the "Gogs" (the Welsh word for *north* is *gogledd*). The south has been industrialized and anglicized and has a kind of Bible belt stretching almost a hundred miles from Chepstow in the east to Haverfordwest in the west. More than two million people live there, while less than a million live in the much larger farming area of middle and north Wales. Aberystwyth is where these two halves of the country caress. That suited us and our families well. Iola came from Blaenau Ffestiniog in the north, and I came from Merthyr in the south.

Aber was a fishing village that goes far back into history. The top of the hill south of the town known as Pen Dinas is encircled by a number of embankments. This was an Iron Age fortress inhabited before 400 BC. In other words, while the prophet Malachi was speaking of the coming Messiah (433 BC), and Ezra and Nehemiah were encouraging the exiles who had returned from the Babylonian exile to keep rebuilding Jerusalem, a bustling community thrived on the edge of the present town we know today as Aber.

The first Christians who came to Wales would have been among the tradesmen—Phoenician entrepreneurs and sailors who sailed from Israel across the Mediterranean and through the Strait of Gibraltar, and then north along the Spanish and French coasts and on to Cornwall and Ireland and Wales. They came trading with their holds full of wine and fine materials and garments. The purpose of their voyage was to buy such things as gold from Welsh mines and animal skins. We know of them from the mapped archaeological records of the Middle East potsherds that litter the coastal settlements of the countries with which they traded, indicating the wine that was sold by these first traders. Would they not also have brought the gospel with them if they were in the first generation of Christians who went everywhere preaching the gospel? After the deals were done, the goods exchanged, hands shaken, and the next voyage spoken of, if there were those gripped by the Christian message who lived at the same time as some of Jesus's apostles, these Phoenicians would have shared what had become new and vitally significant to them—the life, teaching, atonement, and resurrection of Jesus of Nazareth, the Son of God. They were the first Christians to speak of their Savior in Wales' "green and pleasant land," particularly here at the heart of Cardigan Bay, where the Ystwyth and Rheidol rivers run into the sea. The wine later became used for the first Communions and Lord's Suppers. What joy for people in Cardigan Bay to see a copy of some page of the Gospels or apostolic letters that the master mariner owned and treasured. Copies were constantly made and sent from one church to another and copied out by individual literate disciples. It was thus, via the sea route, that the gospel would have first been heard in Wales in the earliest days.

The following centuries were known as the "age of the saints" in Wales, famed especially for zeal in taking seriously the Great Commission. The Welsh took the gospel into Ireland and south to Cornwall and Brittany. Portions of the Bible were first translated into Welsh and printed from the sixteenth century, but the most widely used was the 1588 translation of William Morgan, the Welsh Tyndale, at the orders of Queen Elizabeth I. The following century was the period of Puritanism in Wales, and little fires were kindled in different places, though no inextinguishable blaze.

The eighteenth century was the time that the preaching and the living out of the New Testament gospel transformed Wales, when the Christian message then began to wake up the dormant folk of Aberystwyth. In one of Thomas Charles's marvelous letters, there is a description of the preaching at a Sunday school of two young men, an apprentice saddler and one who would become a grocer, whose ministry impacted hundreds of people in the town and which led to the building of the first of five Calvinistic Methodist churches in town (four in the Welsh language). The great 1823 Confession of Faith of the Calvinistic Methodists was drafted and approved in Aberystwyth itself. The site of the building where it was drawn up, in Great Darkgate Street, the main street of the town, is now a shop of a popular pharmaceutical chain. But a little plaque hangs on the wall in the Welsh language announcing this accomplishment. The confession was approved in Tabernacl Chapel. The vital growing Calvinistic Methodist church prospered mightily and planted scores of churches in Cardiganshire. The focus and engine of the 1859 revival in Wales was from the churches of the Aberystwyth area. Modern histories of that awakening will contain a map of the principality, and there at the heart of things is this town and its environs.

The Railway Arrives

In the 1860s an enduring transformational change occurred in this village by the sea. Its geographical isolation was tempered by the arrival of two institutions. First, the Cambrian Railways line from Shrewsbury via Newtown and Machynlleth arrived in Aberystwyth in 1864. The town was to become three hours away from Birmingham and five from London by train. And in 1867 the Cambrian line linking Aberystwyth to Carmarthen and Swansea also opened. The opening day was a Good Friday and the very same day that the new Royal Pier that still stands today was opened. The town bustled; seven thousand visitors were present on that day, far more than the population of the town, as the people had seen and discussed the lengthening pier as it thrust out into Cardigan Bay. Farms and villages all around emptied, and the town was full of horses. Aberystwyth had become a resort.

Then the grand mile-and-a-quarter-long promenade was begun, stretching from Constitution Hill southward to the harbor where it was completed in the 1900s. The river Ystwyth was diverted so that it flowed into the sea along with the river Rheidol at the harbor mouth, the flow of the two rivers keeping the harbor entrance from silting up. A Cliff Railway was erected, whose top station overlooks the town quite spectacularly. There is now also a narrow gauge railway that takes passengers twelve miles up the Rheidol Valley to the waterfalls at Devil's Bridge.

The First Welsh University Commences in 1872

The 1860s was a time of transformation for the town, a tourist boom when hotels and townhouses were erected. The Castle Hotel was opened in 1865 but immediately ran into financial difficulties and was never completed as a hotel. It was bought as a site for the first Welsh university college—the second feature within a few years of the railway coming to town that transformed the community. Henceforth Aberystwyth was divided into "town and gown." The first university college of Wales could be established neither in the south, as the north of Wales objected, nor in the north for the south's loud protest. Aber was chosen, and in 1872 the University College of Wales was opened eight years after the railway arrived. A university women's hall of residence was erected at the northern end of the promenade, Alexandra Hall, and other buildings were purchased and became halls of residence, particularly on the promenade. Later, at the top of Penglais Hill, a large student village was built alongside the new university campus with its Great Hall. The "college by the sea" became "the college on the hill."

Every August two weeklong evangelical conferences are held at the university, one in English at the Great Hall with thirteen hundred people attending, and the following week, one in the Welsh language with two hundred people attending. Leading preachers from around the world give the four morning addresses in the English conference. It is held under the auspices of the Evangelical Movement of Wales. The only year it was not held was 2020 because of the coronavirus pandemic.

Subsequently, many other institutions arrived. The largest seminary in Wales, the Calvinistic Methodist theological college, was erected on the promenade right next door to the university, signifying the national prominence of this denomination. After World War

II, the students training for the ministry there included a number of older, battle-hardened veterans of Europe and North Africa, and from the list of university student presidents in the second half of the 1940s, it appears that these men wielded some influence in the student affairs of the university.

The National Library of Wales Is Erected

The foundation stone of the National Library of Wales was laid on July 15, 1911, and was in use from 1916, but the central block of this imposing building was not completed until 1937. All the schools of north Cardiganshire were closed for the event in 1911. A small boy named Martyn Lloyd-Jones (whose parents had a shop thirteen miles away in the hamlet of Llangeitho) could remember coming with the school and being given a small Union Jack flag to greet King George V and Queen Mary, who were laying the foundation stone. The crowds were there cheering at this conspicuous new development. "The king was forty-five minutes late in appearing," Lloyd-Jones told me, still remembering being miffed at the delay, as every small boy would have been, as they all wanted to go down to the seaside, but the speeches came first. Lloyd-Jones's literary remains—they are not all that many—are now preserved and accessible to readers within this building. They include, to my surprise, a letter of mine that I sent to him in the late 1960s when he had his cancer operation, sympathizing with him and assuring him of our prayers. He kept it—imagine that! Several of the recent national librarians of Wales have been evangelical Christians.

Other institutions came to the town: the Royal Commission on the Ancient and Historical Monuments of Wales, the headquarters of the Welsh teachers' trade union, the Farmers' Union of Wales, the Welsh Language Society, the massive Institute of Grassland and Environmental Research, the Books Council of Wales, the Welsh government offices, and the Ceredigion County offices. The Bronglais Hospital has over two hundred beds and is the center for medical care for a large area of mid-Wales. What was a fishing village

160 years ago is a self-conscious center for education, culture, health, and government today, the queen of Cardigan Bay.

Many English-Language Churches Built

Back in the 1860s, Christianity flourished as never before in Aber. The churches all asked, "Wouldn't the trains bring non-Welsh-speaking tourists?" Yes. "Wouldn't the university draw non-Welsh-speaking students and staff?" Yes. "What are we going to do about it?" These were the questions all the denominations were asking. A giddy anticipation arose and, naturally, some good-hearted competitiveness. No answer from the churches came in to make such a response as "Then we will encourage the development of Welsh-language schools." No, the answer was in anglicizing the people of Ceredigion. So, from 1867 onward, more than half a dozen new English-language church buildings were planned, funds were raised, loans obtained, and those meeting places were erected. The Wesleyans, the Congregationalists, the Baptists, the Presbyterians, the Anglicans, and the Roman Catholics all put up sturdy new English-language chapels within a decade. Initially they were full for the few summer months of vacation time but with some very small congregations for the rest of the year. One hundred and fifty years later, the very reverse is the situation: the Welsh-language churches have declined numerically, but there are a couple of numerically strong English-language causes. Another seminary was erected in Aberystwyth, one to train Roman Catholics, though it has also closed. Nonetheless, Aberystwyth was a religious community for decades, with special emphasis on Christian morals, the family, and the Sabbath.

Today Aber in the 2020s is a middle-class, educationally self-conscious resort on the sea, surrounded by beautiful countryside and mountains. It is very dependent on government money to survive and is internationalist in its outlook, but currently the Ceredigion constituency has a Welsh Nationalist Member of Parliament, currently with a large majority. The town prospers financially with a few homeless people, as in most places, begging at the heart of town. It lacks free enterprise businesses. It has suffered greatly through the economic consequences of the COVID-19 pandemic. Of course, its isolation from the nearest large town, which is more than sixty miles away, has resulted in the coronavirus barely affecting the people of the town. Aberystwyth is the end of the line, its critics say savagely—"back of beyond."

One of its central main streets, North Parade, was reported to be the most expensive street in Wales in 2018. The town has an abundance of restaurants. All that is very alluring for a preacher who has a love of his country, whose desire—with every evangelical Christian in Wales—was that every university town in the principality should have a free-grace pulpit (and now it does), but dangerous too because it was all a rather easy place to be a preacher compared with the places where some holy and powerful preachers have labored long but, alas, to dwindling congregations. I can admire the desire of C. T. Studd (1860–1931) as to where he wanted to preach the gospel: "Some wish to live within the sound of church or chapel bell. I want to run a rescue shop within a yard of hell."[2]

I like Studd. I need his singlemindedness. He once looked at a group of preachers and missionaries and said to them, "Let us not glide through this world and then slip quietly into heaven without having blown the trumpet loud and long for our Redeemer, Jesus Christ. Let us see to it that the devil will hold a thanksgiving service in hell, when he gets the news of our departure from the field of battle."

It is hard to say specifically the size of the population of this community. One gets many answers. In 2001 the town's population according to the census of that year was 16,000, but ten years later the census announced the impossible figure of 13,000. How do 3,000 people vanish? There are 10,000 students at the university, so does that make the population 23,000? The Office for National Statistics says that the built-up area of Aberystwyth is 18,749.[3] You make your

---

2. Charles Thomas Studd, "Quotes," European-American Evangelistic Crusades, accessed November 8, 2021, https://www.eaec.org/faithhallfame/ctstudd.htm.

3. Nomis, "Aberystwyth Built-up area," Office for National Statistics, accessed February 23, 2021, https://www.nomisweb.co.uk/reports/localarea?compare=W37000398.

choice. It is a small but vibrant town. The average summer temperature is around sixty-five degrees and the average winter temperature thirty-five. You will scrape the frost and ice off your car or spray its windscreen just a couple of times a year on those infrequent freezing days.

The language. Yes, the Welsh language, which is so important for our generation. It has been spoken here for many centuries, and now the task facing the people of Ceredigion is to keep it alive and relevant, not to lose it but use it. Aber has two high schools, one of an estimated 1,100 pupils and that educates mainly through the English language, and one of around 600 pupils that educates mainly through the Welsh language. What is the state of the Welsh language in Aberystwyth today?

The large county of Ceredigion, almost fifty miles from north to south, was majority Welsh-speaking until the 2011 census. In Aberystwyth over a century earlier, 52 percent of the town had been bilingual, and 26 percent spoke Welsh only. The county of Ceredigion was 95 percent Welsh-speaking, with three quarters of the inhabitants speaking only Welsh. By the middle of the twentieth century, only half the population of Aberystwyth spoke Welsh, and by the end of the twentieth century, the figure had dropped to just under 40 percent, though this is still double the percent of Welsh speakers for Wales as a whole.

Let me return to small-town America. One August I brought Pastor Don McKinney from such a community in Louisiana to Aberystwyth to preach. We walked down the main street, passing all its small shops and crowds of people. He took it all in and finally turned and asked me, "Why do people in Wales have any need to travel to Disneyworld?"

CHAPTER 9

Christianity in Aberystwyth in the Twentieth Century

What was the spiritual state of the churches within this religious community where a certain young bull was about to enter a certain china shop? Had its pulpits and congregations succeeded in bucking the trend of twentieth-century Wales? Was Aber in any way different? Some individual ministers were different, and in a number of congregations, there were discerning Christians who read books, prayed, and thought deeply on the nature of true religion. But the overwhelming narrative of Wales in those one hundred years was one of the initial spread and triumph of rationalistic religion (or *liberalism* or *modernism*) and then the beginnings of the reemergence of historic confessional Christianity. The century ended witnessing the death throes of the professing church because of modernism, evidenced by dwindling congregations and closing churches and the dearth of preachers entering the ministry and the disappearance of theological colleges. The light was being removed in the land by the grieved Spirit of Truth Himself. He does not give energy to error.

The Fulcrum of the Spread of a New Religion

Liberal religion is the faith of man focused on man himself, on his wit, resources, and abilities. The most highly regarded preachers had become the men of "personality." Genesis 3 tells us that Adam's wife, Eve, chose to put her own views of God above the divine self-disclosure that the Lord had given to her. Hence the phrase you heard most frequently by her followers in the twentieth century was this: "Well, I think of God like this...." The lecturer and writer Saunders Lewis (1893–1985), the most esteemed and creative Welshman of this generation, whom some hoped would be awarded the Nobel prize for literature, came from a famous Calvinistic Methodist family. He must have grown so weary of all this man-centeredness that he proceeded to abandon Presbyterianism completely and became a Roman Catholic.

That confidence in man is utterly different from what is found in confessional Christianity, that is what is summarized, for example, in such documents as the Thirty-Nine Articles, the Synod of Dort, the Westminster Confession, the 1689 Confession of the Baptists, and the 1823 Confession of the Welsh Calvinistic Methodists. These truths were acknowledged by the first principal of the University College in Wales, Thomas Charles Edwards, though he was not as discerning of the consequences of the higher critical movement as he should have been. His statue stands in front of the university on the Aberystwyth promenade, and the sculptor has captured him accurately in his preaching, his arms open wide with a Bible in one hand.

Thomas Charles Edwards was born in Bala in 1837, son of the founder of the Bala Theological College. His mother was the granddaughter of Thomas Charles, the primary founder of the Calvinistic Methodist denomination. He went to his father's college in Bala and then to Oxford, where he attended Wesley's old college, Lincoln College. He preached during his college vacations in the open air to the navvies, the thousands of unskilled men, many from Ireland, who had been building canals and roads. Now they were building railways across Wales. Then after his years as a pastor-preacher in Liverpool (which some described as the capital of North Wales), he became the first university principal in the history of Wales. He wrote two commentaries, a scholarly commentary on 1 Corinthians and a popular, more homiletical one on the epistle to the Hebrews. Until his resignation as principal in 1891, he took a pastoral interest in his students, engaging in correspondence with those who became missionaries and preachers, until finally he died in Bala in 1900.

Coming from Germany and Embraced in Aberystwyth

The historic Christian religion of Thomas Charles Edwards was steadily and stealthily replaced by modernism even while he was in Aberystwyth and Bala. It was spreading like a virus from Anglesey in the north to Monmouthshire in the south, with few leading voices being antibodies providing immunity to its killing influences. Local gospel pulpits and congregations provided islands of health as the sickness spread. This religion had emerged and flourished in Germany where Friedrich Schleiermacher defined Christianity as a collective expression of religious feeling, a sense of dependence. He was followed by men who were more radical in their scorn of historic Christianity, men who came to be dubbed "the masters of suspicion."

Then from Germany this new movement came across the channel, and in the 1880s it became boldly aggressive in Great Britain, where it was resisted by C. H. Spurgeon in London and by John Kennedy of Dingwall in Scotland and in the twentieth century by R. B. Jones of Porth in Wales. They and others like them warned of the "downgrade" of belief in the Word of God that was emerging everywhere. In time it crossed the Atlantic where it was being opposed by Carl Walther in the Lutheran church, and during and after the First World War, J. Gresham Machen wrote and spoke incisively against it. It took longer to reach the Southern Baptists and Southern Presbyterians, but get even there it did. Most theological students and preachers tended to accept the theories of German professors as if they were writing unassailable truths.

Modernism was nourished first by the upper classes—by the Bloomsbury group in London, the art lovers and cafe society of Berlin, and the Left Bank in Paris. What disdain it showed to the Christianity of the Bible! In 1928 Virginia Woolf, the novelist, wrote to her sister, "I have had the most shameful and distressing interview with poor dear Tom Eliot who may be called dead to us all from this day forward. He has become an Anglo-Catholic; he believes in God and immortality, and he goes to church. I was really shocked. A corpse would seem to me more credible than he is. I mean, there is something obscene in a living person sitting by the fire and believing in God."[1] She later drowned herself, filling her pockets with stones before entering the Ouse River. It was three weeks before they discovered her body.

This atheism continued to spread through the decadent bourgeoisie, but not until the 1960s did it profoundly affect the working classes, their popular music, and their fashions. The movement was nourished by the universities' philosophy departments. Then the science departments were affected by Darwinism and its sympathy with genetics and the superiority of the white race. Finally, the arts faculties embraced it. The quality press first promoted it followed by the tabloid press. The media were initially respectful to the Christian ethic, such as BBC radio under Lord Reith, but after his days, both radio and television became its medium. Atheistic spokesmen were given airtime, voices on the *Brains Trust*, firstly men like Bertrand Russell and A. J. Ayer and then the popular atheists: Richard Dawkins, Polly Toynbee, Christopher Hitchens, Carl Sagan, and Sam Harris. They tended to be treated with kid gloves by BBC reporters and were given columns in the weekly *Radio Times*.

Its Main Characteristics

What, then, were the characteristics of the spirit of unbelief as it entered the churches? Gary Dorrien has a three-volume work on the subject entitled *The Making of American Liberal Theology*. Kevin DeYoung has helpfully listed seven of Dorrien's principal marks of rationalistic religion.[2] I summarize and apply his points thus:

1. *Christianity is not based on external authority.* (The 1823 Confession of the Calvinistic Methodists, like all the great confessions, supported each of its statements with a reference to suitable Scriptures.) Reformed orthodoxy stressed

1. Virginia Woolf, *A Change of Perspective*, vol. 3 of *The Letters of Virginia Woolf 1923–1928* (London: Hogarth Press, 1994), 457–58.

2. Kevin DeYoung, "Seven Characteristics of Liberal Theology," TGC, September 26, 2017, https://www.thegospelcoalition.org/blogs/kevin-deyoung/seven-characteristics-of-liberal-theology.

that the Bible was the sole and infallibly sufficient rule of faith and was inerrant in all that it asserted, but liberal theology claims that Christian theology could be genuinely Christian without being based on an external authority. It was modern knowledge and experience that in the twentieth century was to teach the people of Aberystwyth what they were to believe.

2. *Christian thought was to be brought into organic unity with the evolutionary worldview* in an expectation of creating a better society. The kingdom of God was going to come on earth as Christians and churches cooperated with Caesar, accepting many of the findings of Darwin, Freud, and Socialist writers. Jerusalem would be built in England's green and pleasant land.

3. *Christianity had to be open to the verdict of modern intellectual inquiry,* to the authority of reason and experience. Jerusalem bowed to Athens. The professing church heeded the spokesmen of the public square. Christianity was to be understood as a moral way of life and so tolerated and socially relevant.

4. *Christian truth could be known by stories, pictures, and signs.* People had been confused for centuries, said the modernist, by treating the symbols of supernatural and miraculous pictures as being truths themselves. The new religion tells the world that, rather, they are pictures of truths.

5. *Christian discussion about theology is a matter of language; it is not about truth.* Christian debate was not about belief but about language use. Religious terms are analogies and mysteries that are significant when they are taken as they should be, symbolically. They affirm matters that are bigger and wiser than the words themselves.

6. *The historical accuracies of biblical statements and events are not crucial.* What is important is to meet Jesus in the pages of Scripture. The biblical narrative is impressive as it presents to us the extraordinary figure of Jesus. He is the vehicle of God and is salvation to the human race.

7. *True Christianity is the way of Christ, not any particular doctrines about Christ.* It is the morally regenerative spiritual power claimed in Christ's spirit. The true religion is the way of Christ. Christianity is essentially a life, not a doctrine.

This became the overwhelming voice of hundreds of pulpits in twentieth-century Wales, and Aberystwyth, far from being different, was in fact among the leading centers from which this new religion spread. The men called to be pastors in the town had been baptized into this liberal world and life view by the lecturers and recommended books of their denominational seminaries. Not a single conservative denominational seminary was in the whole principality, save for the Bible colleges in Barry and Swansea. Therefore, ministers felt at ease in this university-influenced community; they were coming home, protected by the inborn respect for the office of the minister and covered from evangelical criticism by the umbrella and degrees of the University College of Wales that God had ordained should be established in their small town. There these modernist attitudes were accepted by church-attending staff and taught openly to the students by the Student Christian Movement's weekly meetings. The ministers called to serve churches in Aberystwyth believed that the college staff sitting in the pews and serving as chapel leaders, deacons, elders, and Sunday school teachers overwhelmingly believed the same ideas they as ministers had been taught in their modernist theological colleges.

So, in a spirit of harmony, town and gown merged within each congregation in believing that this new religion was making Christianity relevant, credible, beneficial, and humane to twentieth-century Wales and its future intellectual leaders. They were not going to be country cousins falling behind the English, Scots, and Germans. They all knew how the claims they just occasionally heard from the pulpits were to be interpreted, such as that "Jesus Christ is God," "the Bible is to be trusted," "Christianity is true." An obvious liberal interpretation of Christianity was put on those phrases as they were declared on Sundays and received by hearers. When it was claimed that the minister believed the Scripture, then it was this sort of Scripture he believed, a Bible that did indeed contain inspired words "but, of course, not exclusively so." They were certainly not fundamentalists. When they said that Jesus Christ was God, then they filled that word *God* with their understanding of God. Thus, pulpits and pews all came into agreement in those assertions, with each one giving his own interpretation to the words used. The weekly denominational papers supported and promoted a studiously vague understanding of Christianity. The reality was that what they were defending was something quite different from that which historic Christianity confessed, whose biblical words, pictures, stories, and hymns had been hijacked.

The one thing all were agreed on initially was the Christian ethic. It was believed that it was quite possible to discard the biblical doctrines while maintaining biblical morality. So there were the strictest rules for the university halls of residence. They were either male or female, and no male students were allowed to enter female students' rooms at the cost of expulsion. No theological student was permitted to marry until his course was over. The university believed it had a duty to protect its predominantly young people from potential pregnancies and abortions. It stood *in loco parentis* and was conscious that it was acting on behalf of the parents who had sent their children to study in Aberystwyth, who certainly would not tolerate such intimacies in their own homes.

All this changed at the arrival of the "swinging '60s" when the halls of residence were swiftly mixed with men and women sharing the same floors and bathrooms. The change that followed was not slow or gradual but like an avalanche—and just as catastrophic. Sexual acts are now openly discussed in school classrooms and mainstream broadcasts. Television features a program with a line of naked men or women, both homosexuals and heterosexuals, being chosen by other naked people for a date. The astonishing swiftness of the change has been compared to the crumbling of an Egyptian mummy to dust as fresh air rushes into the long-sealed tomb chamber. That has been one of the features of my lifetime. Biblical morality was initially being sustained in educational organizations, not by their love for the Lord who had given to His creatures His good and wise laws but by the momentum of an earlier grace in society and by custom and inertia. There was no affectionate attachment to the commandments of Sinai, no singing, "Oh, how I love Your law! It is my meditation all the day" (Ps. 119:97). Consequently, there was no energy or discernment to resist the tsunami of the values of the modern atheistic age as it kept flooding in. It has not yet stopped flooding in, nor can one see it ceasing.

Unknown to the people in the pews of the Aberystwyth churches, the great redemptive religion known as Christianity had been drawn into conflict with a totally diverse kind of religious belief destructive to the Christian faith. They were unaware of this because modernism made use of traditional Christian terminology. The professing pulpits' egregious "progressive" bias was completely out of touch with the desires of sincere believers in the congregations. How many of the saints would light up with delight when the old gospel was preached!

The Burial of the 1823 Confession

After the First World War, a reconstruction commission of the Presbyterian Church of Wales claimed it had summarized the 1823 Confession in a very brief set of declaratory articles. Thus, a creedal-based system of doctrine found in Scripture was substituted by a theological minimalism. This action was based on thin and vague Welsh communal ties of education and culture. The Welsh were not going to fall behind the rest of the professing churches. The argument that justified doing this was that some of the time-honored "rigidity" of the scarcely known 1823 Confession "surely appears obsolete to many Presbyterians in this twentieth century." The declaratory articles became part of the constitution of the Presbyterian Church of Wales, a binding law. To the minority of evangelical ministers in the denomination who ministered largely in the industrial areas of South Wales, this was a grievous move from full-orbed Christianity. They were spectators watching their beloved church spending its energies in a vain attempt to lower its testimony to suit the ever-changing sentiment of Welsh ideas.

Seth Joshua (1858–1925) was the main evangelist in Wales in the early decades of the twentieth century. He became the preacher in the Neath Forward Movement, following his brother, Frank, and addressed some twelve hundred people each Sunday. He knew Wales and the working men of the principality as well as anyone in the country. In December 1924 he was interviewed by E. W. Evans, the editor of *Y Cymro*, the most prominent Welsh-language weekly newspaper. It is a fascinating interview. Seth Joshua was not without hope for the future, but he saw a thick darkness spreading across Wales extinguishing the light of the gospel of Jesus Christ. Joshua, now an old man, having experienced the slaughter of the First World War, described Welsh society at that time thus: "It is a mixture of materialism, militarism, bolshevism, socialism, pharisaism, indifferentism, devilism, spiritualism arising from the bottomless pit. The night is dark, but the morning is coming." But fifteen years later the Second World War broke out, and forty years later, the swinging '60s.

One of the advocates and spokesmen for this metamorphosis from the 1823 Confession to minimal statements of the declaratory articles was the first principal of the Theological College in Aberystwyth, Owen Prys. Prys served as principal from 1906 to 1927 and was appointed as moderator of the Calvinistic Methodists in Wales in 1910. He had gone to Trinity College Cambridge where he got a first honors degree and soon spent a year studying in Germany, mainly in Leipzig. He taught divinity, religious philosophy, and ethics. No one of weight stood in an Aberystwyth pulpit resisting this, explaining to the congregation what was going on, warning or protesting.

The other advocate of abandoning the confession was R. J. Rees, the minister of the largest congregation in the town (and probably in all of Wales), Tabernacl Calvinistic Methodist Church, the preacher in the actual building where the 1823 Confession had been accepted by the denomination. A plaque to that effect hung on one of its walls before the empty building (no longer used for worship) was destroyed by arson on July 11, 2008. Rees was the first Welshman to get a first-class honors degree in Mansfield College Oxford in theology. He became minister in Aberystwyth in 1903 on the eve of the 1904 Welsh revival and remained there for nineteen years, from whence he moved to Cardiff where he administered the Forward Movement for twenty-five years.

The Hwyl

When preachers like R. J. Rees wanted to display the fact that they had the Holy Spirit, then in the peroration of their sermons they entered into what was known as the *hwyl*. This reassured the evangelical element in the congregation that God's blessing was resting on them. They were one of the anointed ones. They had what the 1904 revival was all about: "See! Look! Hear!" The hwyl was a form of impassioned utterance halfway between a speech and song, rhythmic and emotional, the sense giving way to the intonation and pathos. I faintly remember it in Bethania, Dowlais, quite infrequently in the 1940s, for example, once in an appeal for financial support for a woman who was a member of the denomination's missionary society working in India with street women. The children were vividly described in their poverty; the abuse they suffered was hinted at, and then we were appealed to give generously. The medium of the appeal was the hwyl. Initially it might have been strangely moving and impressive, when there were greater truths declared from the pulpit and received in the pews, but when I heard it deep in the silver age of Welsh oratory, people would smile to one another after the service as they talked of the rhetorical outburst they had seen and heard. It was by then quietly considered to be a technical trick, part of the stock-in-trade of the more confident or more desperate pulpiteer and on its way out.

R. J. Rees's son Goronwy became a journalist and even a Marxist for a while before reacting against the pact that Hitler and Stalin made. There was intense Russian espionage in Britain before and after the war. The so-called Cambridge Five, recruited in the 1930s, sent back reams of intelligence from positions of power inside the establishment, resulting in many brave Russians being tortured and shot. Goronwy Rees was a friend of some of them, especially the spy Guy Burgess, and finally became the principal of University College of Wales from 1953 to 1957. He lived his life "in moral and spiritual revolt against Calvinism," said his daughter Jenny—that is, in a revolt against the purest form of Christianity itself.

Goronwy could remember his father preaching when the old man "caught the hwyl." It was an unhappy memory:

> One saw before one's eyes a man, whom one had taken to be a man like any other man, quite suddenly transformed into a kind of witch-doctor, demoniac and possessed; it was as if, without any warning, he had gone off his head. As a child born in 1909 I saw this happening on innumerable occasions and in a variety of forms; indeed, among our preachers it was the rule and not the exception. Sometimes the trick was performed by one of the great popular artists of the Welsh pulpit, a man with the looks, the exquisitely arranged and silvered locks, the beautifully modulated voice, of a tragic actor; sometimes by men who had the violent passion and bitter eloquence of prophets; sometimes by some naive, unlettered minister from an isolated chapel in the hills of Cardiganshire, whose sermon was quaint and touching like a primitive painting.
>
> But whatever form it took, the *hwyl* inspired fear and terror in me, and a kind of shuddering shrinking from such bare-faced, bare-breasted display of real or simulated emotion; and also a kind of alarm, because my father also could become, whenever he chose, a victim of this kind of possession. I resented it because in my heart I felt him to be a great man, too good for this kind of thing.[3]

The Evangelical-Ecumenism Conflict

The liberals had inherited all the pulpits in Aberystwyth and knew what was expected of them if they were to hang on to them. They had to please the undiscerning conservatives and not disturb the growing bourgeoisie. They gloried in the fact that their denominations were malleable and capable of adjusting to new cultural developments in Europe and so also in the principality. Their approach was to boast

3. Goronwy Rees, *A Bundle of Sensations: Sketches in Autobiography* (London: Chatto & Windus, 1960), 25.

that the church was always at its best when it laid aside an emphasis on its different interpretations and rather stressed a spirit of unity. So, the ecumenical movement briefly flourished in the 1950s and 1960s in Aberystwyth and then fizzled out. It affirmed that no professing Christian was to judge and condemn what other ministers taught, and everyone's views were to be respected and accepted as equally valid as anyone else's. The prophet Jeremiah could see in his day how the covenant people of God had turned away from Him and followed other gods, bringing leanness and judgment on themselves. This is what any observer would see in Aberystwyth churches from 1900 to 2000 as they shrank and dwindled and merged and closed, except for those congregations where historic Christianity was honored. Jeremiah cried, "How the gold has become dim!" (Lam. 4:1).

The Lord Christ of the Bible, the Son of God, who claimed that He was the truth, used the strongest language in condemning the moralistic religion of the Pharisees. His apostle Paul also, in censuring the teaching of the Judaizing legalists who had crept into the Galatian congregation, was filled with concern. "Let them be accursed!" he wrote about those Trinitarian, moral men who believed in the deity of Christ but did not preach salvation by grace through the work of Christ alone. The legalists were indeed preaching faith—but plus circumcision in order for a believer to be declared righteous. When Paul heard of their insistence that men's works were necessary as their personal contribution to their justification, Paul says, "I could wish that those who trouble you would even cut themselves off" (Gal. 5:12). In other words, the Holy Spirit is wondering through Paul why the Judaizers didn't pick up a knife and instead of circumcising make a complete job of it! A woman once said to B. B. Warfield that she was fearful of divisive disagreements in the coming General Assembly. Warfield told her he rather welcomed such arguments but did not expect there to be any division in the General Assembly. "You cannot split rotten wood," he told her.

In most of the nonconformist congregations in every town were handfuls of evangelical Christians. Their presence was welcomed, their piety admired—just as long as they knew their place. Alfred

Place had a number of such families in the 1960s, some having gone through Inter-Varsity Fellowship during their college years. Such people were shining stars in the church. They led the Friday night youth work, taught in Sunday school, prayed in the midweek meeting, gave generously to support the church's work, and soon became deacons and officers at the first election of officers.

The ecumenical movement was pressing for the structure of a "united church." Its doctrinal basis was a single sentence. Virtual limitless liberty was afforded both of doctrines chosen to be believed or rejected, and a wide range of acceptable practices were permitted—that is, except in just one area, and that was regarding the doctrine of the government of the church. Episcopacy was nonnegotiable. The coming united church had to be governed by bishops. There was no way that Presbyterian church government or Independency would be tolerated. The planned union of Methodists and Anglicans foundered and sank on the rock of the Anglican insistence that the Methodist ministers were required to submit and kneel before the bishops who put their hands on Methodist heads to maintain an "apostolic succession" (though the very teachings of the apostles as laid out, for example, in the letter to the Romans were rejected). How the gold has become dim!

Evangelical opposition to ecumenism was strong, and the spokesman of an analysis of its concerns became Martyn Lloyd-Jones. I had been the pastor of Alfred Place for eleven months when on October 18, 1966, the sixty-six-year-old Lloyd-Jones and forty-five-year-old John Stott came together on the platform of Westminster Central Hall, London. Lloyd-Jones had been invited by the National Assembly of Evangelicals in a meeting organized by the Evangelical Alliance to outline his vision of evangelical unity, and John Stott was the chairman. Lloyd-Jones's views were well known, explained already to the Alliance's evangelical unity commission. On this occasion, what was to become the most famous of his addresses, he called believers for some visible unity among evangelicals to match their spiritual unity. He told the full congregation of the anomalous situation they found themselves in, structurally separated from one another while

Dr. D. Martyn Lloyd-Jones

being united in their denominations with people who denied gospel essentials. There was some uncertainty as to what Dr. Lloyd-Jones was urging by his words "a fellowship, or an association of evangelical churches." He probably intended a network of local independent congregations.

The chairman of such occasions has a limited responsibility of simply ensuring that the event runs smoothly and to express thanks to the speaker at the close. The address would have been largely forgotten if it were not for what happened next. When John Stott rose to announce the closing hymn, he expressed his disagreement with what had been said, history being against Lloyd-Jones. When evangelicals in previous generations had tried to establish a conservative denomination then, Stott said, those attempts failed. Scripture was also against Lloyd-Jones because the faithful remnant in the Bible were within the visible church, not outside it. The final hymn was not sung enthusiastically. Stott later apologized to the Doctor for his anger in what he had blurted out, but the division over the Anglican attitude to ecumenism and that of nonconformists was now clear. The cat was out of the bag.

John Stott could plead that the doctrinal framework of the Church of England was sound in its Thirty-Nine Articles. The evangelicals held the "legal deeds" of the Church of England. He might also plead that churches in the New Testament itself were doctrinally and morally confused. The Anglican church also provided many gospel opportunities for evangelicals. Six months after this London meeting, the first National Evangelical Anglican Congress was held in Keele, and here there was a rededication of Anglicans to the structures and synods of the Church of England. Soon the younger generation came to emphasize their Anglicanism more than their evangelicalism.

But some in the Church of England were alarmed by the theological trajectory of the Keele congress. They were sympathetic to the call of Lloyd-Jones for a more robust ecclesiology. About twenty vicars resigned from the Church of England, including some nationally known leaders like Herbert Carson (author of *Farewell to Anglicanism)* and Bertie Rainsbury, while Reg Burrows later wrote a book on the situation and why he had left the Church of England, called *Dare to Contend!* He founded the Reformed church in Newcastle. The Baptist pastor Basil Howlett considered the issue from a Free Church perspective and wrote a helpful book on the ongoing implications of these tensions over church unity, *1966 and All That: An Evangelical Journey.* Other concerned Anglicans who remained in the Church of England argued that commitment to the evangelical faith must always trump denominational allegiance of any description. Most of their energy was later channeled into parachurch conferences.

The Birth of the Aberystwyth Welsh Evangelical Church

Christian discussion in the United Kingdom buzzed with the events of that night, and one consequence in distant Aberystwyth was a measure of encouragement given to the formation of a Welsh-language congregation. Eight months after the address of Dr. Lloyd-Jones in the Central Hall, Westminster, four men came together in Aberystwyth, in June 1967, to discuss the situation in the Welsh-speaking churches and to pray for God to direct them. Three of them attended different congregations, and the fourth was a Wesleyan minister named Gordon Macdonald, a Welsh pastor. He had become gripped by the doctrines of free and sovereign grace. There was simply indifference to these truths in the churches where he preached. He came to the inevitable conclusion that as the denominational structures of his ministry were opposed to what he believed as the essence of the Christian message (he was thinking of the great *solas* of the Reformation—Christ alone, the Bible alone, grace alone, faith alone, and the glory of God alone), then this rejection was inevitably driving him to separate from those structures.

For three years a fellowship meeting had taken place in the home of my cousin, Professor Bobi Jones, and Gordon had led that meeting. But after he seceded from the Wesleyans, he had to face the fact of the absence of a Welsh-language confessional church, not just in Aberystwyth but in all of Wales. So where could he and his family worship on a Sunday? Thus, the four men had come together and shared their concerns and prayed about them. All came to the conviction that they should establish a Welsh-language church with Gordon as the minister. The first services took place on Sunday, October 1, 1967, in the YWCA building in the heart of town. They were joined by my sister-in-law Rhiain Lewis and her teacher-husband, Keith; a local doctor, Dr. John Williams; my cousin Bobi Jones and his family; and a number of others.

The church grew, and at one time a spiritual awakening among some of the Welsh students at the university swelled the congregation so that the church needed to move to a larger building, the second of four buildings where they have been meeting during their fifty-year existence. All those four men who came together and decided to start a Welsh-language meeting have subsequently gone from a state of grace to a state of glory. But their brave and revolutionary stand to commence a Welsh-language congregation in Aberystwyth over fifty years ago has been fully vindicated. I wholeheartedly understood and supported the decision to start this new charge, and Alfred Place Reformed Baptist Church has welcomed joint bilingual meetings with the brethren in the Welsh Evangelical Church a couple of times a year, and Alfred Place's building was always available to them for any special functions. I was no longer alone in my testimony or in my creative disaffiliation from ecumenical activities.

In 1967 at the end of the spring term, a significant event happened in the Presbyterian Theological College in the town. Seven evangelical students, about a quarter of the student body, resigned from the college in rejecting the liberalism of the lecturers. I knew two of them well and still count them among my closest friends, but the decision they took was not through any advice I gave them. They withdrew because of their commitment to the denomination's 1823 Confession of Faith. Richard Holst was the most eminent of the seven, along with Irfon Hughes. Both served Presbyterian churches for many years, and years later Richard lectured in the Wales Evangelical School of Theology (Union Seminary) and in the new Westminster Seminary in Newcastle. Because of Richard's resignation, he was refused permission to sit his final bachelor's degree exams in the next semester or in his request to being transferred to Bangor University. The theological college was told by sympathetic Christian staff at the university that the bachelor's degree was a university degree, not a college degree, and no one had ever been denied access to an exam for reasons of a student's conscience. The college responded that Richard was "academically" unsuitable even though he had won a scholarship in the previous year. Without the oxygen of evangelical students from conservative churches, the college tottered, and it finally closed in 2003.

One of the Roman Catholic priests in Aberystwyth, John Fitzgerald, had a brilliant mind and was most engaging. He once sent me a superb Welsh hymn on the greatness of God that he had written. It was very impressive. Other ministers in the town thought that he and I would be close, but neither of us felt that. His view of Scripture was higher critical, that of the documentary hypothesis of Graf-Wellhausen; the Bible was not to be taken as plain truth. I mentioned to him the Lord Jesus's reference to Jonah being in the fish's belly for three days, but he felt that that was just a literary device and did not necessitate we were to believe it actually happened. He also believed that grace came via the church and the sacraments rather than in regeneration by the sovereign work of the Holy Spirit giving a person the transforming inward energy of a new birth, making that person a new creation and enabling a favored person to exercise saving trust in the Son of God. A huge difference exists between evangelicalism and sacerdotalism.

There is a widespread assumption that religious solidarity is admirable—Protestant and Catholic, rationalist and conservative.

Sometimes it might be. The willingness of all religions to help the disadvantaged and frail and unborn is good. But solidarity has always come in two forms. There is the solidarity of mutual faith in the Scriptures and the great doctrines and confessions of faith. Then there is the solidarity of intolerant conformism. That was Rome's response to Luther and Latimer and Calvin and Knox.

The battle with modernism has taken 150 years. Skirmishes won too easily are too easily forgotten. We are not to forget and discount the threat of the spirit of an age. We are also forced to face up to our own inadequacies as soldiers of Jesus Christ, such as our follies, bluster, cowardice, and ignorance. We fail too much in our chief vocation as pastor-preachers. We can also undervalue the help we receive from men of different ages and continents and denominations.

All these things must drive us to the final great weapon: "all prayer" (Eph. 6:18). There is nothing like trials and opposition to make us prayerful; it is then that the pages of Scripture shine and become sweetly satisfying. It is in our testings that our graces are polished; it is then that our desire for the glory of heaven is strengthened. Hard-fought protracted warfare is our future, with too speedy a deliverance being quite detrimental to our hopes of success. No deliverance that encourages us to forget the trials we have gone through is valuable. Our prayer to the Lord of hosts in our contemporary conflict is found in the psalmist as he contemplates the strength and cunning of the enemy: "Do not slay them, lest my people forget; scatter them by Your power, and bring them down, O Lord our shield" (Ps. 59:11). That is what I witnessed in Aberystwyth and Wales in the fifty years in which I preached the Bible there: tottering churches eventually brought down.

CHAPTER 10

Alfred Place Baptist Church

Some people will tell you that when you are the minister of a congregation you should have no special friends within that assembly. And they also say that when you leave a congregation and move away, you should put it behind you—or at least simply retain sweet memories (mortifying the bitter ones) but to forget about the people you have left behind. Certainly my closest friends have happened to be people not in the congregation. They are my sister-in-law, Rhiain, and her husband, Keith Lewis. My indebtedness to them is enormous, and I feel just as close to them today as ever. We went on vacations together even to America and France. We celebrated the Christmas season with joyous family parties, and every Sunday night around ten, Keith and I would call and talk about our Sundays in the Welsh Evangelical Church and in Alfred Place. We each had three children of the same ages who all came to faith around the same period in their lives and went to camps together and attended one another's weddings and married fine Christian partners and raised their children to love the Savior and their cousins.

I finally retired from Alfred Place, and my grandson Rhodri Brady, who had been a member of our congregation for five years, was called to follow me. He moved into the manse, a home he had known all his life. I soon left Aberystwyth—for my own sake as much as for his—and moved to London and became a member of a church there, but I cannot forget the friends I had made in Aber. Being a pastor is not just a job. It's not only a calling. It's a relationship. I gave them the Word, yes, but I gave them myself too, and they gave themselves to me. That giving cannot just be consigned to the dustbin of history. Yes, things fade. Yes, new people will be sitting in the old pews, those "who knew not Joseph," whom you hear about on the grapevine and think you might meet one day (and you hope it happens). I am no longer the pastor of Alfred Place, but I will always care for the life and testimony of those people in that congregation in that small town by the sea. I return, for example, for the funeral services of those I esteem as my friends, and one day I suppose I will be buried there, awaiting the day of resurrection.

I moved to Aberystwyth in the autumn of 1965. My salary was £12.50 a week, plus the manse was mine rent-free and its utility bills paid by the church. I was given twelve free Sundays in a year. That was typical of most churches. The money from those churches for preaching in them was considered a means of enhancing one's salary. I took a sabbatical in 1971 and did a pulpit exchange with Al Martin, but I did not find a few months away from the church profitable. I received invitations to preach in many parts of the world, and speaking to a new congregation and hearing other preachers became a mighty refreshing experience. The opportunity to preach to a new congregation can be a means of grace to a pastor.

The Building

My growing impressions of Alfred Place Baptist Church were quite positive. The building erected in 1870 was just the right size, seating a possible two hundred people comfortably, though we certainly did not reach that number. We knew growth as well as decline. The chapel was in the right place in the midst of the town one block from the sea. The building had a gallery at the back and a basement fellowship room. An organ had been installed forty years after the church was built. Until the introduction of the organ, there was a wonderful balance and harmony about the structure of the 1870 auditorium. The pulpit originally had been surrounded by pews on three sides so that it stood out toward the center of a cube that was twenty yards or so in width, twenty yards up to the lovely ceiling, and another twenty

Alfred Place Baptist Church (Independent)

yards to the clock on the gallery that had the solemn words, "The Time Is Short." There reaching out toward the center of this cube was the pulpit and the Bible. But the symmetry had been destroyed around the First World War by setting a large pipe organ on one side next to the pulpit, blocking out light from one large window.

The Congregation

The congregation was always full of young people, children, families, and students. People would carry their hymnbooks to Welsh churches in order to sing the great hymns of the principality in four-part harmony. They also dressed appropriately as for a meeting with God of some obvious significance. John Piper says,

> In corporate worship, let every man and every woman, as he or she dresses Sunday morning, think something like this:
>
> I want to be totally non-distracting in my presence in worship today. I will not, as a man or a woman, try to stand out—not by style, not by expense, not by cleverness, not by offensiveness, not by sexiness, not by what I reveal or how tight my clothing is, not by how elegant or trendy my hair is, not by how perfectly

> coordinated my colors are, not by how free from taboos I am, not by how solemn I am. My aim will be to dress and act in a way that simply does not attract or distract from what should be happening here.[1]

That is how the Alfred Place congregation appeared.

Hymns

After ten years there was a choice of a new hymnbook. Two excellent hymnbooks had become available, and we narrowly voted in favor of *Grace Hymns*, which was quite superb and lasted for forty years. Later we were given copies of *Christian Hymns*, which we used in the midweek meeting. We added sixty or seventy new hymn tunes to the words-only edition that the congregation were given as they entered. We learned four hundred hymns so that through the year we did not need to repeat a hymn (though of course we did), and we were always open to new tunes. We sang metrical psalms from the time of Moses, New Testament paraphrases, and hymns written in the medieval period such as those written by Bernard of Clairvaux. We also sang Martin Luther's hymns, those of the Puritans like John Bunyan and John Mason, hymns from the great period of the evangelical awakening, and the wonderful hymns that erupted at a time of great poetry by Charles Wesley and others. Joseph Hart, Horatius Bonar, and William Gadsby were some of the nineteenth-century hymnists we preferred; Margaret Clarkson, Vernon Higham, Timothy Dudley-Smith, Faith Cook, Stuart Townend, and others in the twentieth century were hymnists of choice.

Children's Talks

Then there was the practice of the children being addressed after the second hymn on Sunday mornings. Alfred Place does not start with Sunday school. The church starts with thirty minutes of prayer, 10:30

---

1. John Piper, "How Should We Dress for Church?" May 1, 2020, Desiring God, https://www.desiringgod.org/interviews/how-should-we-dress-for-church.

through 11:00 a.m., and then the normal morning service begins. The children used to be given a verse to learn, and they stood up one by one and repeated it. Over a couple of years, they memorized and repeated the Westminster Shorter Catechism. To find justification for such a practice is quite difficult—that is, to select one group in the congregation and speak to them for ten minutes. But I have thought of our Lord stopping on His way to Golgotha and His cross work and pausing to address not the silent crowd that pityingly looked at Him and the other two condemned criminals facing an unutterably cruel lingering death but instead the women of Jerusalem, singling them out with His warning and exhortation.

I had inherited this practice of a children's talk, as it had been part of the church service for many years. It is still done in churches all over the United Kingdom today. In some congregations the children come to the front to do it. This episode is saying to them that they are important enough for the minister to address them and for the congregation to notice them during the seventy-five-minute-long service. Traditionally, the attendance at the evening congregation had been larger as "the gospel service," but this changed, and the morning was always the largest in Alfred Place. Steadily the congregations that have continued to hold an evening service have become a minority. The midweek prayer meeting has long disappeared from many churches, followed soon after by the evening service.

Women Officers

Shortly after I began serving in Alfred Place, I met with the deacons for the first and only time. I did not recognize some of them from my earlier visits, but I knew that two of them were older women. Dr. Marjorie Sudds had been one of the town pathologists in the local hospital. She had been a missionary doctor in India with Amy Carmichael, whom she held in the highest regard. Her father had been an officer in the Indian army, and her mother had just passed away. She had been one of the esteemed "old ladies" in the congregation. Mrs. Pierce-Price was the widow of a Baptist minister who had served in a church in mid-Wales. She was one of the organists; we met often and were big friends.

Both women were sympathetic to my convictions. I regarded these women highly, but my own conviction was and remains that the office of a deacon must be reserved to men alone, those who are "the husbands of one wife" (1 Tim. 3:12) or those who had that intention if it is God's will. In other words, I believe that it is the Creator's purpose for marriage to be exclusively of one man and one woman, that parents are the head of their children, a husband is the head of his wife, Christ is the head of man, and God is the head of the man Christ Jesus. The church is to teach the headship of Christ, and that conviction is to be expressed and reflected in the congregation's structures, in the significant place given to male headship. The apostles, commissioned by the Lord Jesus Christ and inspired by the Holy Spirit, teach that clearly. We creatures are not wiser than our Creator.

One old friend who entered the ministry in the same year as I did was called by a church and confronted with the same issue, and he held those identical convictions. He explained his views to the church officers before beginning his ministry there, and the women resigned from the diaconate. He had a long and fruitful ministry and got on well with the women who for a brief time had been deacons. In Aberystwyth, at my commencement, I would have had the support of just one of the deacons to share in my own views. So, I was not going to start by raising an issue particularly when the women feared the Lord. They would come to see this in time. When people plead that "yes, elders and preachers are to be men exclusively, but women may be deacons," then they must understand the particular place deacons experience in Baptist churches and particularly in the mind of the Welsh. Baptist deacons are virtually elders. Within about seven years we had deacons that were all men, and then we appointed three elders. Reforming work is usually patient work.

The chairman of the deacons whom I met at that initial one-off meeting was a senior lecturer and reader in the philosophy department, the late Dr. Oswald Thomas. He had made the eighteenth-century philosopher and polymath Richard Price his life's work. In 1977, long after he had left the church, Oswald Thomas published his definitive life of Price, *The Honest Mind*. He was fascinated by the eighteenth century, and so this gave him a certain understanding of where I was coming from. When a small group of church members were restless with my ministry, they approached him to ask if he would speak up and resist the direction I was taking the church. He refused. He was not in favor of my becoming the pastor, he told me, but he could sense the strength of desire that a formidable group of serious people had for inviting me, and he did not relish a split, and so he voted for me too. He soon wrote me a fine letter of resignation, telling me of this and that he could not get involved in church politics. He acknowledged that he was a Unitarian. I met with him in future years on a few occasions as he and his wife, who was a doctor, were concerned about helping those with learning difficulties and the elderly in the town. We got on very well. I liked him as a man, and he would have been warmly welcomed to attend our worship services any time. The sign outside the church says, "All Are Welcome," and *all* means all. Oswald later became chairman of the Conservative Association in Aberystwyth.

Godly Officers

Within seven years the church had changed, as some people were waiting to see if I was called to be the pastor, and when I was ordained in Alfred Place, they then applied for membership. At the first officers' election, men like Ieuan Davies, Ira Mills, Michael Keen, Ron Loosley, and Terry Loosley were appointed to office, and several of them were still officers when I ended my days in Alfred Place. What stability was thus given to the church.

Theologically and ethically, we were one both in our commitment to the 1689 Confession and in the law of God being the rule Christ has given to believers to glorify and enjoy Him. These church officers were men of prayer and were dedicated to the climactic aspect of Sunday worship services being the declaration of the Word of God. They supported our home for those with learning difficulties as well as our Christian bookshop, which they also worked in. Their voices were always heard in prayer in the weekly meeting. Their counsels were biblically sensible. They were never mere "yes-men."

The Students

One notable presence in the congregation over the decades was that of the university students. The number peaked in the next ten years with up to fifty students attending, but then the numbers declined as other churches became evangelical. Bertie Lewis became the vicar at St. Michael's and over the years wrought considerable changes there, transforming the congregation. At the beginning he had no evangelical students in attendance. After one weekend visit of John Stott, I received a call from the London All Souls vicar asking me whether I would encourage some of the students who worshiped in Alfred Place to go along to St. Michaels to support the work of Bertie there. But that congregation needed no support from me, and soon it was getting far more students than our congregation.

I once was speaking to one of the history staff at the university, the late Professor Peter Thomas, and he told me he had been interviewing a prospective student who had applied to study history at Aberystwyth. He had asked the student what had drawn him to Aberystwyth, and the reply he got shocked him. "I want to go to the Baptist church to sit under the preaching of Geoff Thomas," he was told. Such an attitude to the importance of a preaching ministry was totally alien to his thinking. When his own son became a Christian and often preached (and now has a column in *The Evangelical Times*), he would accompany him and his family to worship in Alfred Place. Its pastor also conducted his funeral service.

The Demise of the Student Christian Movement

At the university there had been a Christian Union of the Inter-Varsity Fellowship for forty years. In 1910 at Cambridge University, the evangelical students of the Student Christian Movement disaffiliated themselves from the SCM and founded the Cambridge Inter-Collegiate Christian Union (CICCU). There was an awareness of one another's existence for almost a decade until, in 1919, ten representatives of the Student Christian Movement met with two members of CICCU to listen to their concern that the SCM was promoting a liberal view of Christianity and wondering if there were any possibility of reunification through the SCM emphasizing what was central in the New Testament gospel. The apostle Paul writing with all the authority of God said that of first significance he declared to men and women that Christ had died for our sins and that He was buried and rose again on the third day according to the Scriptures. Paul assured his readers that he was determined not to know anything when among them save Jesus Christ and Him crucified. Though the message of the cross was foolishness to the world, yet to those who were being saved, it was the power of God.

One of the CICCU representatives, Norman Grubb, a student at Trinity College, challenged the people from the SCM at this 1919 meeting with this direct question: "Does the Student Christian Movement put the atoning blood of Christ central to its teaching?" After a brief deliberation came the answer: "We acknowledge it, but not necessarily as central." This marginalizing or optionalizing of what the Scriptures put at the very heart of the Christian message resulted in the permanence of the division between SCM and IVF and the bifurcation of a religious testimony to the universities across the land. The message of Jesus Christ crucified, whose blood cleanses from all sin, could not be separated from another central doctrine, the historic view of the entire trustworthiness of the Bible. The SCM desired the foundation of Christian unity to be "in Christ," but the infallible Christ of the Bible has given His followers an infallible Bible. "Your word is truth. It cannot be broken. It is written," He says repeatedly and refers to all parts of the Old Testament as truth. Few, if any at all, in the SCM believed this. An emphasis on the central importance of personal evangelism and mission existed in the IVF as well.

The division spread through the universities, and for many years there were two religious societies meeting on most of the campuses in the United Kingdom, but during the 1960s the Student Christian Movement withered away and died out so that the one movement extant today is what used to be called the Inter-Varsity Fellowship but later changed its name to Universities and Colleges Christian Fellowship (UCCF). A hundred students of the UCCF in Aberystwyth used to meet each Saturday night, and in my first twenty years as a minister, I addressed these Christian unions in the four major university colleges in Wales every year—Aberystwyth, Bangor, Swansea, and Cardiff—and then also in Lampeter and the new redbrick universities that opened in Pontypridd, Newport, and Wrexham. The Aberystwyth student leaders initially were invariably worshiping in Alfred Place.

Sunday nights back at the manse was my main time with them, from around eight o'clock until I made popcorn for them and told them at half past ten it was time for them to go to their beds. Someone has described it like this:

> Every Sunday night is different. Sometimes psalms are given to them in different groups to make a metrical version, and then the various groups have to sing their compositions to us. Those from overseas are subjected to long and sometimes embarrassing interviews. An article from the *Reader's Digest* might be read and dissected. More normally, a topic is introduced for discussion. Geoff will lean back on his chair further and further so that he is almost horizontal, and it gives the suggestion that he is one of us, ready to listen as an old friend before praying and disappearing into the kitchen to make the popcorn. He usually stays there for the last half hour while we chat and laugh. In the kitchen he will make a bacon sandwich for himself and his wife, Iola. He then also calls his wife's brother-in-law. Appointments are made to see a student the following week, or some students are invited to lunch the next Sunday.

They certainly were delightful meetings.

Those Who Entered the Ministry

A number of men with this background of Christian Union and Alfred Place became ministers and missionaries. The following is an incomplete list. Some of them went to the Welsh church for one service.

Chris Pegington, 1967, Royton, Hemel Hempstead, Austria, Cwmbran
Irfon Hughes, 1967, Rhymney, Sheffield, Boston, Grove City, Pennsylvania
Austin Walker (Mai), 1968, Crawley
Keith Underhill, 1968, Kenya, Thika, Nairobi
Graham Heaps (Sue), 1971, Dewsbury
David N. Jones (Ruth), 1973, Crickhowell, Grove London, Tasmania, Brisbane
Chris Rogers (Eleanor), 1973, Coedpoeth, Saron, Knotty Ash, Carmarthen
Richard Davies (Lynette), 1973, Tollington, Yately, Gwersyllt, Machynlleth
Derek Thomas (Rosemary), 1974, Belfast, Jackson, Mississippi, Columbia
Trefor Jones, 1974, Andover
Iain Hodgins (Christine), 1975, Blaina, Cambridge, Penclawdd, Gower
Timothy Mills, 1976, Manchester, Bradford
Gareth Edwards (Ceri), 1979, Lampeter, Clarbeston Road, Haverfordwest
Spencer Cunnah (Wendy), 1979, Gorseinon, Sheffield, London
Stephen Turner, 1980, New Zealand
Gary Brady (Eleri), 1980, Child's Hill, London
Keith Hoare (Janice), 1980, France, Herne Bay
Stephen Mills, 1980, Carmen
Alan Davey, 1980, Deeside, Bordeaux
Mark Pickett, 1984, Nepal, Bridgend
Malcolm Firth (Ruth), 1987, Latvia
Jim Sayers (Helen), 1987, Suffolk, Abingdon, Didcot
Dafydd Hughes, 1989, New Zealand
Ian Hughes, 1992, Caergwrle
Richard Killer, 1993, Japan, Stornoway
Mark Vogan, 1993, Ecuador
Philip Morgan, 1995, China, Chinese Church Bristol
Peter Hughes, 1995, Llandrindod Wells
Mark Rowcroft (Abigail), 1996, Deeside, Darlington

Dan Peters (Hannah), 1999, Newcastle
Jonathan Hodgins (Caroline), 2000, Abergavenny, Mancot
Jim Day, 2001, Ingleton, Yorkshire
James Allan (Esther), 2000, Dowlais
Richard Baxter, 2001, Carey Reading
Ian Middlemist, 2001, Hill Park Haverfordwest
Gerard Charmley, 2002, Ebenezer, Headingley Leeds
Oliver Gross, 2002, Welshpool, Buckingham, Bristol
Ed Collier, 2003, Sheffield
Tom Hayward, 2003, Old Hill, Cradley Heath
Luke Jenner, 2005, Halifax
Peter Hilder (Demelza), 2006, Little Mill
Emyr James, 2007, Cardiff
Geoff Lloyd, 2008, Wyndham, New Zealand
Rhodri Brady (Sibyl), 2014, Aberystwyth
Dafydd Williams (Claire), 2015, Newport
Reuben Saywell (Cathy), 2017
James Sibley (Lydia), 2021, Bridgend

Despite all the weaknesses and inadequacies that they were aware of in me, they became preachers, missionaries, and church planters.

Then there were also some awesomely godly women: Olwen Jones, who was a missionary maternity nurse in Bethlehem for forty years; Ann Brown, who works with her husband, Lindsay, in leading the work of the International Fellowship of Evangelical Students; Megan Patterson, who went with her husband, Jim, to Benin in West Africa for decades; Fiona Adams, who went once with her husband to Nigeria and then as a widow with her children went to teach in a Christian school in Sierra Leone with WEC, for whom she continues to work in the United Kingdom.

The presence of the students was one of the rich encouragements to me in the first decade. I was a student myself. I understood the mentality and spirituality of students. The full congregation that their presence created protected me from unhappy members. They encouraged me with their interest, questions, and the books they would read. As the years passed, there was more distance between us. I became a father figure, even a grandfather figure, but through most of them my spirits were lifted, and they have been my friends.

There were the students, and then there were about ninety people on the membership list of the church. A third rarely if ever attended. A third came once on a Sunday, and the remaining third were the people who made the church buzz. They came from a variety of religious backgrounds. Some were the finest people I have ever known.

Heresy Accepted in the Baptist Union

After I had been in Aberystwyth for six years, an ultimatum concerning its future associations was presented to the church by a meeting that took place in the annual Baptist Union Assembly held in Westminster Chapel in April 1971. The principal of the Northern Baptist College, Michael Taylor, spoke on the deity of Christ. He asserted, "I believe that God was active in Jesus, but it will not do to say quite categorically, 'Jesus is God.'" He imagined himself being asked to draft a modern replacement for the article on Christ in the Nicene Creed, and his emphasis would be on the humanity of Christ.

The following year, at the 1972 Assembly, a debate ensued regarding Principal Taylor's claims. The case for censuring him was put forward by evangelical men but was rejected. The overwhelming majority of the assembly voted in favor of the right of Baptists to assert that Jesus is God, but they also voted that Taylor and those who agreed with him had every right to their beliefs and that he should remain as the principal of the Northern College, training men for the ministry. This decision was applauded years later, by Dr. Nigel Wright, the principal of Spurgeon's College in London, as a positive step showing that "it was possible to maintain faithfulness for a doctrinal tradition while not stifling the proper freedom that belongs to theological enquiry. The essence of Baptist identity included freedom of religious expression." What a tragedy!

This issue then came to our congregation, as to every church in the Baptist Union. A number of us evangelical ministers and churches felt that the denomination had crossed the ultimate Rubicon. We were in total agreement with the views of Charles Haddon

Spurgeon when he resigned from the Baptist Union over similar issues at a time when the denomination was far more biblical in its convictions than it is today. Spurgeon's view was as follows:

1. For Christians to be linked in association with ministers who do not preach the gospel of Christ is to incur moral guilt.
2. A union that can continue irrespective of whether its member churches belong to a common faith is not fulfilling any Scriptural function.
3. The preservation of a denominational association when it is powerless to discipline heretics cannot be justified on the grounds of the preservation of "Christian unity."
4. It is error that breaks the unity of churches, and to remain in a denominational alignment that condones error is to support schism.

When it was put to Alfred Place Baptist Church at a members' meeting in the autumn of 1972 whether it should remain in fellowship with the Baptist Union, with the exception of one woman the entire church voted to secede from the denomination.

CHAPTER 11

Beginning as a Preacher

What a privilege Alfred Place gave me to become a full-time preacher of the gospel. At a basic level, it delivered me from many of the same tensions and temptations that the men of the congregation I meet with each Sunday constantly confront. They work with their minds and bodies in this evil world and give their hard-earned cash to the preacher so that he may spend his days—think of it!—in the quiet of his study, in the Bible, in evangelism, and in pastoring God's people. I hope I will never join with those ministers who sit in fraternities or ministers' conferences and stoop to grumbling about the alleged hardships of being a preacher. What a marvelously privileged life we lead. I want to thank the Lord at the end of each day that He put me in the ministry in Aberystwyth.

Systematic Expository Preaching

I began in Alfred Place with an introductory Sunday in which I preached on the duties of the preacher-pastor in one service and the duties of the congregation in the other service. I then commenced "properly" the next Sunday, preaching in the morning on Genesis 1:1 and in the evening on Matthew 1:1, steadily continuing through Matthew and Genesis at those services for a couple of years. It was a personal statement as to my own convictions concerning the Bible, a Christocentric statement facing overwhelming rejection by town and gown, telling them what the Lord Jesus Christ believed. He said, "But from the beginning of the creation God 'made them male and

female'" (Mark 10:6). He also referred to Lot's wife, the judgment on Sodom and Gomorrah, and Noah's flood. We could never be more knowledgeable or smarter than the Son of God, who claimed, "I am the truth" (see John 14:6).

My preaching through the opening chapters of Genesis was also a moral statement concerning what our ethical standards are to be

as God's creatures under constraint to acknowledge the basic teaching of redemptive history. It was an ecclesiastical declaration about what this congregation needed and where I would be taking it if permitted. It was a political statement to the polis of Aberystwyth after having lost its way over the last century, meandering into the various *-isms* that sprang up like mushrooms, gained some support, and then dwindled. "Consider the Bible," I was saying. "Heed the Word of God. You have lost the Scriptures, and so you do not know God. You do not know yourselves, who you are. You do not know how you should live. The book of Genesis tells us. God is not silent."

I love that young man of 1965 for all his personal failures, who wanted to see a confessional Christian church built in Aberystwyth and believed that one essential way of doing that was by drawing the attention of the people to all the Scriptures week after week. I now have some misgivings, however, with that approach of mine on several different levels. One is regarding my own ability to do this. I was full of graduate and undergraduate biblical studies: university life at Cardiff and then three years of Westminster Seminary, Philadelphia. I had head knowledge and some grasp of the original languages. But there was also the challenge of my ability to communicate with this congregation, many of whom were not from or in such an ethos.

I think I had picked up the idea from William Still of Aberdeen that the work of the minister was to preach through books of the Bible. All the men I admired did this—Martyn Lloyd-Jones, John Stott, the Scots who were followers of William Still, and the men I generally heard about who were regarded as fine preachers (but I did not know their ministries and their success or their churches). Systematic expository preaching was generally commended everywhere in our circles. But was there anyone as committed to it as defiantly and unyieldingly as myself as I started with the first verses of Genesis in the morning and the first verses of Matthew in the evening?

Looking back, I think I should have given them a taste. "Do you like this?" Then another taste, for example, of some New Testament preaching for those who came only on Sunday mornings. I would preach on the Beatitudes and on the life of Elijah or the life of Joseph.

Give them more variety. I have twice preached through the book of Genesis, and the second series thirty years later was far more balanced and lucid than the first time when I began my ministry. I do love the book of Genesis. It is utterly foundational for Christianity.

To start my ministry I now think that I should have done a Lloyd-Jones in the morning—that is, a number of briefer systematic expository series in the mornings—and then in the evenings done a Spurgeon—that is, preached more evangelistically, opening up the "big texts" of Scripture, cutting my teeth on learning to preach on the greatness of God, the plight of man in his sin, the entreaties and invitations of the gospel, the beauty of the person of Christ, and so on. The gift to do what John Calvin did in his preaching and what Lloyd-Jones did twenty years into his ministry is a gift slowly attained, but only attained by doing it. I was better prepared later on. That sort of ministry is an enormous challenge to the greatest preachers, let alone the novice. The sermons can easily shrink into "glorified Bible studies" that no longer engage with the whole of the gathered people in all their needs and personalities.

Its Strengths and Weaknesses

One of the greatest perils that face us confessional Christian preachers is the problem of hyperintellectualism—the constant danger of lapsing into a cerebral form of proclamation that falls exclusively on the intellect. Men who become obsessed with doctrine can end up as brain-oriented preachers. Consequently, a fearful impoverishment dwells in their hearers emotionally, devotionally, and practically. Such pastors are men of books and not men of people; they know the doctrines, but they know nothing of the emotional side of religion. They set little store on experience or on constant fellowship and interaction with almighty God. It is one thing to explain the truth of Christianity to men and women. It is another to feel the overwhelming power of the sheer loveliness and enthrallment of Jesus Christ and communicate that dynamically to the whole person who is hearing of our Lord accomplishing a change of such dimensions that he loves the Savior with all his heart and soul and mind and strength.

Geoff preaching with animation on the Monday morning of the annual August Aberystwyth Conference around the year 2000

It is in the midweek Bible study and prayer meeting that the messages must be particularly characterized by pathos. That is an area of failure for many of us. We bring together two meetings, a preaching service and a praying service, because we are too small to have two distinct services. We need experiential, warm, encouraging messages, not too long, that will lead to intercession. To do that is a great gift, and there may even be men in the congregation more gifted in this than the preacher himself.

But I must not be too severe on myself. We are not to think of ourselves more highly, nor lowlier, than we ought to think. Those students who were to go on to spend forty years of their lives preaching the Word of God, like Austin Walker, Keith Underhill, and Chris Pegington, who sat in the congregation those first Sundays when I began my ministry, have told me the sermons helped ground them in the truth of the Bible. "It was our meat and drink," one of them said.

I must acknowledge that there were times when I was helped by God, and the congregation grew. After a few months in the pulpit, I had reached Matthew chapter 3, and I spoke to the congregation one night on the sermon of John the Baptist under the theme "The Preaching God Blesses to Awaken Sinners." That sermon did immense good, especially to one American who subsequently has become a dear friend and is now a professor of history in the United States. He had given up the faith when utterly disillusioned with his pastor father's unfaithfulness and abandonment of his mother. Through the providence of God, his older brother discovered this very sermon on a cassette and, concerned for his brother, sent it to his sibling. My preaching was to him the grace of repentance, restoration, and consecration, and for years he has been an elder in a PCA congregation. We regularly correspond, and he came to Aberystwyth forty years after that message was first preached there to sit in a pew one Sunday with me and our wives, listening to my grandson preach, and thanking God for His mercy.

David N. Jones commenced his ministry in Crickhowell and then had a notable ministry in Grove Chapel in London before receiving a call to Tasmania for the rest of his life. He worshiped in Alfred Place when he was not preaching and says, "I was struck not only by the consistent standard of preaching content but by the searching application and the rapt attention of the congregation. His preaching was Christ-centered, doctrinal, expository, warm, accessible, challenging, God-glorifying, and always fresh."

It is almost unbelievable to me to read that sort of thing. I remember the frequent struggles and regrets, the feeling that you ought to apologize to everyone as they left the church. To me it sounds as if they are talking about someone else. I was encouraged to read the words of R. L. Dabney: "My preaching seems to human eyes to be utterly without effect; bad for me, and bad for them."[1] I know that feeling well.

Dare I quote the words of another student, Dan Peters, now the pastor of Newcastle Reformed Evangelical Church? They are so dangerously ego-inflating. Is this bragging? If you knew how I agonized over printing these sentences. They would be all right coming from the pen of a biographer, but this is my choice to insert a paragraph of the thanks of another. My plea is the feelings of failure so common among all of us pastors that we did not engage with our congregations nor minister to them, leaving them cold and unfed. These words are saying, "I did help someone once."

This is what Dan Peters wrote:

> I learned that students and others particularly engaged in the marketplace of ideas need to be hearing preaching that is deep, serious, logically coherent and intellectually credible. The fiercest assaults my Christian faith has ever faced were in the lecture theatres at Aberystwyth, and its survival through that period was due in no small part to the weekly preaching at Alfred Place. It's not that Geoff self-consciously preached "apologetics" or that he necessarily addressed the specific issues that were being raised during my university course but that he preached a Christian faith that was every bit as robust and reasonable

1. Thomas Gary Johnson, *Life and Letters of Robert Lewis Dabney* (Richmond, Va.: Presbyterian Committee of Publication, 1903), 110.

> as the ideologies to which I was being exposed. The gospel as it was preached at Alfred Place didn't look flimsy alongside the sophisticated hypotheses of Jacques Derrida and Michael Foucault. Geoff set forth the doctrines of original sin and the incarnation and justification by faith just as carefully and rigorously as my lecturers set forth post-structural literary theory.

Wow! That unsought-for response is moving for me to read, and I am humbled. If Dan could read my heart, there would be times when he would want to spit in my face. I can scarcely believe what he wrote, but I foolishly dwell on my pulpit's barren times and groan.

I do want to challenge my own singular commitment to systematic expository preaching. It can make us lazy in our wrestling with God for His will on which text we should take on a given Lord's Day. It can dull the appetite of God's people for the Word by simply continuing the next Sunday where we left off the Sunday before. Doesn't preaching from different texts demonstrate well that all Scripture is given by inspiration of God? We must never give the impression that we have "done" a gospel, or an epistle, or a prophetic book so that we will never preach on it again. Have you "done" London if you have thoroughly seen some of its biggest attractions? Finally, by preaching through a book of the Bible, we may well end up giving an extended commentary on Bible passages.

The Values of Spurgeon's Approach

A friend of mine suggests that we take a volume of Spurgeon's *Metropolitan Tabernacle Pulpit* to sample six sermons preached within a six-week period, four Sunday evenings and two Thursday-night lectures. He points out that all are superb; all are powerfully expositional and spiritually enriching. Any one of them would make a contemporary preacher think he hadn't even begun to preach, and all of them together would be a feast on a desert island.

In Spurgeon's preaching, there is no series, no plan, no cohesion—two of these sermons are from the New Testament, and four from the Old Testament. The themes are the love of God, the angels' protection, fearing God, power with God, ministry and service, and the nature of forgiveness. Any one of the volumes of Spurgeon's Metropolitan Tabernacle would yield a similar display of ministerial power and influence within the compass of a few weeks. When Spurgeon advised his students on choosing texts for Sunday sermons, he said,

> Many eminent divines have delivered valuable courses of sermons upon pre-arranged topics, but we are not eminent, and must counsel others like ourselves to be cautious how they act. I dare not announce what I shall preach from in six weeks' or six months' time, the reason being partly this, that I am conscious of not possessing those peculiar gifts which are necessary to interest an assembly in one subject or set of subjects, for any length of time.... I have a very lively, or rather a deadly recollection of a certain series of discourses on the Hebrews, which made a deep impression on my mind of the most undesirable kind. I wished frequently that the Hebrews had kept the epistle to themselves.[2]

So, what was Spurgeon's counsel? "Wait upon the Lord, hear what he would speak, receive the word direct from God's mouth, and then go forth as an ambassador fresh from the court of heaven."[3]

When Lloyd-Jones began his ministry, it was essentially a Spurgeonic approach to preaching on texts that moved him. One of the most powerful ministries in Scotland was in the Free Church in Stornoway in the 1940s and 1950s under Kenneth Macrae. Sometimes in his diary he would comment on his own preaching, hesitant about continuing through a chapter of Scripture and then finding great help in his proclamation. Again, his ministry was essentially Spurgeonic, and many said it was the finest preaching they heard in their lives. It made for comprehensive Bible learning. Are there no snags? Of course there are. Isolated texts need to be found week after week. Isolated texts do not capture the flow of redemptive history. They

2. C. H. Spurgeon, *Lectures to My Students* (Grand Rapids: Zondervan, 1945), 94.

3. Spurgeon, *Lectures to My Students*, 96.

also can become hobby-horse texts for preachers who are obsessed with certain themes.

I am challenging my own approach, questioning whether I became a slave to a certain methodology. I took up a style that was prevailing in the evangelical circles in which I moved. I did not have sufficient role models in what I have called the Spurgeonic tradition. Great profit can be reaped from systematic expository evangelistic preaching, but the danger to be avoided in that approach is making a sermon a plain Bible study lacking pathos, passion, and pleading. Even Lloyd-Jones himself did not avoid that in some of his Friday night sermons on Romans. One can significantly benefit from preaching on isolated texts and be touched, in one's daily devotions, by a passage that speaks to your condition and convinces you that preaching on this particular text will help the people.

CHAPTER 12

My Journal

My father kept a diary throughout his life. He wrote four little lines each day, and now we have all his journals in a sealed container. When he died in 1977, I began a diary, but I chose a page a day in a diary the size of a Bible. It took a year or more to get into the rhythm of not missing a day, like daily brushing one's teeth. But for forty-three years I have written roughly two hundred words about the events of most days. It is not, alas, like Andrew Bonar's fragrant diary. So many days are mundane, ordinary days unmarked by any particular drama. But that it might reveal more of myself as a saved sinner, husband, father, pastor, evangelist, and preacher, I thought I could share some extracts in these pages, though I don't come out of it all that well. It is too judgmental at times. Evaluations that should have remained thoughts or quiet words shared with my family and soon forgotten have been given permanence by being written. So, I took down at venture from the shelves full of these journals one particular year, which happened to be 1981. I will quote some excerpts from the pages to indicate the life of a minister and his family at that particular juncture in my life in Aberystwyth after sixteen years of ministry there.

Thursday, January 29. I went to a debate in the University Hugh Owen building at 7:45 between Dr. Margaret White, the president of the Society for the Protection of the Unborn Child, and Dr. John Hughes, the local general practitioner who is a leading spokesman for abortions. There were sixty people present. In the local hospital, between 150–170 abortions occur each year. She was splendid dealing with the debasement of language in abortion, the discrimination against size, challenging the phrase "poor quality of life." She mentioned a man she knows whose name is Nigel Hunt who has Downs Syndrome. He has written a charming book called *The World of Nigel Hunt*. She compared his achievement with what Hollywood stars display. She said that there was no proof of increase in backstreet abortions when a country refuses to legalize abortion. One can make similarly falsely "compassionate" arguments about killing fathers or grandmothers with slogans—"Every Granny a wanted Granny," and the answer is not abortion but waiting, caring, struggling. If it were baby seals that women carried in their wombs, there would be an outcry about aborting them. Then Dr. Hughes presented the abortionist view. He spoke of a "potential child" and that 19 percent of all first pregnancies end in spontaneous abortions. He had not seen the life of a pregnant mother endangered in twenty years of medical practice. Dr. White said during the debate that it was broken homes that caused social problems, not unwanted pregnancies. Most of the young men locked up in Borstal for stabbings and crimes of violence were wanted babies.

Friday, January 30. It is Iola's fortieth birthday, and at 8 a.m. the light came on in the bedroom and three singing daughters came in carrying a tray with toast, marmalade, tea, and coffee. We opened cards and gave Iola gifts. The day ended with my mother joining us for tea with lasagne, water-cress, bean shoots, and corn. We finished it with cheesecake.

Saturday, January 31. Robin Wells, the head of UCCF, came for the weekend. He was speaking at the CU in the university tonight. He talked about Michael Griffiths turning down the leadership of UCCF because he considered any such appointment should be a joint appointment and that UCCF was providing nothing for his wife. She would have been a "mere appendage."

A Communion season at Alfred Place

Sunday, February 1. I think I spoiled things a little in the morning service by choosing two or three heavy hymns with high notes; the sermon was a bit heavy too. I should listen to a tape of it tomorrow to see how it sounded, but of course I won't. Harry Kilbride does that on discouraged Mondays, and he finds that when he is utterly depressed about the sermon that listening again to it lifts his spirits. Again in the evening service I believe that I preached better than the morning, but alas not deeply or feelingly enough. I have been in Alfred Place too long. Do they and me also need a change?! The best part of the service was around the Communion table afterward.

Tuesday, February 3. Esther Jones was a tonic to visit even with her heavy new caliper. She spoke of the wonder of God's love in saving her. So fresh, so real, and quite profound. A tramp called at the manse and told me such a painful story evidencing its truth with documents. I gave him a couple of pounds and some food. Iola later questioned me in giving him money, and I was foolishly *angry!* We had an excellent prayer meeting with thirty-three present. We are doing a short series on Jerry Bridges' *Pursuit of Holiness*.

Thursday, February 5. Esther hasn't been well. The new caliper chafed her leg, a huge blister formed. It burst and bled. The blood stuck to the leather support to her leg. A nurse eased it away and dressed it. Finally, Mr. Southern the specialist came to see her. He insisted that the caliper will have to be worn for ten months again. She was depressed by this, but when I was with her, I could see her spirits lifting. She bounces back faster and higher than any other Christian I know.

Friday, February 6. I rang Iain Murray, and he spoke of the continued interest in Arthur Pink and that there was a Benedictine monk who was very interested in him. He had read fifteen of his books. There was also a philosopher at Cambridge who would only read the works of A. W. Pink!

Saturday, February 7. James Fox the actor wrote to say how much he had appreciated my booklet *Reading the Bible*. He would try to learn from it. He was intending to speak on this theme at a Navigators' conference in London a week today.

Sunday, February 8. I started this new series on the blueprint of the church, and it went well. It was long, but I think it was interesting. My mother never says much about my preaching, but today she said, "Simpler than last Sunday, you know. We could all understand it." Thank you, Mam! I spoke at 4:45 at Bodlondeb old people's home. It was a rather depressing experience because I feel no care or love for them. Do I patronize them because they are old? Ugh! I am an impatient man, alas.

Monday, February 9. A man called from Glasgow. He had heard my lecture on "The Origins of Christianity in Wales" that I gave at the Aber Conference. He was to give a lecture on Saint David on March 1 in Glasgow. He wanted to borrow my notes. I wrote out the first draft of them and sent them to him. Bill Haley of "Rock Around the Clock" died today.

Friday, February 13. Eric Hughes, the Penparcau Labour councilor, had phoned social services reporting one of our members, Miss Lingard, for her bizarre behavior. I do not think she has ever been to church or leaves her flat. He alleged she was catching wild birds and plucking off their feathers and that her milk bottles had not been taken in for a few days. He wants her to go into an old people's home to live. So I drove there to see her. The milk bottles were all gone. I knocked the door and heard the familiar "Just a minute. I'm coming." She duly appeared, dirty, a bit breathless but pleased to see me, and in I went. She told me that she had a problem. The front door had swollen because of the heavy rain, and it was jammed for a few days so that she could not open it and bring the milk in. Then she had heard the milkman coming, and she had called to the milkman, and he had pushed open the door. The man in the flat above her had reported the bottles of milk to the police who had called. So I returned with a plane an hour later and planed away the part that had swollen, and at the end I got the door opening and closing easily. She was delighted, and she gave me £2! A health visitor will now call and see her.

Wednesday, February 18. I went up to the Students' Union, and Ron Goodfellow accompanied me. The room was packed. Two hundred were sitting and thirty-five standing. Leith Samuel was speaking on the resurrection. It was a very traditional biblical statement illustrating what he said from John's gospel, the raising of Lazarus after three days buried. He was a bit rushed for time. By the end of the evening, he told me that over the past week twenty people had come to speak to him about personal faith in Jesus Christ, and there were a lot more conversations going on through Lindsay and Ann Brown and the other workers.

Monday, February 23. The girls came into our bedroom early, excited by the sight of the first snowfall of the winter. It was a slight covering but enough for snowballs and slides. Gwennan their cousin came down and played in the snow for a while until they got cold

The Manse, Buarth Road, our home for over fifty years and now the home of my grandson Rhodri Brady, who succeeded me to the pastorate.

and moved into the parlor. There they began to play puppets with four dolls that were held high above the settee by Fflur and Catrin. The puppets danced to Beethoven's Fifth Symphony. They later were to put on a performance for their grandparents in Blaenau Ffestiniog. Student David Smalley called to see me in the early afternoon concerned about his lack of love for the Lord Jesus and his coldness toward the Bible. Then at 3 p.m. we and the Lewises drove up the mountain behind Penrhyncoch where there was an abundance of snow. We took our sledge [sleigh] and plastic sheets. Keith Lewis tirelessly played with Carys, Eleri, Catrin, Gwydion, Fflur, and Gwennan. I pathetically gave up and nursed my aching ears, forgetting completely my track-suit top had a hood. Austin Walker called from Crawley in the evening. He had been to the Westminster Fraternal where R. T. Kendall had spoken on universal atonement but had not made his argument from the exegesis of Scripture at all.

Tuesday, February 24. Buckingham Palace announced the engagement of Prince Charles and Diana Spencer. She becomes the first Princess of Wales for over one hundred years. She could be "Princess Dai" in Wales! A good Welsh name. The children, but the oldest especially, Eleri, were excited. Catrin discovered to her pleasure that she shares the same birthday as Princess Diana. [They were to comb the newspapers in the next days to find out everything about Diana.] Then off I went visiting, Mrs. Doris Evans, John Ling, Aubrey Davies, and finally Esther Jones, who was eager to see me, longing to hear all my news but knowing most of it already, and giving me some.

Thursday, February 26. We went for the day to Portmadoc. A cold day. I looked through a stand of beautiful sheet music by Mozart, Beethoven, and Schubert. It was for new players graded for the young pianist. I handled it for ages, but it was £1.50 a sheet, and I had only £2 in my pocket, so I didn't buy anything. I will probably regret it for a few months, but I know it's a folly, just wishful thinking. I dream of going to the piano instructor Mr. Deverill and starting some piano lessons again AND speaking Welsh fluently AND reading through the *Institutes* in a year AND go jogging in the summer AND playing tennis with Eleri twice a week AND building a cupboard in the kitchen—AND, AND, AND. This dreamer will do some of those things, no doubt, but I will certainly strive to do the only things that eternally matter, to have a heart that obeys and loves God and appreciates the beauty and excitement of such a life.

Sunday, March 1. Dr. D. Martyn Lloyd-Jones died this morning at 7:30 after a long illness. John Griffiths phoned at 1:40 p.m. with the news that he had heard from Hugh Morgan. But it had been broadcast on the 1 p.m. Welsh news. I immediately phoned Ieuan, Mike, Gordon, Keith, David Bugden in Canada, Irfon, David Boorman, and David Kingdon. Then Stuart Olyott called from Liverpool to tell me the news. Later Mari Jones called from Llanymawddwy, and she wanted any photographs of him that I had. Arthur Murray came to the front before the service to tell me in case I had not heard. Others heard about his death on the radio, and it was announced in Heath Church at the morning service. What mighty meetings he annually held there. He had been very ill through the week and lost his voice in the last few days. He could only communicate through writing, and the last word he wrote was "Ready." He finally sank into a coma last night. In the evening service I spoke about him for five minutes quite inadequately. What can one say about such a decease? One is glad for him and sad for his family. Iain Murray has completed eight chapters of the biography of the Doctor. How I look forward to reading the completed work.

Friday, March 6. The funeral service of Dr. Martyn Lloyd-Jones. I didn't sleep very well thinking of all that was ahead of me today. John Edwards came by at 11 a.m. We had soup, and off to Newcastle Emlyn we went, thirty-five miles away. We were there by noon for the 2 p.m. service. Cars of minister friends were driving round and round looking for a parking place. It was market day, and the market is held in the car park. I hurried through the streets, John trotting at my side, to get a place in Bethel. It was down an alley, a broad tarmac square in front of the Wedgewood blue chapel. A cluster of ministers were talking outside, and soon Iain and Jean Murray joined us and Eluned Thomas. Inside the chapel were a mere half dozen people. I had expected hundreds. I wandered about and spoke to Gary

Brady about Kenya. By 1 p.m. the chapel was half full, but even at 2 p.m. when the funeral service commenced, there were some empty places. I had envisaged more than a thousand coming with crowds standing outside. So Wales regards so faintly her greatest son. The funeral service was good, two Welsh hymns, and the one in English was, "The God of Abraham Praise!" Hywel Jones prayed well, and Vernon Higham spoke with his usual simple touches. The family in their vulnerability and unity, from grandchildren to older members, were lovely to consider. What a privilege for the Catherwood men to carry out the coffin of the Doctor. We drove to the Gelli cemetery, and the atmosphere was a family occasion with Mrs. Lloyd-Jones at the hub, but all of us spreading around from the graveside. I am sure she was blessed by the service in the chapel and at the Gelli graveyard. We sang some hymns, which were pitched horribly low so that some sang an actual octave higher. Omri Jenkins pronounced the benediction. Then someone took Mrs. Lloyd-Jones to see the flowers. "Aren't they beautiful?" I heard her say, appreciative and composed. I went to preach in Corsham Bible Witness in Wiltshire that evening and described for a short time to them the funeral. Dr. Lloyd-Jones always commenced the Friday night, autumn-to-spring sessions in September each year.

Monday, March 9. A student from Borneo came to see me. He is in his second year and is an alcoholic, his life in utter ruins. He had gone to the Pentecostal minister last week. He had anointed him with oil. The student had gone out and immediately got drunk again. I asked him had he been born again. Did he know God? I told him so plainly that he was going to hell. No drunkard would inherit the kingdom of God. He had a fine Christian grandmother who had prayed for him and helped him. I must help him. I wrote a long letter to him to point out the thing that must be done to break the chains that tie him to alcohol.

Sunday, March 29. It is Mothers' Day, and the girls came into our bedroom with gifts and cards. Eleri had bought a nice French tray, and Catrin a super candle in a metal ball. The cards were funny and put on display in the kitchen. I took to Mam in Tanygraig some spiced tea that Iola had made.

Monday, March 30. The Leicester Banner of Truth Ministers' Conference. Someone tried to kill President Reagan, and some of us found a TV set and watched a report on the attempted assassination on the ten o'clock news. One of the speakers commented to me, "How much is Western democracy worth? The Communists don't let the people shoot their leaders." That was an unusual political comment at a gathering quite indifferent to governments. One thing about this conference is the manliness and attractiveness of those present. Few vegetarian beard-sprouting cranks, no sandal-wearing poets! No need in this gathering for Rupert Hart-Davies' reproof of Archbishop Fisher's excessive geniality, "Sir, this merriment of parsons is mighty offensive." Iain Murray spoke on the last eighteen months in the life of Dr. Martyn Lloyd-Jones. The world says that it is a mercy when someone dies suddenly. They want to just slip through death. It is not at all a mercy. You must look at death and observe it. You must prepare for it and gain the victory over it. Dr. Lloyd-Jones was very serious when he spoke of death, but he was also animated. His face was alive, almost glistening.

Friday, April 3. Al Martin called from New Jersey about a man from his church going out to Keith Underhill in Kenya. Peter Master from the Metropolitan Tabernacle also called about the September School of Theology there. I visited Esther and then went to the hospital to visit the Plymouth Brethren professor of mathematics at the university, John Heading, but he had been discharged.

Saturday, April 4. I went to a wedding of two former students. They asked me to give a closing word at the reception. I sat near a five-year-old bridesmaid and chatted happily to her. Then I happened to mention her name in the introduction to my closing little message. Alas, she howled when she heard her name! She would not be pacified as she went sniffing to her mother for comfort. I carried on, pretending I was not put off by her wails but in reality feeling guilty and tense, condemning myself for embarrassing a child in front of others. It is never easy speaking in a wedding and being light and luminous and spiritual and serious all at the same time. I can understand why Dr. Lloyd-Jones announced his stand that he never spoke at weddings, and he never did. I have no idea how I did today. At the end of the day, the children watched the European Song Competition, which was won by Britain, much to Catrin's excitement, while Eleri was more sophisticated, doing some school homework and watching at the same time.

Monday, April 20. I went to Brynygroes in Bala to speak to twenty-five men doing the ministerial training course. I spoke on Dr. J. Gresham Machen, recounting to them his visit to Wales to speak for R. B. Jones in Porth, and his correspondence with R. B. Jones' son. Machen had a fine Cesarean head, cut so vigorously that one thinks one can still hear the thud of the hammer on the chisel. He was single-minded and uncompromising because he saw so clearly the issues at stake and the implications of modernism in the loss of the gospel and the glory of Christ's person and work. Yet he was a most human Christian, enjoying watching Princeton play American football, and delighted by the most slapstick student stunts on stunt night, in which he participated and led out of sheer enjoyment. He combined great *joie de vivre* with a commitment to the Westminster Confession.

Saturday, May 23. The opening of Plas Lluest, Aberystwyth, the home for people with learning difficulties. We arrived at 1:45 with 130 other cars crawling down the drive. It was raining, and the meeting was in the open air. The mayor arrived. The rain temporarily stopped. We started by singing "Great Is Thy Faithfulness," but I pitched it too high. David Potter spoke very well. Then it started to pour, and I got up and spoke, the rain running down my neck. My notes got wet and stuck to the desk. Then Grace Wyatt spoke. She was excellent, and it stopped raining again. Finally, she cut the ribbon that symbolically announced the opening of the new home, and the crowds, 350–400, slowly wandered around the place. A bus of 25 came from Liverpool. Tons of food seemed to be left over. We loaded the chairs onto a lorry [i.e., truck] in renewed rain and unloaded them at 7 p.m.

Friday, June 26. Fflur's ninth birthday—she had written this information down in my pocket diary in large script. The three girls piled into our bed at 8 a.m. Eleri gave her a Mickey Mouse mug, Catrin gave her a zipped pink purse, Nain and Taid gave her a bedside cabinet plus £10, and we gave her a bedspread and Bible. Seven children came to her party—Gwennan, Karen, Esyllt, Wendy, Carys, Nerys Morgan, and Nerys Parry. After tea I took them to Tanybwlch Beach where they climbed rocks and ran to the lighthouse at the end of the jetty to wave at a fishing boat returning with its haul. They went into the old concrete pillbox through a tiny window. They then went to look at the donkeys that take children for a ride on the prom. They are kept in a field nearby. They all began to bray loudly when their field was invaded by eight nine-year old girls. Then we drove across to the promenade, and I bought each of them a candy floss. We returned to the manse and played Pass the Parcel and ate Maltesers with a knife and fork. I collapsed into bed, quite joyful in my spirit, at 9:15.

Wednesday, July 1. Catrin's thirteenth birthday, so now I have two teenage daughters. She merely underlined this date in this diary. They came into our bed at 7:30, opening presents and cards. She had a lovely waistcoat from Iola, which she had finished yesterday. Eleri gave her a Charlie Brown sticker and felt pen. Fflur gave her another Charlie Brown sticker and a plastic straw of wondrous shape. She also had Eine Kleine Nachtmusic. Twelve of us were at her party, but it was more subdued by Catrin's present poor sight and her migraine.

Wednesday, July 29. The royal wedding, and TV on much of the day to watch the procession and crowds. Runcie's sermon was pathetic—God mentioned once and not Jesus at all. The children were engrossed with it all and delighted at the two mistakes, Diana

My beloved daughters, Catrin, Fflur, and Eleri.

putting Charles' names in the wrong order and Charles omitting the word "worldly" in promising her all his worldly goods. Kiria Te Kanawa, dressed like a peacock, sang like a lark. Gary and I spent the afternoon taking tracts around the Morolwg flats. In the evening I preached in the open air on the promenade. I spoke on the parallel about a wife being joined to her husband in marriage and a Christian being joined to Christ in salvation. Gary preached well.

Wednesday, September 9. I went to meet Fflur from school. I watched her come out. She saw a dog tied to the school railings and talked to it, stroking it, talking to the dog's owner. I watched it all with quiet pleasure. Then she straightened up and walked on—and spotted me. Her face lit up, and she put her arms out and ran, jumping up into my arms. It was enormously enthralling. My heart leaped, though that run and leap will soon end, for many years until, maybe, a certain Grandpa Thomas will meet his granddaughter outside another school.

Thursday, September 17. Eleri's sixteenth birthday. Into our bed the three gathered at 8 a.m. to open her cards and presents. She had a Hanimax camera from Nana and a Scottish kilt that Iola made. Catrin gave her a poster of four piglets and *Holiness* by Hugh Morgan. Fflur gave her sweets, the Lewis family gave her a Jogger t-shirt. She had a black scarf from Ann Eleri, notelets from Bethan, a notebook and container from Elin, recipe book from Carys, a little ornament from Menna, a ribbon from Austria from Eirian, a picture cube from Sian James, a plastic picture holder from Mabli, writing paper from the Keen family. Eleri was playing netball in Aberaeron and was sick in the bus, and her team lost, and she did not get back to her party until 6:40.

Thursday, October 15. My forty-third birthday. The children made hilarious cards. "Getting old? No way, Dad. He is fun for the whole family. You are only 43, stop worrying! A young bright-eyed Dad!" I had bars of chocolate and two-color pens, a Charlie Brown calendar, and a telephone pad. Miss Patterson sent me a frozen trout. A totally spoiled man.

CHAPTER 13

Key Brothers and Formative Influences

As a preacher, one must make choice of a number of role models. In other words, it is a mistake to choose just one and absolutize his strengths while ignoring his inevitable inadequacies. See the vitality of a variety of men. They are more accessible to us all today than at any time in Christian history. I was influenced by many anonymous men and women, students and contemporaries and older people, who at different times were brought into my life. God greatly blessed and helped me through their example. He has done that again in the closing years of my life with the many humble members I have met in Amyand Park Chapel and the folk in my new wife's Independent Presbyterian Church.

It was an anonymous man whom God spoke to at the time of Gideon; "The LORD sent a prophet" (Judg. 6:8). An anonymous boy gave Jay Adams a New Testament in school, and in reading this Scripture, Jay became a Christian. An anonymous working man was preaching on January 6, 1850, in the Primitive Methodist Church in Artillery Street, Colchester, after a heavy snowstorm. Fifteen-year-old Charles Haddon Spurgeon could not walk the miles to his own church, and so he popped into this chapel, and there he heard an awakening sermon from "a thin-looking man." He often referred to the event and blessed God that no one could later identify this man. God blesses us through simple people who love the Lord.

Some young men are favored with the example of their own pastors, while many others can build up a composite picture of an all-around minister through reading the Bible, and by the study of preachers and missionaries in church history and in the providence of God through the men we come across, whose messages we have listened to or watched, whose books we've read, and whose conferences we've attended. We add to those initial preachers others who come to impress us as the decades go by. God pours out gifts to men continually. New men are raised up, and then enthusiasms from friends commend to us a new voice that "you must hear." There have been great men whom I have had the privilege of knowing. They have all changed me for the good. I cannot imagine my past without them, though none was a perfect man. That is why we have all needed the Lord Christ.

I can commend several men who have helped me enormously in different ways, and I believe that any preacher could be mightily assisted in the life of the pastor through becoming more acquainted with their ministry online or in their books. Some of these friends have been involved in public controversies, and have faced a variety of accusations, some of which were false and some of which at times contained some truth. Please do not assume that because I acknowledge their mighty gifts and the help I have received from them that I judge that they have been always in the right. Those who belong to Christ are my brothers even when I have heard about falls into grievous sins. "If You, LORD, should mark iniquities, O Lord, who could stand?" (Ps. 130:3). My own sins may well be worse than any of these men's or even worse than all their sins put together. I am thankful for brothers who, knowing my many failures, have continued to count me among their friends.

Dr. Martyn Lloyd-Jones (1899–1981)

I was fortunate to hear Dr. Lloyd-Jones on a number of occasions. I heard that he had resigned from Westminster Chapel, and one of his purposes in retirement was to teach a course in preaching to theological students (so he had written to his congregation). I immediately sent an airmail letter to the president of Westminster Seminary and told him of Dr. Lloyd-Jones's intention, urging him to act fast. "Write in order to book him to teach that course in preaching in Philadelphia," I wrote. Ed Clowney told me that he did that immediately, and the rest is history. The church now has the freshest book on preaching of the twentieth century, *Preaching and Preachers*. I have read it numbers of times. When I have had an assistant, we have met once a week and sat together and read alternate paragraphs of a single chapter and discussed it. That is a particular delight, and I always see something fresh and helpful. I hope I put its counsels into practice.

I chaired Dr. Lloyd-Jones's last preaching in Wales in the early summer of 1980 in Baker Street Congregational Church, Aberystwyth, that was used for that Wednesday evening. He preached in Welsh in the afternoon and then in English in the evening. For the first ten minutes of the latter sermon, I had ordinary thoughts as I sat in the congregation and watched him, thinking, "Isn't it wonderful that at eighty years of age he is preaching so well?" Then I became

Dr. and Mrs. Martyn Lloyd-Jones after having lunch with Professor Bobi Jones, May 1980 in Aberystwyth on the last occasion he preached in Wales, in Welsh in the afternoon and in English in the evening to a packed congregation.

gripped by the message and forgot all about such inconsequentialities, God engaging me through His Word, and the message of the gospel was everything. The time flew by. How often I have heard him say after fifty minutes, "Well, we must draw to a close; the time is going by," and upon hearing that, someone in the congregation says aloud, "Go on!" Yes, don't stop. There are not many men who could preach for fifty minutes and an entire congregation longs for the sermon not to end.

The Doctor sat in the big seat afterward, and people waited in a little line to introduce themselves to him and talk. He seemed delighted with each one. How his face lit up. No one was in a hurry to leave, and even when we moved out onto the silent street on that warm evening, we hung around and greeted one another, wanting the atmosphere and the sense of the presence of God to abide.

Terry Virgo writes well of one of the occasions he heard Dr. Lloyd-Jones preach at Westminster Chapel: "He started his sermon from a passage in Acts but was drawn into Romans 1 and concentrated on the three places where the apostle states, 'God gave them up.' I hadn't heard such preaching before or since. I had never felt the sense of awe and fear of God that I felt during that sermon. He concluded, and we had the closing hymn, but, having sung it, everyone sat in silence for long moments. No one hurried to leave the building. It was perhaps the most awesome moment I have ever known in church. That experience was not simply personal to me but was being felt across the whole hushed congregation." My own second wife, Barbara, was there on those occasions when it would be just as Virgo well describes it.

I remember on an earlier occasion, my ten-year-old daughter Eleri was with me when Lloyd-Jones had visited Aberystwyth, and we finally walked home together hand in hand. "Well, what did you think of the sermon?" I asked her. She replied so naïvely, "It was like Sunday mornings—only simpler!" I told his daughter Ann that dialogue. I was anxious that her father should receive the encouragement of such artless appreciation.

When Lloyd-Jones was becoming increasingly influential as a London doctor, he felt a call to become a gospel preacher. The Forward Movement, Bethlehem, Sandfields, in Port Talbot, having heard him preach a couple of times, spoke to him publicly after the evening service when he was present with them that day officially "with a view" to being invited to become the minister. At that meeting they asked him if he would consider coming to them as their pastor, and he spoke to them saying, "I feel this is the place I would like to work in. Will you have me?" They held another meeting and voted unanimously to call him to become their new minister. He returned to preach there on December 12, 1926, and then on Monday took the train back to London.

On the Tuesday he went back to his work in St. Bartholomew's Hospital. A note was left in his pigeonhole requesting him to meet immediately with his chiefs Spilsbury and Horder. When he entered their room, they were pouring over the morning newspapers, which carried such headings as "Leading Doctor Turns Pastor: Large income given up for £300 a year" and "Harley-Street Doctor to become a Minister." He saw their concern and apologized to them, acknowledging that there had been a press leak and that his intention was to inform them first of his decision. "But is it true?" they asked him. He acknowledged that it was, and then they began to plead with him to reconsider his decision. They reminded him of all the usefulness of being a physician, the people he would be able to help, the Christian work he could do, and so on. Though he listened patiently to them, he was unyielding, and then they became more argumentative, begging him to think again of all he was giving up—what in their minds was just foolishness. Finally, he addressed them and said, "Yes, we can do much good, but after you and I have done all we can to help people, they are still going to die." He believed that his calling was to preach to people this message of eternity, of receiving eternal life, that God so loved the world that He gave His only begotten Son that whosoever believes in Him should not perish but have everlasting life. Not without difficulty he continued to work in Bartholomew's Hospital until early February 1927, when he moved to Sandfields to begin his notable ministry that was soon known throughout the whole principality.

Most of his hearers were working men, colliers and steel workers, and so it was too when he was the minister in Westminster Chapel. The congregation was not exclusively middle-class office workers, medical students, and businessmen. There were many people who were employed for wages that were earned especially in manual or industrial work. This was illustrated for me one Tuesday morning in December around the year 2000 when attending the Westminster Conference at Westminster Chapel. My two sons-in-law and a friend and I walked into the courtyard at the side of the chapel in our coats and hats. The chapel was getting a new roof and was covered in scaffolding. Descending from a long ladder was a "hard hat," a roofer dressed in boots and jeans. A wide leather belt (from which hung a number of tools) was around what appeared to be a beer gut, and he wore his yellow hat. He arrived on the ground and turned around to see we four men soberly dressed in our suits walking toward him alongside the entrance into the chapel. He spoke to us. "So, what's going on there?" Ian Alsop, my son-in-law, answered on behalf of us all as we paused: "We are going to a lecture on Sandemanianism." The hard hat looked back at us and replied, "Oh, yes. I heard the Doctor speak on that—must be thirty years ago. I had such a blessing whenever I heard him preach." We smiled, nodded, knowing from where he was coming, for we had traveled that same route. The lecture we were about to hear that morning was not simply an intellectual and historical exercise. It dealt with truths and practices truly relevant for one big issue facing the Christian church everywhere in the world that day. Children and working men heard him gladly.

Many people would choose as the best example of the Doctor's preaching to be the sixty sermons transcribed, bound, and entitled *Studies in the Sermon on the Mount.* I would concur with that. One of the reasons I chose to begin in Aberystwyth by preaching through Matthew was that I could soon take advantage of this book and the help it gave me. A. W. Pink has an earlier book on those same chapters in Matthew's gospel, and they would have been a help to Lloyd-Jones. I love Dr. MLJ's volume because locked into these beloved chapters is an explanation of such peerless truths that speak to the conscience and set out the righteous life in all its beauty so that one longs to live like that.

However, a fine introduction to Martyn Lloyd-Jones for someone who has never read him is a collection of nine sermons preached on his last visit to America in 1969 at the Pensacola Institute of Theology. They have been transcribed and published as *Setting Our Affections Upon Glory*. The book contains his evangelistic preaching at its most powerful. It is also a good refresher for people who have not read him for some time. For a deeper examination of Lloyd-Jones, anyone would benefit from reading Iain Murray's *Lloyd-Jones: Messenger of Grace.*

There was just a single occasion I heard him preach on a Sunday at Westminster Chapel. It was on Whit Sunday in 1965. He preached on Pentecost on that Sunday morning and in the evening on Acts 3:19, "So that times of refreshing may come from the presence of the Lord." I wanted the service to be as one of those I had experienced in Wales, or as one Terry Virgo remembers in the chapel, but it was not to be. We thought it was good, but we were not moved as invariably as we had been in the past. When his series of sermons on Acts was published, that very message appears in the first volume. I read it with profit, noticing how well he had developed the theme and approached the text, applying it to the contemporary situation in the church and in the world. It is a very fine sermon; I got more from reading it than hearing it that night—which rarely occurs. Somehow, sitting in the congregation that evening simply lacked for us the touching and moving of our affections that we had known at other times. There is a romance about preaching that Lloyd-Jones would often acknowledge. For one person, a message is life-changing, indiscriminating saving grace, while to another it is merely interesting.

I felt that Dr. Lloyd-Jones was a little interested in me in the late 1960s. I was preaching outside London on a holiday Monday at a Bible rally. I had spoken in the afternoon on Lot lingering, and in the evening, I preached a sermon entitled, "Remember Lot's Wife."

As I was in the ministers' room awaiting the start of the evening service, who should get out of his car and walk past the window but Dr. Lloyd-Jones and his wife. I was petrified. I thought, "He knows J. C. Ryle's *Holiness*, and he will know that I have got help for the sermon from that book. I have a sermon at home on John the Baptist's preaching that he will like, and that sermon is all my own!" But Aberystwyth was far away, and I had to give what I had prepared. He was kind to me afterward.

I had some little exasperations with the Doctor. For example, in his going through his studies in the epistle to the Romans, he totally ignores some Scriptures of chapter 1, verses 26 and 27, omitting them from his preaching, as though the Holy Spirit had not inspired them. He does not say a word about the sinfulness of homosexual activities that is commented on in these words. And again, there is his strange silence over the killing of the unborn child in abortion.

I mildly argued with the Doctor concerning what he referred to as the "baptism of the Spirit"—the Bichon Frise arguing with the St. Bernard. It was Maurice Roberts who helped me when reading these words of his:

> Ecstasy and delight are essential to the believer's soul and they promote sanctification. We were not meant to live without spiritual exhilaration, and the Christian who goes for a long time without the experience of heart-warming will soon find himself tempted to have his emotions satisfied from earthly things and not, as he ought, from the Spirit of God. The soul is so constituted that it craves fulfilment from things outside itself and will embrace earthly joys for satisfaction when it cannot reach spiritual ones.... The believer is in spiritual danger if he allows himself to go for any length of time without tasting the love of Christ and savouring the felt comforts of a Saviour's presence. When Christ ceases to fill the heart with satisfaction our souls will go in silent search of other lovers.... By the enjoyment of the love of Christ in the heart of a believer we mean an experience of the "love of God shed abroad in our hearts by the Holy Ghost which is given to us" (Romans 5:5).... Because the Lord has made himself accessible to us in the means of grace, it is

> our duty and privilege to see this experience from him in these means till we are made the joyful partakers of it.[1]

I choose to believe that that was largely the concern of Dr. Lloyd-Jones in his abbreviation, "the baptism of the Spirit," and that such a longing to be filled with the Spirit is an eminently biblical one.

I loved him dearly; I defended him zealously and still do. I purchase every book of his as it appears and find them all profitable. I do what he did. I lead the services as he led them. I make no allowances for the shrill demand that revelatory gifts be given opportunity to be exercised in any church meeting—just as he would not permit that. I wish I had been more like him in wisdom, kindness, and graciousness. I yearn for an ounce of the authority he had in his preaching. It was an immense blessing to have known him. I loved his openness in giving me his opinions of preachers and institutions and theology. He spoke to you as a fellow pastor, as an equal. He spoke to you as one Welsh head of a family to another head.

Iain Murray knew Dr. Lloyd-Jones as well as any other human being outside of his family. This is his evaluation of him:

> I came to know Dr. Lloyd-Jones in the early 1950s. He was then at the height of his powers and labours, and I was an unknown student for the ministry. Nonetheless he gave me time and counsel as generously as he did to countless other young men. Hundreds will never forget what his friendship meant to them. He was a truly self-effacing Christian who sought to live for the approval of God, and one could scarcely leave his presence without being moved by a like concern. Any moderation of fundamental truth in order to gain influence was anathema to him. Here he was stern and unbending. Yet he stressed love as an imperative for all witness, and on secondary issues no-one was a stronger believer in the need for Christian unity. He was a Calvinist not simply in belief but through and through. He saw man-centredness—whether in evangelism or in the

1. Maurice Roberts, *The Thought of God* (Edinburgh: Banner of Truth, 1993), 57–58.

Dr. Lloyd-Jones between Geoff Thomas and Stephen Turner of New Zealand in Llanymawddwy, North Wales.

> theological scholarship approved by secular universities—as the root of modern evangelical weakness and he did not believe the churches would see a better day until they learned to "cease from man" (Isa. 2:22). Although trained in one of the highest schools of scientific learning, his life as a Christian depended on simple faith in the word of God, and he died, as he lived, magnifying the grace of God. We all loved him and thank God that in very many languages around the world today his ministry reaches far more than ever heard him preach.[2]

Dr. J. I. Packer spoke soberly of Dr. Lloyd-Jones's preaching, saying,

> What was special about it? It was simple, clear, straightforward man-to-man stuff. It was expository, apologetic, and evangelistic on the grand scale. It was both the planned performance of

2. Iain H. Murray, "Endorsements," MLJ Trust, https://www.mljtrust.org/endorsements/.

a magnetic orator and the passionate, compassionate outflow of a man with a message from God that he knew his hearers needed. He worked up to a dramatic growling shout about God's sovereign grace a few minutes before the end; then from that he worked down to businesslike persuasion, calling on needy souls to come to Christ. It was the old, old story, but it had been made wonderfully new. I went out full of awe and joy, with a more vivid sense of the greatness of God in my heart than I had known before.

Packer's conclusion about him is this:

We are all together in regarding Dr Lloyd-Jones as, warts and all, one of the greatest Christian men of the twentieth century, a man whom God used powerfully to recall British evangelicals, both individually and corporately, to their true roots in the Bible, in the gospel and in theology—in other words, in Christ—at a time when such a recall was badly needed. Seeing him so, we join in honouring his memory, and in hoping that English-speaking evangelicals will continue to honour him as he deserves long after we ourselves are gone.[3]

Iain Murray (1931–) and the Banner of Truth

Iain Murray was a member of a Scottish church-going family attending a Presbyterian church in Liverpool. As a teenager he heard the gospel preached through Tom Rees, the founder of Hildenborough Hall Conference Centre, and he professed his faith in Jesus Christ. He grew in discernment during his years of national service in Singapore. There, in 1951, a lady missionary pointed him to the life and writings of Robert Murray M'Cheyne. Then as a history student in Durham University, he came across the books of the Puritans and introduced them to his friends. He felt increasingly that his life was to be spent fully in the service of God. He lived in what was called

3. J. I. Packer, foreword to *Engaging with Martyn Lloyd-Jones: The Life and Legacy of "the Doctor,"* ed. Andrew Atherstone and David Ceri Jones (Nottingham: Apollos/IVP, 2011).

Iain and Jean Murray

the Foreign Missions Club in Highbury, London, and worshiped in Westminster Chapel. One weekend spent with Sidney Norton in Oxford helped him to see that "golden chain" uniting the teaching of the Reformers, the Puritans, and the leaders of the Evangelical Awakening with those in the next century, C. H. Spurgeon, Robert Murray M'Cheyne, J. C. Ryle, until finally there were J. Gresham Machen, Louis Berkhof, Martyn Lloyd-Jones, and John Murray in the twentieth century. But along with Iain Murray's acquaintance with the continuity of historic confessional Christianity was the supreme relevance of the teaching and stature of these men to the Christian situation in today's world.

Iain Murray preached along with Sidney Norton in St. John's Church in Oxford for a couple of years, and in September 1955 they launched a magazine through a legacy of £30 that a lady in the congregation left them in her will. They called it the *Banner of Truth*. I received issue number 17 in 1959 and became a subscriber.

Dr. Lloyd-Jones invited Murray in late 1956 to come and assist him at Westminster Chapel by teaching a gathering of church members on Wednesday evenings a survey of church history. There his lectures were heard by an acoustics engineer, Jack Cullum, who saw the same relevance of this historic Christian testimony to the religion of the needy millions of London. He increasingly wanted the books commended by Iain to be made accessible again. It was being done in America by Jay Green with his Sovereign Grace publications. After much serious thought, discussion, and prayer, these two men in July 1957 launched the Banner of Truth Trust, with John Murray and W. J. Grier of Belfast as two of the other trustees. Thus began the publication of Banner of Truth books, and early on they had some surprising best sellers such as Thomas Watson's *A Body of Divinity* and Louis Berkhof's *Systematic Theology*.

There was a general sense of surprise in gospel circles at the interest taken in these books. The publication of a book of the barely known Puritan John Owen on the doctrine of effectual definite atonement entitled *The Death of Death in the Death of Christ* created a buzz in the evangelical world with correspondence about its thesis in popular religious magazines. This centered on the lengthy foreword by Dr. J. I. Packer, who zealously defended this thesis that Christ loved the church and gave Himself for the redemption of that vast number of His people, as we sing, "Till all the ransomed church of God be saved, to sin no more."[4]

Sixty-five years have gone by, and the Banner continues to publish books reflecting the same convictions. Each month the magazine appears under a series of sympathetic editors, as Iain Murray has retired as editor. It once experimented with a different format to the magazine but then returned to its traditional size. It has brought out a series of miniguides, little books on great themes of living the Christian life from the very best of the Puritans. It also once organized a family conference, but that was all. It is willing to experiment. Its annual ministers' conferences in England and America, a biannual one in Australia, and its Borders' Conference and youth conference in the United Kingdom were all put to one side in

4. William Cowper, "There Is A Fountain," 1772.

2020 by government decree, with all religious gatherings worldwide, because of the coronavirus threat. Its absence for some of us was like missing the oasis on a journey through a desert. The anticipation of new books, especially by Iain Murray, and attendance at these conferences have become part of our happy annual routine.

I remember being given some insight by one of the early Banner of Truth catalogs in how it had divided up its publications chronologically. For example, the sixteenth century was represented by John Calvin's studies of the prophet Joel. The seventeenth century by such Puritan authors as Joseph Alleine, Thomas Manton, and Thomas Watson (precursors of a tremendous series of Puritan paperbacks). The eighteenth century displayed George Whitefield's sermons and his *Journals*, John Newton's *Letters*, and *The Early Life of Howell Harris*. The nineteenth century saw a reprint of the life of Robert Murray M'Cheyne, Spurgeon's *Revival Year Sermons*, some of J. C. Ryle's books, and Charles Hodge' s *The Way of Life*. The twentieth century was represented by John Murray's *Redemption Accomplished and Applied*, W. J. Grier's *The Momentous Event,* William Hendriksen's commentaries, and Iain Murray's *The Forgotten Spurgeon*. Soon sets of the sermons of Lloyd-Jones on Romans and Ephesians appeared as examples that in our day this historical Christian position was vital and being blessed by God.

But the Banner of Truth's publications were not simply a statement of confessional Christianity summarized by the Westminster Confession of Faith, the 1689 Baptist Confession of Faith, and the Savoy Confession of the Congregationalists. The Banner of Truth had a strong emphasis on personal piety, on God-honoring worship, on Christian godliness and the devotional life, on family devotions, and the walk with God, honoring Him in all that was done. The Banner has also put a priority on evangelism, in publishing books that have been evangelistically challenging and those helpful for novices to be introduced to the Christian faith. There was also a wise sympathy in the Banner of Truth toward the history of redemption, or biblical theology. A new edition of Geerhardus Vos's *Biblical Theology* was produced with paragraph headings and an index. Other books evidencing the help of these insights were by Frederick Leahy, with his warmhearted publications on Christ's redemptive work, and by Noel Weeks' *The Sufficiency of Scripture* and *Gateway to the Old Testament*. These books all show the contributions to our understanding of covenantal redemption.

A considerable emphasis on revival resides in the Banner of Truth publications. Some of the Reformed tradition in Anglicanism, some Dutch theology, and some modern Presbyterianism in the United States have had their suspicions of the concept of revival. Some conservative Presbyterian critics have not written altogether kindly about Iain Murray's careful distinction of *Revival and Revivalism*. But the Banner, though critical of Charles Grandison Finney's theology and methodology on revival, and properly so, has always been deeply serious and exegetical in commending true great awakenings, times of the sovereign work of the Spirit of God when many have come to confess Christ as their Lord and Savior.

The Banner of Truth has also emphasized the climactic aspect of the sermon in Sunday worship services. Its great concern is to see awakening ministries springing up everywhere. How can our preaching be improved? Where is the pathos, and were the great truths proclaimed in power and in the Holy Spirit and with much assurance? Books like Charles Bridge's *The Christian Ministry*, a definitive issue of *Lectures to My Students* by Spurgeon, and Sinclair Ferguson's *Some Pastors and Teachers* have been published. There has also been an emphasis on history and the lessons we must learn from the lives and gatherings and councils of Christians in the past centuries.

So, one meets the Banner publications everywhere—on the shelves of students in halls of residence, in Scottish crofts, in the front rooms of terraced homes in Welsh mining villages, on Long Island in the library of a commuter to a Wall Street bank, and in the homes of blacksmiths, farmers, and lorry drivers. And of course, they are there in the manses and parsonages of any preacher of the gospel. Where there is any serious God-centered pulpit, there you will find a delight in reading these books. In camps teenagers are told to look for the image of the little man preaching, which they will find at the bottom of the spine of a book, and that in spotting that, the purchaser will be safe to buy and devour that book. What comes home to me whenever I pick up a new Banner of Truth book is the seriousness with which the subject is approached.

I can understand what Peter Hitchens says about his response to listening to the cadences, rhythms, and contents of seventeenth-century language, how disturbing it is:

> It is the voice of the dead, speaking as if they were still alive and as if the world had not changed since they died—when I had thought that the world was wholly alterable and that the rules changed with the times. Now I am comforted greatly by this voice, welcoming the intervention of my forebears into our lives and their insistent reminder that we do not in fact change at all, that as I am now, so once were they, and as they are now, so shall I be.[5]

But Iain Murray is more than an author of many books. He is an inspiring speaker about history, theology, and ethics. He can reach the affections through the mind. At the beginning, he and the Banner of Truth publications and its readers were misrepresented as those encouraging a Christian ethos that was totally out of date and out of touch, having a pining for the past, a real nostalgia. The Banner of Truth is not a conservation project. Its purpose is to strengthen, enlighten, and sanctify contemporary Christians in order to make them more usable as servants of the Lord Christ today.

It was suggested that Iain was defending and embodying European reformational and cultural attitudes and an English and Scottish national identity. But in Europe, abiding biblical attitudes had been deliberately marginalized, and crucial values had been lost. Iain was in part raised to express and defend our collective Christian memory and freedoms. For him, the alternative to the killing fields of liberalism and modernism was the vitally relevant "whole counsel of God" found in the Word of God that lives and abides forever. The long

---

5. Peter Hitchens, *The Rage against God: How Atheism Led Me to Faith* (London: Continuum, 2010), 28.

march of humanism through education, the arts, the media, entertainment, and politics has steadily undermined such core values as spiritual vitality, consecration, seriousness, and modesty.

So, Murray has his heroes; that much is evident—the Reformers, the Puritans, the leaders of the Great Awakening, the giants of the nineteenth century in Scotland, England, and America. The articles and books on those men and religious movements of the past are not simply an exercise in escapism or restorative nostalgia. The present lacks the very things that made evangelical religion strong and attractive in years gone by. Thus, both Iain's study and his eager hearing of a range of preachers today has resulted in his invitations to new voices from all over the world to address the Banner of Truth ministers' conferences, usually to our great benefit. The pilgrimages and ministries of these men have highlighted different aspects of experiential Protestantism.

The Banner of Truth's publications have brought to the church's consciousness forgotten events—councils, controversies, personalities, publications, confessions of faith—all of crucial significance and contemporary relevance. The appearance of the first few Banner of Truth magazines initially created a sense of pity in some quarters, and a mild hope to numbers of people who had witnessed in their lifetimes other attempts to fan the flames of the embers of free-grace doctrines in the United Kingdom. Those British men and women were the salt of the earth, people who were trying to live by the Scriptures, raise their families, and enjoy a breadth of Christian fellowship. They were keeping one day each week sanctified and more focused on the Lord of resurrection. They were longing for better days and adopting a modest, settled, and affirmative way of life. The continued appearance of the magazine followed by the steady publication of new books resulted in their being surprised by joy.

Iain and his wife, Jean, were given to hospitality, but Iain has been generally known through what people read in the magazine or what they heard on cassettes of the addresses he has given at the Leicester ministers' conferences. On those unforgettable occasions, as I looked around and chatted to people during mealtimes, we seemed at times to resemble a flotilla of ships from another age, buffeted by tempests and mountainous seas! For some it was hard to dispatch the feeling that despite the huge book room and the hundreds of men gathered there and the blessing of God on some of the speakers, the forces of darkness were powerful and the light from glory often seemed to be flickering.

Iain's exceptional character has shone through his long life. Humble and self-effacing, he has rare qualities of generosity of spirit and a good sense of humor. We are quite able to judge theological truth and Christian ethics, but Iain is also a fine judge of character and an encourager of younger men and is a magnificent writer. That will remain in our lives, and it will continue through his recorded messages and the books that are yet to appear. They will all surely enlighten future generations. They will learn about the importance of truth, godly living, love for the Son of God, and what it is to be made in God's image that is restored through the indwelling Spirit of Christ.

Over a long life I have gathered convictions, which Iain has reassured me most of were right! I learned from him that the Reformed faith is the theology of God's love for me and that it comes to sinners biblically, covenantally, evangelistically, personally, dynamically, experientially, and Christ-centeredly through the means of the saints of God, both alive and dead, and demanding a decision. No one in their right mind could accuse Iain Murray of having lived the quiet life of an author ensconced in his study.

He has given me so much to love and admire in the British Christian idea of the home (there was always a dog in the Murrays' house). I have loved him for his seriousness, his learning, his difference from me, his discovery and insight into the relevance of older ways (that had seemed to have died and gone) far superior to today's flashier mores. God has given him a complete life and has fulfilled his purpose not only for the UK but for Christians in every continent. Dr. Lloyd-Jones and Jack Cullum passed on a baton to him, and he has passed it on to us. He is one of those who has given to evangelicalism its steel. He also gave it its thinking by encouraging its historical momentum when it was barely moving at all except by looking to the movements and men of the United States for some kind of temporary push. He also gave us heart not only by what he has written but by giving us himself, by his generosity of spirit, and his piety and love of righteousness. How he appreciates gospel evangelism. I have been blessed to have had him as a counselor and friend. He has ever been as intelligent and generous in my company as he is on the page. One day his autobiography will appear, and I long to read it. Now I reread any or all of his magnificently helpful books.

Albert N. Martin (1934–)

In 1967 I went to the Banner of Truth ministers' conference in Leicester. I learned that the largely unknown speaker was an American. That disappointed me a little because I had recently spent three years in the United States and had not heard many inspirational preachers during that time. I had met many fine God-fearing ministers, but I felt that there were more inspiring preachers in the United Kingdom. Why bring a man from America to teach us about preaching? Ah, my prejudice!

The American was thirty-four-year-old Albert N. Martin, and I was humbled and ashamed hearing him opening up Scripture at that conference and preaching God's free grace in a most challenging way. It was a thrilling few days. What we were praying for—that God would raise up in our generation younger gospel preachers—was taking place, and we were witnesses to this. How little we are aware of the spread of the kingdom of God and what the Lord is doing day by day all over the world.

Al was raised in the Christian home of George Albert and Mildred Sophie, mainly in Stamford, Connecticut. He was the second of eleven children, one of those dying in infancy. The family attended gospel churches, and when he was sixteen, his family left the Salvation Army and began to attend First Baptist Church. He graduated from Stamford High School in 1952. Because of the influences of his parents, he never doubted the basic teachings of Scripture, that there is one living and true God who has revealed Himself in creation and man's conscience but uniquely through prophets and apostles and especially in His Son, Jesus Christ. So, Al Martin was always convinced that the God of the Bible is and that Al existed in a moral universe with his final destination being either heaven or hell. He went through times of conviction when he felt that all was not well between him and his Creator. He would have nights of lying in his bed crying to God for mercy because he knew that if he were to die in the next hour, he would go to hell.

In the Salvation Army where they first attended, he was taught that a sinner could be saved but then could lose his new salvation, only to be saved again and lost once more! And so a number of visits to the mourners' bench at the end of services was a part of his growing up. But the effects never lasted more than a day or two until a different period arrived during his high school years when he began to sense the emptiness and futility of living a life without a personal relationship with his God. What was he going to do with his life if there were no overall meaning or purpose? During that time God used the testimony of some of his friends in their senior years of high school to explain the way of salvation to him, something so crucial that somehow he had never grasped before these months. As a result, sometime between late 1951 and early 1952, Al was enabled to turn from sin and lay hold of Christ and His grace. From that time God gave him a hunger for His Word. He saved his money from a little after-school job and bought a large Bible and read it constantly.

Al Martin worked part time for the Western Union Telegraph Company delivering telegrams and would often attach a gospel tract to the envelope. Was this the reason the manager sent a message to him one day telling him he wanted to see him? It was nothing to do with that. Someone had heard about this movement toward religion in Stamford High School led by a boy named Albert Martin. He had written an article about it and sent it to *The New York Times*, and they had printed it. The manager asked Al if he were this boy, and discovering it was, he then commended him for doing something worthwhile.

Some elderly Christians in a gospel mission heard about Al and invited him and his friends to address their midweek meeting. The leaders would sit on a chair to the left of the pulpit, occasionally uttering an "Amen!" and then, if something very searching was said, would say, "If that's not the gospel, I don't know what is!" They would then exhort the young people to preach in the open air in the main streets of Stamford. This took place in February 1952 as Al was approaching his eighteenth birthday. He walked the mile and a half to the appointed place outside the drugstore on a snowy night. He met up with his friends while the old men were in the mission praying for them. They enthusiastically sang some hymns and choruses, and then Al stepped forward, his *New Testament & Psalms* in his hand, to give his testimony and preach. He opened his mouth and began to speak. He says, "Much to my surprise, although I was natively a timid young man, I was made conscious of dynamics that profoundly affected what I said and how I spoke on that memorable night. In a real sense that occasion was my 'coming out party' where I confessed my attachment to Christ before my peers. It was also my 'spoiled for life' party in that I experienced on that occasion what I knew to be the immediate agency and operations of the Holy Spirit during the act of preaching."[6]

Al Martin went on to study in a couple of Christian colleges and was well drilled in New Testament Greek, and in the following four or five years, he exercised an itinerary ministry. His wife, Marilyn, accompanied him on a number of these visits, and on one such occasion they were in Chicago and were able to spend some hours with A. W. Tozer. They discussed the "deeper life" teaching that Al had been exposed to in one Bible school he had attended. Finally, they kneeled to pray, and Tozer prayed like this, "Lord, save my young brother from pride, save him from women, and save him from the

6. Albert N. Martin, *Preaching in the Holy Spirit* (Grand Rapids: Reformation Heritage Books, 2011), vii–viii.

hierarchy of the 'deeper life,' Grubb, Fleece, Tozer, and the whole bunch of us. Save him and keep him fresh."

These years of itinerant preaching gave him an acquaintance with the state of fundamentalism in the country. All was not well, and in that period he discovered some splendid literature that more fully explained the whole counsel of God and the history of Christianity. It was while reading Thomas Boston's *Human Nature in Its Fourfold State* that he saw that some Scriptural doctrines, such as those found in John 6, John 17, Romans 9, and Ephesians 1, were being neglected by alleged "Bible-believing" churches and that the Word of God was indeed revealing that those truths that men have labeled "Calvinism" are in fact the message of the Holy Scriptures. He remembered one of his teachers at Columbia Bible College used to say that Luther and the other Reformers believed that repentance and faith were not the cause of our regeneration but rather the result of the sovereign work of God in their hearts. Now he understood the point that they had been pressing home. Reading Charles Bridges's *The Christian Ministry* was enormously helpful in giving him some understanding of what the vocation of the pastor-preacher entails.

In 1962 Al was invited to become the pastor of a small church in Montville in northern New Jersey, an hour away from New York. Little did he know when he accepted the call that for the next forty-six years he was to be the preacher in that vicinity. Its tape ministry increasingly went around the world. A training school for pastors was established, and Al taught a course on preaching, now published in three essential volumes of enormous importance entitled *Pastoral Theology: The Man of God.*

Joel Beeke urged him to put a heavy emphasis on writing some books in his senior years. At that time Al tried to distance himself from Joel's exhortations by asserting that he had no gifts to write, no computer skills (or computer for that matter), and no idea how to go about the whole publication process. Joel told him those were just excuses, that he should get a computer, learn how to use it, and with the help of editors and publishing houses, he would soon learn he had gifts for writing he didn't know he possessed. Al often thanks Joel for "helping me discover a gift that I didn't know I had." Well done, Joel, and well done, Al, for responding and for producing these three volumes full of wisdom and a dynamic for increasing usefulness in preaching the Word of God. We believe that they will never go out of print and will be on the shelves of every gospel minister and in every seminary as companions and teachers for coming generations.

Al Martin has the acquired discipline of assimilating the best pastoral and evangelistic writing of the past centuries, making it his own, rehearsing it vividly, and then applying it to his hearers in an utterly contemporary way. In addressing the lives of men of God, he often has an awakening ministry, speaking to their consciences from the Scriptures without crushing them. His sermons can also have a pastoral richness in comforting and renewing, like those preached after the death of his first wife and have appeared in his book, *Grieving, Hope and Solace: When a Loved One Dies in Christ*. I found it helpful when my own wife died.

Al has a mighty evangelistic gift. I remember him preaching in Sandfields, Port Talbot, in the former pulpit of Dr. Lloyd-Jones, on the words of Jesus Christ, "Then He will also say to those on the left hand, 'Depart from Me, you cursed, into the everlasting fire prepared for the devil and his angels'" (Matt. 25:41), under the title "The Most Terrible Words a Man Can Hear." I believe it to be one of the most searching sermons I have ever heard, causing me to regret that I could not preach with the authority and convicting power of this minister. Or again I chaired the final Friday night session of the Evangelical Movement of Wales Conference in Aberystwyth when Al Martin was preaching in four mornings on sanctification and then preached on John 3 and the new birth to a packed congregation. What a listening! The sermon had exegesis, context, application, edification of the Christian, and saving power for those in the congregation who were not yet believers. All his books and booklets are helpful: *The Forgotten Fear, You Lift Me Up, Preaching in the Holy Spirit*, and *What's Wrong with Preaching Today?*

Pastor Edward Donnelly describes an event that occurred at the Southeastern Reformed Baptist Family Conference in the summer of 1990 at William Jennings Bryan College:

> The main auditorium was filled with six or seven hundred people, and he was preaching on Jesus in Gethsemane. Toward the close of his sermon, all the lights went out, and Pastor Martin finished preaching in the dark. As he led in prayer at the end, the lights came on again. It was discovered that the building was equipped with a motion sensor system for switching off the lighting when no one was detected in the auditorium. The large audience had been so gripped by the preaching that there was literally not a single movement among them. The engineers had not calculated that it would be possible for people to sit so motionless, and the instruments were calibrated accordingly. When Pastor Martin had announced the closing prayer, we must have leaned forward in our seats and triggered the lighting. It was a startling example of the power of the Word.[7]

Ronald Jones expresses the convictions of many other people when he talks of how it was principally Al Martin's tape messages that had assisted him in his journey from Anabaptism to Dispensationalism and finally to a decidedly Reformed Baptist position: "Our family was first blessed by his public ministry when we heard him preach a three-sermon series on sanctification at a family conference in 1970. Now, more than forty-three years later, I can still recall those sermon titles, though I made no intentional effort to do so."[8]

---

7. Quoted in John Reuther, "Biographical Sketch of Albert N. Martin," in Albert N. Martin, *Pastoral Theology: The Man of God: His Calling and Godly Life* (Montville, NJ: Trinity Pulpit Press, 2018), 1:xlv.

8. Quoted in *Pastoral Theology*, 1:xxxix.

Joel Beeke (1952–)

The bare facts are these: Joel R. Beeke was born in 1952, and he is an American Christian pastor and theologian. He is a minister of the Heritage Reformed Congregation in Grand Rapids, Michigan, and president of Puritan Reformed Theological Seminary, where he is also the professor of systematic theology and homiletics. He is editor of *Puritan Reformed Journal* and *Banner of Sovereign Grace Truth* and editorial director of Reformation Heritage Books. He studied at Western Michigan University, the Netherlands Reformed Theological School, and Westminster Theological Seminary where he obtained his PhD. Dr. Beeke is an acknowledged expert on the Puritans.

That is all true, but terribly academic. It does not reveal to us that there is no one in the world so willing to travel to any group, large or small, anywhere in the five continents, to promote the gospel of Jesus Christ—and then send fascinating reports on what he has observed to hundreds of his friends.

This man has come to Aberystwyth three times to preach at the August Conference of the Evangelical Movement of Wales to thirteen hundred people and on two other occasions to preach in Alfred Place Baptist Church, once to help celebrate my fiftieth anniversary there. He was not invited because of his academic credentials or his historical and theological knowledge but because of our friendship and my esteem for him as a reformer, theologian, family man, tireless traveler, and preacher of the gospel of Jesus Christ. One of the last times he was in Aberystwyth, he preached on the words of the apostle Paul: "For to me, to live is Christ, and to die is gain" (Phil. 1:21). He practices what he preaches, and that is why he has been one of the most encouraging influences in my Christian life and as a minister. So, let us look at the man.

Joel spoke to an Australian friend and shared with him his early life:

> I grew up in a very godly home. My father was a ruling elder in the church for forty years. He talked to us as children a lot about our souls and about the need to have a close relationship with God. He was big into what I call "Reformed experiential teaching and preaching," that is, what the Lord does savingly by His Holy Spirit in man's heart (what John Murray defines as "man's dispositional complex" out of which come all the issues of life). My mother [Mrs. Beeke], was not as open as my dad in terms of really speaking out about the Lord, but she modeled it. She was very loving and very prayerful. And so, there was this background to my boyhood, this combination of a father who cared deeply for my soul and a mother who prayed daily for my soul and cared deeply for all my other needs. There was such power in their godliness in those different forms, and that was a huge influence in my life.
>
> Then, when I was fourteen, I came under deep conviction of my sin. I thought I was a reprobate. I thought, I had the best parents in the world, and I had rebelled against them—even though you wouldn't have seen any open rebellion in my life, but I just felt like I was a wretched guilty sinner. The church that I grew up in was good, God-fearing, with lots of wonderful, God-fearing people, but it didn't give much hope for a young person seeking the Lord. Of course, they didn't say that explicitly, but that's how I felt. So when at fifteen I was delivered from my sin and brought to liberty in Christ, it was an overwhelming experience for me. Then I just started talking to people everywhere about the Lord.
>
> What also happened in that year and a half while I was under deep conviction of sin was that I not only read the Bible straight through more than once, but I also read an entire bookcase of Puritan books (including all of the Banner of Truth Puritan paperbacks) that my father had bought. I read the works of John Bunyan and *A Body of Divinity* by Thomas Watson and *Christ Our Mediator* by Thomas Goodwin. I was reading every night from about 10 p.m. when my homework

> was done until midnight, or even one o'clock in the morning. I just loved reading those books. I couldn't get enough of them. I read slowly, looking up every text they referenced in the Scriptures, marinating my mind and soul in this material.

Hence, a large part of Joel Beeke's focus on the Puritans arises from his personal experience, from the time when as a teenager he took books by Thomas Goodwin down from his father's shelves and read them. Since then, he hasn't read anything outside of the Holy Scriptures that so strengthens his soul than their productions. The more he reads the Puritans, the more he is convinced that God the Holy Spirit worked through them with unprecedented clarity and power to bring biblical reformation and revival.

But it was not simply the fact that there were books in the house that were made available to the boys to read but that John Beeke took an active role in instructing his sons in the Christian faith. On the Lord's Day evenings, there would be a special family worship time in which his father would read *The Pilgrim's Progress*.

> He loved *The Pilgrim's Progress* and we did too, and we would literally sit at his feet when we were kids, and he'd read with tremendous expressiveness. He'd finished his schooling at thirteen years of age, but he was a good reader and teacher. We would just be drawn into that story. Then we'd ask questions: "Who's Mr. Talkative? What does that mean? What is the House of Interpreter?" And my dad would put the book down and just talk to us, from heart to heart; often with tears in his eyes, and sometimes with tears streaming down his face. He'd talk to us about the need to be converted and to live a life of communion with Christ, out of union with Him. He'd tell us about his own experiences, and that was awesome. Then he would pray, and he would often weep in his prayers, too, as he said, "Oh Lord, we can't miss any of our children in glory! Lord, help us to be an undivided family, reserved for the heavenly mansions above." And you just felt under such teaching and prayers, "Oh, if I don't get saved, everything is lost!" My dad made spiritual life in Christ so very real. At the time, I thought all dads did this. It was only when I was later in the ministry that I realized that I

> had had a truly unusual upbringing from a teaching father who had to quit his schooling at the age of thirteen.
>
> When my parents had their fiftieth wedding anniversary, and all five of us children thanked each parent for one thing, all five of us chose to thank my dad for those amazing times around *The Pilgrim's Progress.* But what is fascinating to me is that Dad didn't seem interested at all in my daily life. I mean, on a grading scale, I'd give him a D minus for interest in what I was doing every day. But in terms of soul love, caring about my soul, I'd give him an A plus. Like J. C. Ryle said, "Soul love is the soul of all love." What my dad lacked, my mother [Johanna], strongly possessed, so I was blessed. Mom would set out our breakfast things, but we just helped ourselves while she had her quiet time with God in the other room. There she was reading the Scriptures and praying for the family and the church every morning while we had breakfast and went off to school.
>
> Being one of the longest serving elders in the church, my dad taught most of the catechism classes. So, I sat at his feet every week in catechism on the Lord's Day. He was a very good teacher, despite his lack of formal education. He would use the chalkboard to write headings and explanations. He would be really expressive in his teaching, and that resonated with myself and all my siblings as well.

Joel felt God's call to the ministry powerfully as a teenager some months after he was delivered from spiritual bondage by the Spirit's application of Christ and His atoning work to his soul. In fact, God so gripped him that he thought he would have to obey it immediately, but his father encouraged him to continue his studies. Eventually he was accepted by his denomination to study for the ministry at age twenty-one. Meanwhile, he received a low lottery number, and was compelled to enter the army. He enlisted with the US Army Reserves. It seems incongruous—Joel Beeke with a bayonet on his rifle! It is also refreshing that he has been out of a Dutch Reformed Church bubble, seen men unprotected by their upbringing and parental care, and learned from that time. He tells this story that illustrates how all these experiences of life can be turned to our advantage as we walk with Jesus Christ.

> The day I left active duty from the army, my boss came to me and said, "Remember, if Uncle Sam calls you back up to come to battle, and to a war (because I was in the Reserves and had several years of service before me), remember three things: (1) Remember how war should go; you've been taught to fight. (2) Remember how wars do go. They never go the way they should go, because they're bloody, messy, surprising. And then (3) remember the end goal. You're fighting for your country and for freedom."
>
> How did Joel turn that experience to serve his vocation?
>
> Later, I thought, "You know, that's a good definition spiritually, of experiential preaching." (1) The preacher must preach what the Christian experience and life should be like—such as you can find in Romans 8. The ideal Christian walks by the Spirit, remembering that we are more than conquerors in Christ Jesus, for nothing can separate us from the love of God. Thus, the preacher must preach how things should go. But (2) a preacher must also preach Romans 7, how things actually do go—the struggles, the battles of experiencing that the good I would do, I find myself not doing, and the evil that I would not do, I find myself doing. Oh, wretched man that I am! This is the real life of the Christian—a life of spiritual warfare! Then (3) the preacher must also preach Revelation 21 and 22 which present us with the optimistic end goal of the Christian: being sin-free in perfect bliss with Christ and the saints forever in heaven.
>
> So when the Reformers and Puritans spoke about experiential preaching, they were saying, "We need to experience the great doctrines of the truths of Scripture in such a way that it moves us through the real struggles and warfare of the Christian life more and more into progressive sanctification that aims for the ideal, even though we never reach it in this life, with the end goal always in sight—always living with one eye on eternity.

So began Joel's long ministry, from his ordination in Iowa in 1978, on to Franklin Lakes, New Jersey, from 1981 to 1986, and then back to Michigan in 1986 to commence his long ministry in Grand Rapids that still continues now. There the Puritan Reformed Theological Seminary (PRTS) was started in 1995 with the acceptance of four seminary students from the Heritage Reformed congregations. Classes officially commenced on August 9, under the leadership of Dr. Beeke.

The original purpose is still their goal today, to prepare students to serve Christ and his church through biblical, experiential, and practical ministry. Students are trained according to the Scriptures and the historic Reformed confessions. Initially the Heritage Reformed Congregations were motivated to begin the seminary to meet the needs of their fledgling denomination, but from its commencement, they had a worldwide, international vision for the work. They just never dreamed that it would grow and expand as rapidly as it has. In 2019 they had the privilege of serving 224 students in their accredited MA, MDiv, ThM, and PhD programs. The students hailed from twenty countries and thirty-two denominations. By God's grace, they have an excellent faculty and staff. Students apply to attend the seminary from every inhabited continent on the globe. There are eleven full-time professors and about a dozen adjunct faculty. They now also have five campuses for the ThM around the world, one in Brazil for Latin America, one in London for Europe, one in Alexandria, Egypt, for the Middle East, one in South Africa for Africa, and one in Taiwan for South Korea, China, Indonesia, and the Philippines. Their faculty teaches half the courses, and the seminaries they are working with teach the other half. All the graduates then earn their ThM from PRTS.

If you should ask Joel how his experience pastoring the local church benefits him in the seminary and vice versa, he will answer thus:

> As a professor of systematic theology and homiletics, it helps me immensely to have significant experience in pastoral ministry, for it constantly reminds me that theology and sermons exist to serve real people in real life. We do not do academics

for the sake of academics but to serve the church. Vice versa, my doctoral studies and subsequent involvement in teaching theology have greatly enriched my pastoral ministry, both by increasing my understanding of divine truth and by expanding my exposure to the broader Reformed tradition outside my particular denomination.

How, then, do the Puritans assist contemporary preachers? Joel will say this:

> First, the Puritans understand that true holiness arises from vital union with Christ by the Spirit. Hence, they constantly pointed their hearers (and readers) to the Mediator, which kept their approach to sanctification within the grace of the triune God.
>
> Second, the Puritans were eminently practical and realistic. Their view of sanctification did not entail removing yourself from ordinary human life (though it did require separation from worldliness and sin) but instead showed how to bring holiness into the heart and home.

Joel has recently written a book on preaching titled *Reformed Preaching: Proclaiming God's Word from the Heart of the Preacher to the Heart of His People*. Joel summarizes the goal of this book in this way:

> Really it is just a basic textbook on the experiential dimension of Reformed preaching. So, what I'm doing is three things.
>
> First, I'm giving you a definition of what we mean by *Reformed experiential preaching* in a variety of ways.
>
> Second, I'm beginning with the first Reformed preacher, Ulrich Zwingli, and moving through to Lloyd-Jones, looking at two dozen examples or so of preachers from the Dutch tradition, the English tradition, and so on, who preached experientially, which was just about actually every preacher from the Reformation up to the 1830s.
>
> Third, I'm crossing the bridge and saying in the last third of the book, "So, how do we then preach experientially today?" And of course, one of the big thoughts in the book is, you reach people's souls not just by preaching from your mouth, but your

> whole life, your whole being, your whole demeanor, your whole soul needs to be preaching together with your mind to them. So that's why the subtitle is *Proclaiming God's Word from the Heart of the Preacher to the Heart of His People*. So I'm arguing that historic Reformed preaching was not just academic or intellectual. It was, but it reached the whole man—head, heart, hands, and feet—through biblical, doctrinal, confessional, experiential, and practical preaching.

Finally, Joel (together with his assistant Paul Smalley) is presently completing publishing in four volumes his *Reformed Systematic Theology*, which has been his life's dream since he was a teenager. He tells us,

> I gave up the dream for a while. But now I have an able teacher's assistant who's taking my notes of systematic theology teaching. I've been teaching that for about three decades, and he's fleshing out my notes, adding footnotes as well as other details. And then I carefully go over each word of every chapter he completes, editing it thoroughly and suggesting additional ideas and changes. We pray together about it nearly every day.
>
> The first three volumes have already been printed by Crossway. The first deals with the prolegomena, the doctrine of the Word in Revelation. And then the second half deals with the doctrine of God. Volume 2 deals with the doctrine of man and the doctrine of Christ. Volume 3 addresses the Holy Spirit and the doctrine of salvation. Then, volume 4, which we are presently completing, is on the church and the last things—such as death, judgment, heaven, and hell. So it will be a few years, if God spares us, before this last volume is printed and my life's legacy in systematic theology will be complete.
>
> These four volumes address contemporary issues, but they follow the old pattern of doing systematics where ethics is attached to it rather than divorced from it. Throughout, we aim to look at five things, basically, in each doctrine. We look at (1) What does the Bible say about the doctrine being discussed? (2) What does church history say—pro and con? (3) How do you experience this, how can you commune with

God in relationship to this doctrine? (4) What are the major practical takeaways for your Christian life of this doctrine? (5) We then conclude each chapter with a psalter of hymn to move the reader to doxological praise. The goal is that by the end of each chapter, you'll be moved with excitement, and your affections and your mind and your conscience will all be prone to magnify our great, Triune God.

Throughout, we are arguing that doctrine is anything but dry or dead. It's exciting. Luther said, "Doctrine is heaven," so that's what we're trying to show and model. The volumes are written at a beginning seminary level, but a layperson who's interested in Bible truth can make their way through this and find it easier reading than they might think.

We are enormously thankful to God for raising up Joel Beeke in Grand Rapids in this sympathetic congregation, giving him Mary as his beloved wife and giving him health to complete so much that ten other men could not create while working together in harmony. It is the Lord's doing and such a heaven-sent encouragement, particularly to every preacher serving the same kind and generous Savior as the Lord Jesus Christ. He is building His church. The gates of hell are not going to prevail.

Professor Bobi Jones (1929–2017)

There was always my dear cousin Bobi. Our mothers are close sisters, and my being an only child, my cousins were important to me, none more so than Bobi, who was nine years older than me. He would become my best man on my wedding day in 1964, and we would live more than five decades together in the same small town. When the war began, he and his younger brother, Keith, were evacuated for a time, Keith to our home in Merthyr Tydfil and

Bobi to one of his aunts in the Rhondda Valley, Auntie Annie or maybe Auntie Laura. But because there was such *hiraeth* for home and the bombing was so sporadic, after a time the brothers went home, as did many other evacuees, and saw out the war in Cardiff, the capital city of Wales.

When we stayed in one another's homes, what fun we had. The bed was turned into a stagecoach, and our dressing gown belts became the horses' reins, and we shot at the Indians who were intent on scalping us. I was John Wayne. Bobi later built a little go-cart for me. I could hardly sleep that night for excitement as I heard him sawing and nailing in the backyard. I was hoping it would be the Rolls Royce of a go-cart, but it turned out to be a mini. I once locked him in our stationhouse cellar for a prank and went out to play for ages, forgetting all about him. The Bash Street kids from the Beano had influenced me alas. Thank God there were other compensating influences.

Bobi's mother, Edith, and my mother were born in Merthyr Tydfil in the early twentieth century, the sisters coming under the influence of their godly uncle Oliver. On Bobi's father Sid's side of the family, his grandmother was an exceptionally godly woman. My mother stood in awe of her. They lived outside Merthyr in Cefn Coed y Cymmer, but every week she walked back and forth the two miles to the prayer meeting in High Street Baptist Church. There was also a quaint humor about them. She bore six children; Will, Annie, Laura, Eunice, and Sid were the first five—the first initials of their names spelling out the word *WALES*. "Then," said Bobi, "they called the next child 'Glyn'; they had started on 'Glamorgan!'" The family had a thing about names. His father had been born on February 14, and so he was named Sidney Valentine Jones. Likewise, Bobi was born in the month of May, hence his middle name Maynard.

Sidney Jones moved from Merthyr to Cardiff and worked as a draper in Hope Brothers' man's outfitters in the prime shopping street in the city, St. Mary Street. He spent much time in the evenings with his sons, and he was a deacon in a local Baptist church. I wore Bobi's cast-off coats. I loved visiting the Joneses and staying there. They had an air-raid shelter in the back garden, which made a wonderful den, if rather musty. Bobi's comprehensive brilliance manifested itself very quickly. He was an all-rounder, being able to paint (his portrait of a horse hung on the wall) and play the piano, and for his school, Cathays Grammar School, Cardiff, he played rugby, playing against my future school, Lewis School Pengam, where, he observed ruefully, the pitch was ankle deep in mud. His brother, Keith, was the sportsman of the duo, playing rugby for Bath and having a trial for Wales when he had to mark the elusive outside half Cliff Morgan with his famous sidestep, who glided effortlessly past him any time he had the ball.

Keith and I could have been daunted by the effortless achievements of Bobi, setting the academic bar so high for us, but Bobi's own modesty and humility about his intellectual prowess were natural. He was without a grain of snobbery and was earthed into the *werin*, the common folk of Wales. His mother's father, Jack Francis, worked for the Great Western Railway, and he was a zealous Socialist who talked much to his grandson about his social and economic convictions. Thus, Bobi too became a radical in his politics. He had that egalitarian spirit, but with his sympathy for Christian schools, he never fit easily into any political party but always supported Plaid Cymru, the Welsh Nationalist Party. We increasingly spoke less and less about our political differences. Life was too short, and there were so many other themes for the followers of Jesus Christ to talk about.

When he passed the scholarship at the age of eleven, he attended Cathays School where he speedily was constrained to make a little decision that changed his whole life. What languages were he to take in school: French, Latin, Welsh? All the boys had to choose two of those three. Derek Swann, the notable Congregationalist minister, was in the same class as he throughout school, and he chose the French and Latin option. Bobi came from a totally English-speaking home, and so at first he also opted for French and Latin, as did the majority of children in South Wales. The Welsh master, superintending the process, coveted this bright boy and challenged his choice, asking him what he intended doing with the French he had mastered. Bobi was at sea when the option of Welsh was put to him by this advocate, and so the young boy took that option, being persuaded to learn the Welsh language. He loved it from the start. In time he became the most prodigious Welsh scholar Wales has ever known, professor of Welsh Language and Literature at Aberystwyth University. He told me that he had written one hundred books in the Welsh language, the most that anyone has ever written in our precious ancient Celtic language. Among his last major works was one on biblical infallibility and another on the Welsh hymnist William Williams Pantycelyn. His last works are available online. Right to the end of his life he wrote every day, but in those final autumn months of 2017, he returned to his first love, to writing poetry.

Bobi went on from the school in Cathays to study at the university in Cardiff and got his brilliant first-class honors degree. Then he studied in Dublin for a year or two and gained an MA, and soon he had married Beti James of Clunderwen in Pembrokeshire, the local blacksmith's daughter. Their moving, long romance resulted in book after book being dedicated to her: "To Beti." He began his career briefly teaching the Welsh language in two schools. His first school was in Llanidloes, in the county of Powys, and his second school was in the heartland of the Welsh language in Llangefni on the island of Anglesey. There the sixth-formers who were fortunate to take A-level Welsh under his teaching loved him, and through his enthusiastic dedication they attained the best results of any school in all of Wales.

This was a period when he had to come to some commitment to Christianity—or not. What would he do with this Jesus who is called the Christ? It is a question everyone must face. Bobi had been raised in a Baptist church in Cardiff, but his immersion in the Welsh language resulted in his regular attendance in the Welsh Congregationalist Church in Cardiff on Minny Street. There he heard a social gospel and meandered under that influence throughout his teenage years and during his time at Cardiff University. He was aware of evangelical Christianity through people like Derek Swann and the witness of the Christian Union at the university, but he kept its emphases at a distance in some suspicion. When attending the National Eisteddfod in Dolgellau in 1949, he went to a special meeting that the Welsh Christian students had organized in their outreach to the Eisteddfod. On August 4 at 11:30 p.m., this twenty-year-old new graduate heard the forty-nine-year-old Dr. Lloyd-Jones preaching on "Rejoice in the Lord always, and again I say rejoice." In the sermon the Doctor contrasted earthly pleasures with the joys that the grace of God in Jesus Christ could bring. But Bobi was unimpressed and untouched by the sermon.

During his time in Llanidloes, he attended China Street Calvinistic Methodist Church, and there, quite suddenly, at the Lord's Supper one Sunday night he received a personal, saving interest in the Savior's blood. He was henceforth self-consciously a Christian, a disciple of Jesus Christ, and his life from then on was an outworking of the consequences of that. But in the four or five years during which he taught in two small towns, there was no pulpit anywhere near in which the Christianity of the 1823 Confession of Faith of the Calvinistic Methodists was being proclaimed, and when he moved to lecture at Trinity College, Carmarthen, the situation in the Welsh-language churches there was similarly one in which the sermon was a presentation of a very horizontal theology. Man's duty to their fellow man was the supreme theme. The notes of authority, personal repentance, redemption, atonement, and regeneration were absent. It was a frustrating time.

"What of Rome?" he asked himself. Would he find such essential emphases there? The great mentor of modern Welsh scholarship and creativity Saunders Lewis, coming from aristocratic Calvinistic Methodist stock, had forsaken that heritage and become a Roman Catholic, though he was disenchanted when the Latin Mass was abandoned all over Wales for English and so was not often present for the Mass. Bobi felt attracted to take that same route, so he took the claims of Rome seriously. Could there be a coming together of gospel Christianity and Rome? He talked to me and wrote briefly and anonymously about such a union, but he did not find in Rome a spiritual home. I was concerned with this development, being on my own pilgrimage after my conversion in March 1954. When I was a student at Cardiff, I once visited out of curiosity (but to the alarm of my parents) the morning Mass in the Roman church in Barry, just opposite our home, but apart from the numbers present, it was unimpressive. There was a background buzz of constant talking everywhere in the pews throughout the service, and the singing was rare and weak. There was no preaching, nothing like the congregational response of intense concentration and doxology, having heard the Word of God laid on them. There was no power, no spiritual presence, and nothing to grip a person.

In 1958 I gave to Bobi J. I. Packer's *Fundamentalism and the Word of God*, and subsequently he said to me how important was the subject of infallibility. He always read what I gave him. He was delighted that I had gone to Westminster Seminary—and that I had returned! I introduced him to Van Til and told him of the Dutchmen, Herman Dooyeweerd, Dirk Vollenhoven, and Hans Rookmaaker. He could not escape from the writings of Francis Schaeffer and their influence when Schaeffer rose like a rocket in the late 1960s. Bobi appreciated the contribution they all made. We Reformed evangelicals seemed to be a force to be reckoned with because of the great breadth of the biblical vision.

In 1958 Bobi moved to Aberystwyth, joining the education department at the university, moving later to the Welsh department, and in 1980 he was appointed the professor. Soon our parents came to join us in the town. My mother and father lived in the house whose ground-floor flat I now occupy, while his mother lived upstairs in the first-floor flat. When I was seeking a call to the ministry, he gave my name to one of the deacons in the Baptist church in Aberystwyth, and I was invited to preach there and subsequently was called there as minister in 1965.

We lived a fifteen-minute walk from one another for over fifty years. I looked with awe at the flow of books that came from his pen, handwritten and then typed by Beti, novels, short stories, children's books, poems, hymn translations, and books of literary criticism. He wrote monthly columns in the prestigious Welsh journal *Barn* and regularly in the Welsh-language version of the *Evangelical Magazine of Wales.* His scholarly work was published under his given name, Robert Maynard Jones. His children's books had a pseudonym. He will live on in hymnbooks and congregational singing by his moving translations of a number of classic Welsh hymns in the hymnal *Christian Hymns.* All this was done while running a university department, lecturing, marking papers, and superintending PhD students.

Charles, the son of the queen, was given the title the Prince of Wales and so was expected during the preparation for his investiture in 1969 to study for a semester at Aberystwyth. His bodyguard lived in a house opposite the manse. Prince Charles was taught the Welsh language by an old schoolfriend of Bobi's, Tedi Millward, while Bobi taught Prince Charles, one-to-one, each day for more than a month the history and literature of Wales. Prince Charles drove down Penglais Hill each day in his blue MG into the town, and faithfully each day the crowds came out, stood on the pavements, and cheered and waved at him. There was, however, considerable opposition among the students and others to Charles's presence at Aber, and Bobi especially opposed the investiture. As a republican, he still found Prince Charles very intelligent, one of the most able students he had ever taught, one who was forthright in his opinions to Bobi on most subjects even on parliamentary figures, but there was little reaction from the prince to Bobi's lecture on the birth of Calvinistic Methodism in the eighteenth-century evangelical revival. Bobi used the helpful division of Dr. Lloyd-Jones: "Calvinism" and what that signified as the fullest presentation of historic biblical Christianity, and "Methodism" and its expressions of an experiential response to God and its stress on the Bible, conversion, the cross of Christ, and personal piety. His lectures to Charles were published in English under the title *Talks with a Prince.*

In 1968 a "Cultural Olympiad" was held in Mexico City to coincide with the Olympic Games there, and Bobi was chosen to represent Wales. On the plane he had a severe heart attack and was at death's door for some time. The receptionist at the hotel where he was taken had trained as a nurse in a heart ward, and her experience and knowledge were vital in saving his life. Beti and his two children, Lowri and

Rhodri, were utterly helpless so far away. For an hour I cast myself on God and prayed for Bobi, and I was given the strongest sense of assurance that he would get over this, so much so that I got in my car and drove to Beti and told her with the utmost confidence that it was all going to be well and Bobi would be coming home again. Such an experience had not come to me before that time, nor since, and I do not give it a label but recognize it as one of the realities of having God as your Father and Shepherd. From his experience in Mexico, he wrote me a long and wonderful letter, and a poem-saga was later written by him and published—death hammering on the door to be let into Bobi's life with God declaring, "No!" It was almost forty years before God finally permitted death to come to him.

Bobi and Beti spoke well of their minister, H. R. Davies, in Salem Calvinistic Methodist Church in Aberystwyth, but they were deeply concerned as modernistic unbelief was unresisted when, for example, the denomination installed a rota system so that ministers who opposed the blood atonement of Jesus Christ and denied the miraculous and supernatural events of the Bible had to be received into evangelical pulpits. This was the theology dominating the denomination's college for training ministers. It became time to secede from the "Old Body" as the connection was known (*yr hen gorff*).

The men and women who came together from a number of churches during the first year of the Welsh Evangelical Church in Aberystwyth were a significant group of people, and those who identified themselves with them consisted of professors, a local doctor, schoolteachers, and a Welsh detective fiction writer. They were among its leaders. This church planting took place fifty years ago, and the assembly is still standing and has celebrated its golden jubilee. There were times when Dr. Bobi Jones taught the Sunday school there.

The last time Dr. Lloyd-Jones preached in Wales was in Aberystwyth, and he and his wife had dinner with Bobi and Beti in their home, the Doctor's sermons on the book of Romans having been the companions and teachers of them both for many years.

There was a remarkable time twenty or more years ago when a group of evangelical students of the most unusual caliber all studied Welsh, and no fewer than six of them gained first-class honors degrees the same year, and several more gained high second-class honors. The professor at the time was Dr. Geraint Gruffydd, another member of the Welsh Evangelical Church. At Bobi's funeral the mourners were invited, in lieu of flowers, to give gifts to the work of the Welsh Christian Unions of the colleges of Wales. It was by his support and instigation that a separate Welsh-language Christian Union was started with weekly meetings. Many years later Rhodri Brady, my grandson and successor in Alfred Place, became its president, and the following year he was the president of the English Christian Union.

Bobi came to specialize in the methodology of teaching Welsh to adults, playing a pioneering and inspirational role in this for many years. He longed for a mass movement similar to the Ulpan scheme, which the modern state of Israel had adopted so successfully so that Hebrew was restored to Israel. Meic Stephens wrote in his obituary of Bobi in *The Independent*, "He was fond of telling the story of Eliezer Ben-Yehuda and his wife Devora who, after landing in Jaffa in 1881, resolved to speak only Hebrew with each other and swore to become the parents of the first child in modern times to have that language as its mother tongue."[9]

Bobi suffered with a spinal complaint for the last twenty years of his life. He was unable to sit and so stood or lay down. He never complained, but in the last month a cancer spread. He recovered remarkably from one major operation, and two weeks before his death he was in church. What golden hours we enjoyed over the past months talking and praying as Bobi was on the borders of the land of the living.

His funeral was understated just like himself—two hymns, a reading, a prayer, and a brief sermon. It was all over in forty minutes, just like an Isle of Lewis Free Church funeral! The family sang at his

---

9. Meic Stephens, "Bobi Jones: Scholar of Welsh Who Taught Price Charles and Whose Native English Became a Foreign Language," *The Independent*, November 23, 2017.

graveside a Welsh hymn, "We thank you almighty God for the holy gospel. Hallelujah. Amen." He was weary of the funerals of academics from the university when all their achievements were solemnly read out by a senior member of staff. So Bobi insisted that the whole service be in Welsh "without a single word of English" and that not a word about him be spoken. I am unsure about that. The gospel can be made real through hearing of the work of grace in a man's life. A dying person's wishes should be weighed but not necessarily obeyed if the living can be helped and comforted at the service by some references to the deceased. Let me end this tribute to his influence over me with his translation of William Williams hymn, "*Iesu, Iesu, r'wyt ti'n ddigon.*"

Jesus, Jesus, all-sufficient,
Beyond telling is Thy worth;
In Thy Name lie greater treasures
Than the richest found on earth.
Such abundance
Is my portion with my God.

In Thy gracious face there's beauty
Far surpassing everything
Found in all the earth's great wonders
Mortal eye hath never seen.
Rose of Sharon,
Thou Thyself art heaven's delight.[10]

10. William Williams, 1717–91; trans. by Robert (Bobi) Maynard Jones, 1929–2017.

CHAPTER 14

Some Memorable Conversions

The sun rises quickly over the equator, but in Lapland it rises very slowly. In some places, a swift dawn, and in others, a lingering dawn, but nevertheless the morning light comes. That is a picture of the different experiences of the light of the gospel as it comes to men and women. For some, it is sudden and dramatic; we call it a "Damascus Road" experience. For others, they are not sure even of the year in which they had an assurance they were regenerate believers with an interest in the Savior's blood. So, let us consider some of the conversions we witnessed in Aberystwyth.

Wyn Hughes

Wyn Hughes was a student in Aberystwyth, and he was drawn to the company of Christian students. He enjoyed sitting in on their gatherings and listening to their conversation, and those students, for their part, were like the women of Bedford who saw the tinker John Bunyan coming to join them and have his lunch while sitting with them, so they made sure their conversation was about the grace of God in the gospel as a witness to him for whom they were praying. One day Wyn walked back to his room from one of those fellowship meetings, and as soon as he entered his room, he got down on his knees, and this is what he prayed: "O God! Make me a righteous man!" It is all there in that prayer—his helplessness to self-improve, his humbly casting himself on the mercy of God, his conviction of his own unrighteousness, his paramount desire to be clothed in righteousness and longing to live a righteous life, his need to change, and the awareness that only the living God could change him. And God heard and answered his prayer so that sixty years later his one desire is to have the righteousness of Christ and live a righteous life.

Barry Adams

My dear Christian friend Barry and his wife, Jacqueline, have been a great encouragement to me all the years I have known them. Barry was born in Rotherham in 1956 to a steelworker father and a housemaid mother. He had five brothers and two sisters, and he was educated in a typical secondary modern school for those who failed to get into grammar school. Finishing at fifteen there, he went on to Rotherham College of Higher Education to study engineering. His first job was with an engineering company in Sheffield where he served his apprenticeship as a mechanical engineer. Why did he choose this route? It was not that he enjoyed engineering, but it was done to please his father and win his approval. After completing his apprenticeship, he left the industry for two reasons: better pay and a change of direction. His heart wasn't in engineering. He had chosen it to receive a smile and recognition from Dad, but his father didn't show the slightest appreciation for those choices and continued to disaffiliate himself from his son.

Barry then left engineering and became a night-shift worker for ASDA supermarket for double the wage of an engineer with the opportunity of progressing up the chain to becoming a manager. As part of his training, he made a relocation choice and moved to Nottingham as a trainee manager, and from there to Wales, to Merthyr Tydfil, to open an ASDA store in the town. In Nottingham he had met and married his first wife in 1976, and eventually they had eight children of their own.

So, there they were in Merthyr Tydfil, settling into a bungalow first in a village called Heolgerrig, and then they moved down the valley to Quakers Yard where they stayed for twenty-six years. You might think his life was idyllic, living in a large family and working a responsible job. But for Barry, it was stressful. As he says, "I had feelings of failure that would have made my father proud."

In Quakers Yard they became friendly with a neighbor and his family who were Mormons. In 1963 the impressive Mormon chapel had been opened in Merthyr. Before this, they were meeting in a leaking wooden hut in Penyard. Mormons have been in Merthyr for over a hundred years since the early Mormon missionary Dan Jones came to the town speaking and baptizing converts there. There are in fact some sixth-generation Mormons in Merthyr, but the congregation began to grow when the building was opened in 1963.

Mormonism began with an American named Joseph Smith, who in the early 1820s was living in upstate New York. He claimed that in 1823 an angel from heaven had directed him to a buried book written on golden plates containing a religious history of an ancient people. He published what he claimed was a translation of those plates in March 1830, and in the following months he founded the Church of Jesus Christ of Latter-day Saints.

The following is a brief overview of the beliefs of Mormonism as summarized by Justin Taylor for The Gospel Coalition, a mainstream evangelical Protestant organization.[1] Interestingly, these are not the beliefs that are presented to inquirers who begin to attend Mormon services. They are not the beliefs that are hammered home in the evangelical-type, family-friendly, popular music services full of evangelical language with which inquirers are confronted when they first go to a Mormon meeting, getting a warm, smiley, Welsh welcome. The regular one-evening-a-week family focus meetings are also crucial for Mormons. This is what results in the slight growth of the Mormon Church in Wales today and the change in the lives of restless addicted men and women who are encouraged to believe in Jesus Christ and find forgiveness and life in Him. But these are the

1. Justin Taylor, "The 8 Beliefs You Should Know about Mormons When They Knock at the Door," The Gospel Coalition, August 18, 2021, https://www.thegospelcoalition.org/blogs/justin-taylor/the-8-beliefs-you-should-know-about-mormons-when-they-knock-at-the-door.

teachings of the Church of Jesus Christ of Latter-day Saints, and the great question one must ask is whether an angel ever met Joe Smith and directed him to the discovery of the golden tablets that he translated and published. Is that true or a fiction? And are the following teachings of the Mormons true?

1. Apostasy and Restoration

Mormons claim that "total" apostasy overcame the professing church following apostolic times and that the Mormon Church (founded in 1830) is the "restored church."

2. God

Mormons claim that God the Father was once a man and that He then progressed to godhood—that is, He is a now-exalted, immortal man with a flesh-and-bone body.

3. Polytheism

Mormons believe that the Trinity consists not of three persons in one God but rather of three distinct gods. According to Mormonism, there are potentially many thousands of gods besides these.

4. Exaltation of Humans

Mormons believe that humans, like God the Father, can go through a process of exaltation to godhood.

5. Jesus Christ

Mormons believe that Jesus Christ was the firstborn spirit-child of the heavenly Father and a heavenly mother. Jesus then progressed to deity in the spirit world. He was later physically conceived in Mary's womb, as the literal "only begotten" Son of God the Father in the flesh (though many present-day Mormons remain somewhat vague as to how this occurred).

6. Three Kingdoms

Mormons believe that most people will end up in one of three kingdoms of glory, depending on one's level of faithfulness. Belief in Christ, or even in God, is not necessary to obtain immortality in one of these three kingdoms, and therefore only the most spiritually perverse will go to hell.

7. Sin and Atonement

Mormons believe that Adam's transgression was a noble act that made it possible for humans to become mortal, a necessary step on the path to exaltation to godhood. They think that Christ's atonement secures immortality for virtually all people, whether they repent and believe or not.

8. Salvation

Mormons believe that God gives to (virtually) everyone a general salvation to immortal life in one of the heavenly kingdoms, which is how they understand salvation by grace. Belief in Christ is necessary only to obtain passage to the highest, celestial kingdom—for which not only faith but participation in Mormon temple rituals and obedience to its "laws of the gospel" are also prerequisites.

So, the kind and helpful Mormon neighbors of the Adams family taught them about their faith, took them to the chapel, and after a little time that family made the decision to become members of the Mormon Church. In fact, Barry quickly progressed through the ranks of leadership until he was named "stake high priest counselor." Looking back now with regret, he shakes his head and says, "I was always looking for approval."

The singing and smiles and companionship of the Adams family on Sundays were not sanctifying Barry. With all the pressure of work, family, and social life, Barry was frequently despondent with dark depressions, eventually suffering a moral breakdown. This emotional stress led him to make some terrible decisions and actions, for which crimes he received an eight-year prison sentence. He says, "There are no excuses. I acknowledge that I hurt the ones I loved the most. I am desperately sad about this. My wife divorced me, and all my family bar one son wiped their hands of me. And I went directly to jail."

Thus, God dealt with him. He lost everything—his liberty, his work, his family, his friends, his reputation. Samuel Rutherford spoke aright when he said, "Ye will not get leave to steal quietly to heaven, in Christ's company, without a conflict and a cross. I find crosses Christ's carved work that he marks out for us, and that with crosses he figures and changes us into his own image, cutting away pieces of our ill and corruption. So I cry, 'Lord, cut, Lord carve, Lord wound, Lord do anything that may perfect your Father's image in me, and make me meet for glory.'"[2]

What Barry had when the prison doors closed behind him were the memories of hymns and the readings from the Scriptures and the words about what Jesus Christ had done, that He had died for our sins to forgive and redeem us. He took nothing into prison but that, and that is powerful, life-changing, elevating, and saving. In prison he met an acquaintance of mine whom he discovered was a professing Christian. He was a warden who, unknown to Barry, was in fact in need of the same extravagant mercy that Barry needed. One day Barry said to him that he needed to get sorted out. The warden suggested he write to a minister of God's church in Aberystwyth.

So, one day a letter from a stranger in prison was pushed through my letter box. It was long and very moving. Who was this man whom I had been entrusted with? He was clearly intelligent and deadly serious, and I warmed to him. Each week I sent him a full transcript of one of my sermons and answered his questions. The basic problem with Mormonism is their rejection of the sufficiency of the writings of the prophets and apostles. A new revelation, binding on the world, had come directly from God, so it claims, and it must be received by all. Jesus Christ and His apostles had failed to give this message, and so eighteen hundred years after the coming of our Lord, God

---

2. Samuel Rutherford, *The Loveliness of Christ* (London: Samuel Bagster & Sons, 1958), 21.

talks to someone in the United States named Joseph Smith and tells him what He is like, how we can know Him, and what needs to be done for us to be made whole. I think, however, that the Holy Spirit did a pretty good job when He spoke through the four writers of the Gospels and through Paul, Peter, and the other men in telling us everything we had to believe to be saved and how we were to live to His honor. We don't need more revelation; we need understanding and obedience to what we've got.

Barry says,

> With much writing of letters back and forth to Geoff, slowly I was able to see the lies that the Mormon Church had taught me. I read earnestly Geoff's sermons each week, and I joined in all the Christian activities of prison. I felt that I had found a treasure in the dirt of prison life. These words of Jesus are particularly relevant to me: "The kingdom of heaven is like treasure hidden in a field, which a man found and covered up. Then in his joy he goes and sells all that he has and buys that field. Again, the kingdom of heaven is like a merchant in search of fine pearls, who, on finding one pearl of great value, went and sold all that he had and bought it" (Matthew 13:44–46 ESV).

When Barry left prison, I invited him to come and live in a house I own in Aberystwyth and to join our church. He eventually remarried in our church with my officiating and the congregation all working together to provide a happy reception. How he has worked in the church over the last decade and more. What a support he has been to me. He says, "Twelve years on, and I'm still connected to the same church in Aberystwyth. I'm now remarried and accepted into a new family. The arrow-shaped neon light that once shined over my head everywhere I went when I was released early from prison now is shining less and less brightly. But it shines more brightly on the cross where Jesus bore my guilt and shame. Every day I am blessed. Praise be to God my Father and His Son, Jesus Christ."

Derek Thomas

The Rev. Dr. Derek Thomas is the most well-known of the former students who were church members in Alfred Place Baptist Church, Aberystwyth. Everything in his background suggests that his life would be one lived in steady opposition to the Christian faith. He came from a farm not far from Lampeter in an area of Wales known as the stronghold of Unitarianism and greatly lacking in historic Christian pulpits. Among the Trinitarian churches, the Welsh nickname for the area is *y smotyn du*, "the black spot." Although his father had some nominal link to a Congregational chapel and his mother a similar link to an Anglican church, neither of them had any interest in Christianity and had not darkened the doors of a church for decades. They were not close as husband and wife. Derek showed a twinge of interest in Christianity when he was about thirteen years of age, but after a few visits to a church, he decided that religion was not

The two Thomases, Derek and Geoff, July 2003

for him. Derek vaguely believed in "science," in deductive reasoning, and that any answers to what life was all about could be found in the findings of man's knowledge.

He helped his father on the farm milking the cows in the morning and self-consciously went off to school imagining he was carrying the embarrassing smell of the cowshed. What a confined life! He instinctively knew there was much more. He came across classical music, as did his closest friend. He played rugby for the school every Saturday morning, and then often in the afternoons he and this friend would listen to Mozart and Beethoven, even taking the bus up to London and attending the promenade concerts. They parted company after graduation from high school, his friend going to university in Birmingham, while Derek came to study physics and mathematics in Aberystwyth, specializing in mathematics.

One November day a year later, he received a little parcel in the post. It was from his friend, who told him that he had become a Christian and had enclosed a copy of John Stott's *Basic Christianity*. Because it came from an esteemed companion, he did not bin it but tucked it away on a shelf. Then for some reason, at the end of term, he put it in his bag and took it home to the farm. Christmas was not a happy season, and on Christmas night, in the solitude of his own room, he picked up *Basic Christianity* and began to devour it over the next couple of days. What a revelation of another worldview! This world did not come about by chance but by a loving Creator. Man was made in God's image, defied his Lord, and fell into rebellion. Sin and death entered the world. God in His love sent His Son, Jesus Christ, to confirm and elaborate all that had been said to men by Moses and the prophets. The Lord Jesus lived the righteous life of grace and truth. He became the Lamb of God who made atonement for sins by dying on the cross. Without such an atonement, there can be no reconciliation of a holy God to us. That is the nature of God. The third day Jesus rose from the dead. See all the evidence for this! Now we are called upon to repent of our unbelief and entrust ourselves to the Lord Christ.

Derek had never heard anything like it; it had a ring of truth about it. So, what was he going to do? Jesus of Nazareth was a historical figure. Jesus of Nazareth was a living reality. He could not henceforth continue living a life deliberately disaffiliated from Him. On December 28, 1971, he knelt before the God of providence who had orchestrated the arrival of the book and the testimony of his friend. He prayed. He said something like this, "I need answers, and if you exist, I need to be saved." When he rose to his feet in his room, he discovered an overwhelming sense of peace and happiness. He had spoken to a God who hears and answers us when we talk to Him, and now he was a Christian. It was a discovery of the simplicity of truth. God created him. Sin ruined him. Grace restored him.

The next morning, the first thing he did was tell his mother he had become a Christian and, with the knowledge he had picked up from *Basic Christianity*, spoke to her all day about her need to be converted and become a believer in Jesus. At the end of the day, she was so worried about him that she sent for the doctor telling him her son was having a nervous breakdown. He arrived with his little bag and interviewed Derek, asking what was wrong. Derek told the doctor he had become a Christian and that the doctor, needed also to become a Christian. The doctor prescribed some tranquilizers and left.

On Sunday, Derek went to the local Anglican church. He vaguely knew the vicar, and after the service was over, he spoke at the door to him and told him, "I have been saved." "No, you haven't," said the vicar. "Come and see me this week." Derek went to see him, and they had some tea together and spoke about football, politics, sports, and his new car but not a word about religion until Derek stood up to go. The vicar said to him, "Too much religion is a bad thing," and gave him a copy of Paul Tillich's *The Shaking of the Foundations*, which he read. (Many years later he read it again as part of his theological course. It is fiercely opposed to historical Christianity and seeks to undermine every biblical doctrine.)

Derek returned in January 1972 to Aberystwyth for the new term, where the center of student life is the bar. As he walked along the corridor, he saw a notice that had always been there but which he had never seen before. It stated that the Christian Union (which he and others had dubbed "the God Squad") was holding its meetings upstairs. He walked up and entered the room, and to his surprise recognized some of the students as taking the same mathematics course as himself. "Ah, so these are Christians. I have found my brothers and sisters." One in particular, he was soon to discover, would become his future wife.

The other students welcomed him, and he told them that he had been saved. "Oh, good. What church are you going to attend on Sunday?" He mentioned one church he vaguely had heard about. "No. Not there," they said. "We will meet you and take you to church," and that Sunday was the first time I saw nineteen-year-old Derek Thomas. The news of his conversion and rapid growth in grace spread through the Christian Union, then through the congregation and even through part of the university. Two of the professors in the mathematics department were serious evangelical Christians, and one day a month later, one of them, Dr. Ken Walters, announced to the lecture room, "So, you have something to tell the class Thomas," (we were all called by our last names). "No, I haven't," Derek thought, but he got up and walked to the front and gave his testimony to all the men and women in the class. Then the professor went on with his lecture on rheology (the viscosity of fluids). Dr. Walters paused before him at the end of the lecture and said to him, "I always believe in a man nailing his colors to the mast."

Derek began attending the Christian Union meetings, and during this semester their speakers from all over Wales had been asked to speak on one of the communicable and incommunicable attributes of God. Derek devoured it all. A few weeks after he had been for the first time to Alfred Place, I saw him on the road speaking to a vicar who lived three doors away from me, an Anglo-Catholic, later to become a bishop in the Church of Wales. Derek was finding his way through the maze of this professing church dynamic in the confusion of Aberystwyth religion, but God had begun a good work in him and was keeping him.

At this time he came across J. I. Packer's *Knowing God* and loved it. Later on, he met J. I. Packer and still felt a little drawn to the Anglican church. Jim Packer asked him, "What about your future? Where are you thinking of going?" Derek told J. I. Packer that he was thinking about the Church of England.

"Why on earth would you do that? Where are you worshiping now?"

"In Alfred Place Baptist where Geoff Thomas is the preacher."

"Stay there!" he said, "I was raised in the Anglican church, and that is one of the reasons I remain in it."

By his last year at university, he was appointed the president of the Christian Union. I had spoken briefly to him about baptism and then baptized him. Then I asked him to preach instead of me at a country church. Welsh was the language of his home, but he preached there to a very few people in English. The organist was sitting behind him. He is naturally embarrassed at what he might have said to them in his first sermon, but he loved the experience, and they thanked him warmly. Someone urged him to become a preacher, like godly older women are prone to do. When he told his father he was going to become a minister, his father's terse reply was, "What a waste!"

At this time Derek came and lived in the manse with our family. My daughters adored him. When their hamster escaped from its cage and hid behind the freezer, it was Derek with a wooden meter ruler who coaxed it out and grabbed it. He and I studied John Owen together some mornings, reading alternate paragraphs, but Derek is more a student of Calvin than Owen. He was to spend much of his life reading the material of the Genevan Reformer for his doctoral studies. Calvin was a man who wrote the first edition of the *Institutes* in his late twenties, after being a Christian for only a few years and with no seminary education. That is a phenomenon in itself.

I longed for Derek to stay in Wales. Evangelical Christians were thin on the ground, and we lacked theologians and preachers. I thought I might soon move on and he would have been welcomed warmly to the pulpit of Alfred Place. So that is the rationale I use for justifying encouraging him to stay in Aberystwyth and study in the Presbyterian seminary. It was a great mistake. The majority of lecturers were unsympathetic to conservative evangelicalism and utterly unhelpful to Derek. The college has long since closed down. He soon left and did a number of things like preaching in St. John's Independent Church in Oxford. But at a Banner of Truth ministers' conference, John R. de Witt talked with him, recognized his gifts, and arranged for him to get a bursary and place in Reformed Theological Seminary in Jackson, Mississippi. So that same summer I officiated at the Thomas's wedding in Alfred Place, and within some weeks the Thomas's were in Jackson, where they would reside for the next three years. This education did him much good. It also, in the last months there, caused him to acknowledge that he had become a Presbyterian.

Forty-two men went into the ministry during my years at Aberystwyth. A number were students at the Presbyterian seminary but worshiped with us, and at least thirty-five of them are Baptist preachers, though there are few who have the gifts of my dear friend Derek.

Derek returned to the United Kingdom for seventeen happy years to a fellow Celtic nation as the minister who followed the beloved W. J. Grier in the Evangelical Presbyterian Church in Belfast, Northern Ireland. We have remained the best of buddies. I regret he did not have a ministry in needy Wales, though I perfectly understand his pilgrimage and opportunities.

Derek's many books are all valuable, and now he pastors and preaches in Thornwell's old pulpit in what is today the First Presbyterian Church in Columbia, South Carolina. He is also a chancellor's professor of systematic and pastoral theology and a teaching fellow with Ligonier Ministries. God's rich blessings continue to rest on him.

The Troubled Student

The elders had left the manse by nine thirty on that Saturday morning, and I was back to preparing my sermons for the next day. The doorbell rang. When I opened it, there stood a student with red hair, a red face, and red denims.

"Hello," I said to him, "Can I help you?"

"I am being haunted by a spirit that needs sacrifice," he said unsmiling.

"You'd better come in," I said.

And so we went into the front room so recently vacated by the three elders. "What's your name?" and he told me. "Tell me about the problem."

He explained what had happened over the past couple of years. His father had had a heart attack, and as he was recuperating at home, a woman would come to visit him. It was obvious that they had been having an affair, and that upset him greatly, transforming his relationship with his father. He would linger at school after the bell rang to announce its close, and after coming home, he would go straight upstairs to his bedroom. There he built a model farm where a farmer had a happy family—a wife and two children, a boy and a girl.

He refused to eat with his father. He would not go to the city where his father worked. He would not ride in the car with his father. He totally cut his father out of his life. Then he got obsessed with other matters such as the word *evil.* Any combination of those four letters he avoided. He would not wear anything made by Levi. St. Ivel's products he would not eat. He was listening to the radio one day, and he heard a discussion about who God was, and the suggestion was made that God was a woman.

Then his father died, and in the following weeks, he read a review of a film called *The Exorcist*, which spoke of a child being possessed by an alien spirit. He felt his father's spirit was tormenting him, and he needed to appease it and placate its anger toward him.

"So, what did this entail?" I inquired, more than a little concerned.

"When I buy anything, I buy two of whatever it is. Two shirts, two ties, two pairs of shoes—and one of them is for my father."

"What do you do with it?"

"I leave it on the floor in the corner of my room," he answered.

"Why did you come to me today?" I asked him.

He told me that he wanted to know if there was anything in this haunting. Did he need to be exorcized? If I had been a humanist, I might have dismissed his fears or sent him to a psychiatrist. If I had been Pentecostal and believed in "deliverance ministries," I would have laid hands on him, maybe called the elders to come back, and then we might have together done that and commanded the spirit of his father to leave him. But he was very vulnerable, irrational, and needy. So, what did I do?

I had encouragement from Paul's letter to the Romans, where he says to the congregation, "You also are full of goodness, filled with all knowledge, able also to admonish one another" (Rom. 15:14). My desire was to admonish him, but true help would only be his if he knew God and became a disciple of Christ. Only if he for the rest of his life had limitless access to the indwelling Spirit of God and knew the teaching of Holy Scripture for every circumstance he would face, then, and only then, would I have truly helped him.

I said to him that the way he had treated his father was despicable and that he was facing hell for tolerating such an attitude in his heart. The Bible tells us to honor our father and our mother, and he had dishonored his father, even though his father's conduct was evil. But no one need end in the place of woe. There is deliverance. God has loved sinners just like him and placed in his heart a desire to see a man of God and find the truth. It was God's love for him that had brought him to see me this morning, and I was able to help him.

I explained to him how God had loved the world and given His only Son to live here with us, the only human being to live a blameless, obedient, and God-pleasing life in a world dominated by its evil god. But the Lord Jesus was also the eternal Son of God, and so His righteous life was infinite, eternal, and unchangeable. His righteousness was enough to cover every one of the 37.2 trillion cells in the human body and 37.2 trillion stars in the sky—with still more than enough to cover any more, in fact much more than all that could be needed. The righteousness of Christ was to all and upon all who entrusted themselves to Him. "You may be ransomed and forgiven because of Jesus Christ," I concluded, "and you need to go just as you are and ask Him to become your Lord and Savior and start to pray and never stop asking for His mercy until you have the inner witness of the Holy Spirit in your heart confirming that all is well between you and God." He listened gravely.

Then I told him there were four things I wanted him to do:

1. He was to go immediately to the phone booth and call his mother and tell her that he was better, that he had been to see a Christian minister and had had a helpful talk with him.

2. He was to go to W. H. Smith's and buy a Bible, and he was to look up these verses:

    - 1 John 1:7–9, "But if we walk in the light as He is in the light, we have fellowship with one another, and the blood of Jesus Christ His Son cleanses us from all sin. If we say that we have no sin, we deceive ourselves, and the truth is not in us. If we confess our sins, He is faithful and just to forgive us our sins and to cleanse us from all unrighteousness."

    - Acts 16:31, "Believe on the Lord Jesus Christ, and you will be saved."

    - 1 Corinthians 15:3–4, "For I delivered to you first of all that which I also received: that Christ died for our sins according to the Scriptures, and that He was buried, and that He rose again the third day according to the Scriptures."

3. He was to come to church tomorrow morning, 10:30, at Alfred Place.

4. He was to come next Saturday morning and talk to me again.

Then I prayed with him and for him, and he went off. The next morning, I looked down from the pulpit and saw him sitting there paying close attention to what I said. He held a brand-new Bible. I was preaching a series on the Ten Commandments, and that was most suitable for his state. I introduced him to some students in the congregation and urged him to go with them to the Christian Union meeting next weekend.

The following Saturday he rang the doorbell and spent half an hour with me again. He opened up some other troubling thoughts he had, and we dealt with those, and then I think there was just one more time he came to see me. But he was in church twice on Sunday and with the students back in the manse Sunday nights.

Eventually he came to faith in Christ, and during the next year I baptized him. His mother and sister came to the baptismal service, overwhelmed at the transformation that had occurred in him. They were tearfully grateful to me and even told me they were thinking of moving to live in Aberystwyth. They never did.

He met a girl in the congregation, married her, and they moved away. The years went by, and I totally lost track of him, where he lived, and how he was doing. Over twenty years later, a student with her boyfriend was attending the congregation, and one day she casually said to me that I knew her father. Who was he? It was this friend I have been writing about. I probed her gently to see if she knew anything about how her father had been when he came to follow the Lord, but he had never told her, and I respected his silence. Then the young couple asked me to marry them and to preach at their wedding. He was there giving his daughter away, and it was a blessed reunion. God had begun a good work in him twenty-five years earlier in Aberystwyth and was going on faithfully to complete it in the great day to come.

Keith Underhill

In 1964, eighteen-year-old Keith Underhill of Watford was accepted to study for a degree in geography at Aberystwyth. The first-year students had to share a room, and the registrar who determined where each student should live allocated a room for Keith in the finest hall of residence on campus (incidentally, named after the greatest of all Welsh hymn writers, William Williams Pantycelyn). It was God's choice of who was to be his roommate that was so determinative for the future. Brian Williams received him into the room they were to share for the next year, after Keith's long train journey from London.

He soon asked Keith, "Are you a Christian?"

"Yes," replied Keith.

"So, when do you have your quiet time?"

"When I get out of bed."

The reply was, alas, only partially true, although there had been times when Keith had tried to read his Bible. But now he had committed himself to reading the Scriptures first thing in the day, and so began the habit of the early morning rise at six thirty for Bible study and prayer with Brian.

The truth was that they came from quite different religious backgrounds. Brian and his parents were members of the Heath Presbyterian Church in Cardiff, and two years earlier, in 1962, they had called a minister named Vernon Higham to become their pastor. He was a very fine preacher, and soon Heath was packed with even the pews in the gallery around the organ behind the pulpit full of people. Brian was habitually listening to the gospel preached with the Holy Spirit sent down from heaven. On the other hand, Keith went to the local Methodist church where there was considerable difference of opinion as to what the gospel of Jesus Christ actually was.

At the start of their morning Bible studies, Keith read helpful notes from Francis Dixon of Bournemouth. And thus the process began of immersion into gospel influences, all of which were scrutinized and received. There is no single specific experience that could be pointed to in Keith's life as the moment of his conversion, as to when he became a Christian. Keith can thank God that this was so. His relationship with God was gentle at first, steady and growing constantly. Whereas once he was blind, now he could see. He was consistently being exposed to the Word of God, and then through Brian's influence he was taken to the Christian Union in the college.

At the Methodist church Keith attended, the previous minister had been Roland Lamb, a notable evangelical, who had been succeeded by Laurence Churms, also an evangelical. There Keith was given opportunities for ministry. His first sermon at the Methodist church was entitled "A Brand Plucked from the Fire," based on Zechariah 3:2. It was taken from one of Francis Dixon's Bible studies that had touched him. In fact, he read the sermon word for word. There were also such opportunities to speak at the University Methodist Society in the college. Then a Bible study was started on John's gospel using William Hendriksen's commentary, and several people became Christians through this. Some students went on Sunday evenings after the service to the home of an older man in the Methodist church, Henry Miles, a godly bachelor who lived with his mother and was an influence for spiritual good.

The following year I arrived in town to minister in the Alfred Place Baptist Church. Some of the Methodists were not happy with the Methodist church, including Henry Miles and Keith Underhill, who left the congregation and began attending Alfred Place. They soon were immersed every Sunday morning in the book of Genesis and with the gospel of Matthew in the evenings. Keith kindly says how excited they were to hear such consecutive expository preaching, though I have my doubts. He still has the notes of my sermons on index cards.

My preaching, however, was all in line with what they were hearing in the Saturday evening Christian Union meetings. What privileged Christians they believed they were. They were instructed in Scriptural doctrine. For the four years Keith was in Aberystwyth, they had the best men from all over Wales coming to them and teaching them the Scriptures. Austin Walker remembers clearly those Saturday night students' meetings with one hundred students attending. He writes, "In the first year we were working our way through the statement of faith in the IVF doctrinal basis that all office holders and speakers had to sign. Keith and I were exposed to that. You were the first speaker as I recall, and your subject was 'The Need for Doctrine in Wales Today.' I still have the notes somewhere."

The students were also readers. Keith remembers reading J. I. Packer's *Evangelism and the Sovereignty of God*, T. C. Hammond's *In Understanding Be Men*, and A. W. Tozer's *The Pursuit of God*. Keith says, "We heard a rumor that Lloyd-Jones had a message on baptism with the Spirit, and so we looked for it. We wanted whatever the Lord had promised for us in His Word." Keith also did a lot of deductive Bible study, finding all the verses that proved a particular doctrine. All this prepared him for his life's vocation. What with the Baptist church and the Christian Union, Sundays were full and wonderful days. On one really full Sunday, there would be:

- missionary breakfast at 8:00 a.m.
- morning service at 10:30 a.m.
- missionary prayer meeting at 2:00 p.m.
- Methodist society at 4:00 p.m.
- evening service at 6:30 p.m.
- fellowship at Henry Miles' house

At the end, they walked back to their rooms glad. It was having such exposure to the Word of God from the very beginning and such clarity in teaching the historic Reformed faith that made it a smooth journey from Methodism to confessional Christianity. Keith had very few struggles over doctrine. But to be taught is one thing; to understand in the heart is another. Keith still remembers walking back to his room one evening, and it came to him so forcibly that salvation is received through repentance and faith. And he had repented and had believed, and now he could articulate the answer to the question of what someone must do to be saved.

A bigger struggle was baptism as a believer. It was not until 1967 that he was baptized at Wealdstone Baptist Church, the church he attended during vacations when not in college, by its pastor, Peter Hetherington. He was now approaching another issue—the Bible's teaching on the centrality of the local church.

Early in his Christian life, the twin themes of preaching the gospel and missions came to him powerfully. Preaching was thrust upon him, starting with the Methodist church, where the need for a clear gospel was great. Students were given opportunity to preach. But many factors led to the pursuit of missions. By *missions*, Keith was thinking of the preaching of the gospel in other parts of the world outside the United Kingdom. But providentially, in the Pantycelyn

Hall of Residence where he had his meals, he constantly interacted at the tables with students from overseas, especially from Africa. For example, there was Damian Wachira from Kenya, whom later he was able to visit in Kenya after Damian had returned and had become the head of an Agricultural Research Station. What was happening? Was Keith drawn to them because he was interested in overseas ministry, or did he get that interest by sitting with them?

There was a strong emphasis on missions in the Inter-Varsity Fellowship group. Every Christian Union member was expected to join a prayer group for one of the various continents, and Keith joined the small Africa group. "We prayed for needs we came across, and we gave the little we could, but we also had to say, 'Lord, if you want me to go, here I am.'" Keith adds,

> I specifically remember one evening after the Saturday Christian Union meeting. I was browsing through the book table with missionary-type books, and the word "Sudan" jumped out at me. Then turning over some more pages, it happened again. From that moment I was fixed on that country where most people were without the gospel. In God's providence, Sudan was closed to all missionaries in 1965. But I was greatly affected by a book about the work of the Sudan Interior Mission (SIM), *Run While the Sun Is Hot,* and a smaller one also on Sudan, *Dry Season.*

For 1966–1967 he was appointed as the Overseas Students' Secretary for the Christian Union. His work was to encourage involvement in this "mission field" that had come to his doorstep, students from countries where it was hard for missionaries to enter, such as Iran and Malaysia. There was also a house party to arrange. Then because his course of study was geography, he was able to do a unit specifically on the "White Highlands" of Kenya, the area where most whites had settled during the colonial era.

As he neared the completion of his degree course, he had to decide what to do next. He already had a definite conviction that it would be to go to Africa to preach the gospel. He had not yet seen the vital role of the local church in this. He remembers seeking advice from leaders at a Christian Union conference at Swanwick in January 1967. The advice was clear, and he embraced it: train to be a teacher so that you can go to Africa, particularly to one of the newly independent countries crying out for teachers. This is what he determined to do, and he received his teacher's certification in Aberystwyth in May 1968.

During that time, for some reason he applied for a job in a private school in the south of England for the post of geography teacher and field hockey instructor, and that suited him perfectly. It can only have been God's kind providence that he did not get the job. He then applied to the Ministry of Overseas Development for a teaching post in Kenya—because it was next to Sudan, perhaps? He was told that they could only consider him for Tanzania. He went for the interview in London, and at the top of this tall office block with glass sides, he was "interviewed." All he remembers was being asked something like this: "When you go to Kenya, do you want to go to the town or the countryside, to a Protestant or Catholic school?" "Countryside" and "Protestant" were the answers without hesitation, and so it was.

He thanks God for those four years in Aberystwyth that wonderfully prepared him for his future ministry in Kenya. It was the Lord who brought the gospel to him, saved him, and gave him such a grounding in the Scriptures through the Christian Union and Alfred Place. He was exposed to missions in many ways—the preaching he heard, the conferences, prayer meetings, and many of his fellow students from overseas. Alfred Place Baptist Church became the local church that later sent him and his wife and baby son to Kenya, and he and I became lifelong friends and encouragers.

Who can measure the importance of casual conversations? There were, for example, "Geography Practical" classes in 1967, the final degree year for both Keith Underhill and Austin Walker. They both did geography degrees, but Keith did a BSc, and Austin did a BA. Only a few of their courses actually overlapped. The "Practicals" were one of them. Neither of those students found the Pracs very demanding, and they usually finished within three hours. But in those days students had to stay for the full three hours even if they had finished the work, so Keith and Aus sat at the back and "chatted" about the gospel and the doctrines of grace, as Keith was on his journey out of Wesleyan Methodism into confessional Christianity.

Fellow students like Austin Walker were to become some of his great supporters in a variety of ways throughout his ministry in Kenya. There are the four *W*s—Austin Walker, Chris Watts, Keith Weber, Brian Williams—as well as John Pascoe, whose invaluable contributions have included prayer, correspondence, financial support, visits to Kenya, inviting Keith into their churches when back in the UK, sending out his prayer letters, and becoming trustees of TRAIN(Kenya).

Keith taught in Meru, Kenya, for three years, and then went to Westminster Seminary in Philadelphia in 1971 for three years, where in visiting the church in New Jersey pastored by Al Martin he met and then married his lifelong companion, Priscilla. Of course, I urged him to go to Westminster, and so did Austin Walker, who had graduated in 1971, the [illegible]ear that Keith began.

Let me skim over th[illegible]xt forty years of the productive life of pastor and church planter in Kenya, Keith Underhill, and bring us up to date. I had shared a room at Westminster Seminary from 1963 to 1964 with a Kikuyu from Kenya, the late Leonard Kaguru Guchu. And so, in 1975, Alfred Place sent Keith and Priscilla to live in Thika and associate with the Bible Fellowship Church (pastored by Leonard Guchu). That lasted for some years, but in 1978 Trinity Baptist Church was started in Doonhom, Nairobi, and the following year it was constituted as a church.

In 1981, Trinity was officially registered by the government and began to train pastors. They bought a piece of land and built a church building, where they began to meet in 1989. Two years later a manse was built on the compound, and the Underhills and their three children moved in. Contacts began to develop with people from the distant rural areas, the Rendille first, and soon those from Pokot.

In 1997, annual pastors' conferences were commenced, and the following year the Reformed Baptist Association was initiated. The twenty-first century saw a steady stream of missionaries being sent out from Trinity Baptist Church. There are now about forty Reformed Baptist churches in Kenya. In 2010, Pastor Murungi was appointed as an elder, and the heaviest block of preaching in Trinity is now delivered by him as Keith Underhill began to step aside as the pastor-elder in 2018. Keith returned to England to live in Liverpool where two of his children live, but he frequently returns to Kenya to teach in the Trinity Pastors College that he had begun almost forty years earlier.

Ava: From Islam to Christianity

Ava was born in Iran and raised as a Muslim in a loving home.[3] She left Iran in 2009 and came to study for a PhD in Bath University. She knew no one there, and her grasp of English was poor. In the early months, she was conscious of the gulf between life in Iran and life in England. But the first day she walked around Bath, she met a woman on the street named Merry, who wanted to know if she could help Ava in any way. Merry was a member of Cafe International, a student outreach attached to Widcom[illegible]ptist Chapel. "Come to the Cafe on a Wednesday," she suggeste[illegible] and you will make some friends, and they will help you improve your English." Both those promises proved to be true, and the Christians in the Cafe spent a lot of time listening to Ava and talking to her. She even attended some of their prayer meetings, and that blew her mind! She had never prayed like that nor heard praying like that. It was enormously convicting. When one comes to God in and through Jesus Christ, one learns to speak to Him.

The following year Ava moved to Aberystwyth and initially had the same loneliness as she had known in Bath, but the people in the Bath Cafe went out of their way to direct her where to go and who might help her. Carys, a friend of my daughter Eleri, had been a nurse for some years in Bath and had attended the Widcombe Chapel. She met Ava, welcoming her to Aberystwyth. Carys took her to Alfred Place each Sunday night for the first month. She introduced her to Eleri's son Rhodri and to John Noble, one of the elders in

3. Names in this narrative have been changed.

the church, who introduced himself and his wife, Janet, to her. John knew something about Eastern culture, having served in the navy for some years and traveled the world.

These early months Ava was irregular in attending church, as she found the MBA course tough going. But Janet Noble kept contact with her, and they spoke on the phone often. When Ava settled into the academic routine, she began to be a regular in the services. But the lynchpin that held her in the congregation was Janet, who talked to her about the gospel of Jesus Christ and answered well her many questions. Ava looks back on that time talking to Janet with wonder, saying, "She was always happy to answer my questions. I never saw her upset about anything that I asked her." As she was attending church most Sundays, she was discovering more about the message of Christianity, who Jesus Christ is and what He did now for those who trusted in Him. She was given books in the Farsi language that people recommended to her, and she appreciated the concern and patience shown toward her.

When her course was complete, she had difficult financial problems, but she increasingly found that she could take all her troubles and spread them out before the Lord. She said, "The people in the congregation dealt with me like my own family would." She noticed that and was grateful. The Aberystwyth church had been involved in starting a home for people with learning difficulties, and Ava was interested and then got a job helping them there. That, too, had an influence in shaping her faith in Jesus Christ.

In January 2012, she spent a time in London, and when she returned to Aberystwyth, John Noble gave her a recording of one of my sermons on the Lord Jesus Christ speaking to the rich, young ruler. I concluded the message by saying to the congregation, "If not Jesus, then who? If not now, then when?" Ava played that sermon over and over. She does not know how many times she listened to it. *If not Jesus, then who? If not now, then when?* She increasingly felt her need:

> Yes, now is the time, and there is no one else but Jesus. I should trust in him, and I cannot go on pleading for yet more and more

> time. I must respond to him now personally and acknowledge him to be my God and Saviour. I did so, and then it dawned on me that I had become a Christian, a follower of the Lord Jesus Christ!
>
> I do believe in the Lord Jesus Christ. I know he is always with me. He supports me, just as he promised he would. He gives me rest. I did not do anything special. All I did was trust in him. I cast my cares always on him, for he cares for me. Sometimes I am anxious about the problems and the issues that my own pilgrimage has brought to me, but I bring them always to him. I put everything in his hands.

Two relationships were especially important to Ava. She had a fine Islamic boyfriend named Hossein, who was studying in Birmingham, and who loved her deeply and longed for them to get married. But there was the second relationship with her parents. They were grand people. Her father was a respected academic and a member of the mosque, troubled with many of the policies of the ruling political party in Iran. Ava could not think of marrying Hossein without her father's permission and blessing, but at the present time, relations were strained between her parents and herself, as she had left Islam for Christianity. She was in limbo.

I met Hossein on the afternoon of her baptism when they came to the manse for an hour. He read her testimony that she was to give that evening at her baptism and took it very seriously. I liked him enormously. He was not opposed to the Christian faith but knew little about it, and she was helping him.

Soon Ava moved to Shrewsbury and joined the evangelical church. It was a happy time for her. Hossein could easily get there from Birmingham, and under Paul Yeulett's ministry, he learned about Christianity and made his profession to become a Christian. As the months went by, her father warmed to the young couple, and he gave them permission to marry. I preached at their wedding in Shrewsbury, enjoying particularly the Iranian traditions they introduced into the reception, which were delightful and fresh.

In the next couple of years, we all changed our locations. Ava and Hossein moved to London and got good jobs there. I also moved to London after my wife, Iola, died, and I married Barbara. Occasionally we four meet up in our apartment or in theirs. We know the church where they are worshiping and are delighted to see them going on serving their Savior, Jesus Christ.

CHAPTER 15

The Ministry of Mercy in Aberystwyth

The ministry of mercy exercised by Alfred Place Baptist Church involves at least three areas—all of which have meant a great deal to me in my life—that I would like to comment on before concluding this book.

The Christian Bookshop

Alfred Place Baptist Church opened a Christian bookshop. It is going on toward fifty years since the July *Evangelical Times* of 1974 published this report:

> Early one Tuesday morning several men removed the whitewash from a shop window at 3 Western Parade, Aberystwyth, and revealed an attractive Christian Book Shop. Children going to school at 8:30 looked through and said, "Look at those men praying in there." The date was May 7, 1974.
>
> A number of Christians from Alfred Place Baptist Church had discussed the project for several years and made various enquiries. Now their plans had finally come to fruition. In the previous year they had witnessed the followers of the Guru Maharaji opening shops in Aberystwyth to sell health foods, hand crafts and their misleading literature. They had seen four Marxist students selling communist papers in the main streets on Saturday afternoons. They had had the so-called Jehovah's Witnesses calling regularly at the doors with their magazines. But what were Christians doing?

This concern weighed on their hearts increasingly. When some shops owned by British Rail went empty, they made application for their tenancy. The response to the first inquiries was not encouraging, as the shops were already promised to other parties. But the months went by and the premises remained empty.

Finally, British Rail wrote to all who had expressed interest in the shops and asked for tenders. The Christians involved in the earlier application sent in a tender, and there was loud rejoicing when they learnt that British Rail had accepted it. April saw the beginning of intensive and enthusiastic activity. The shop was dilapidated; the back window had no glass and a broken frame, and the skirting board had dry rot.

Then old talents were displayed, and new gifts came to the fore, especially among the deacons. One decorated and painted the inside, an electrician re-wired the shop, another carpenter obtained wood from an old school and a lecturer helped him in its painting and preparation. A fifth deacon designed the shelving, while a sixth painted the sign. At remarkably low cost the shop was transformed.

One of the church elders, who was a lecturer in the College of librarianship, took initial responsibility for the business side of ordering books. Most Christian publishers proved helpful, especially the Banner of Truth Trust.

The shop was opened with a time of earnest prayer in Welsh and English that for years to come it might serve the cause of God and truth in this important educational centre. The shop will be staffed by volunteers from Alfred Place and from the Welsh Evangelical Church. The first morning an enthusiastic nun, lecturing in the University, called in to look around and bought a copy of Herbert Carson's *Roman Catholicism*.

The shop for all these years has been managed by one of the elders of Alfred Place, the late Michael Keen, and his wife, Norma. If you should ask Michael what the essential ingredients of a Christian bookshop are, he would suggest four: (1) a suitable building, (2) sound books, (3) a dedicated staff, and (4) faithful customers.

Let Michael, then, amplify that list in the remainder of this sketch how one local church can open and maintain a Christian bookshop for almost fifty years.

A Suitable Building

The location of the Western Parade lock-up shop was a good one: next to the railway station, with local and regional buses parking outside. One (and later two) display windows were kept lit at night, all in what started out as a row of eight shops. The bookshop's closest neighbor was the Poodle Parlour, where small canines were groomed and noises of barking could be heard by the book browsers through a thin separating wall. That last fact was a blessing in disguise: sometime around 1979 the Poodle business departed, and application was made to the landlord for the bookshop to expand, doubling the shop's size.

This application was successful, so once again hammering, decorating, and installing shelving took place. It was discovered that there was already a lintel in the connecting wall, and a previous pass-through was found behind our bookshelves and opened for use again.

Though numbers 3 and 4 Western Parade gave us a building for twenty years, it had some unsuitable features: an ancient structure with damp walls and a leaking roof and plagued by coal-yard dust (especially when the wind blew from the east). Building redevelopment of the old railway sidings and coal yard had been talked about for many years, and one by one the shops closed with no further tenancies allowed. The unoccupied shops were boarded up, and in the early 1990s half of them were demolished. The boardings attracted graffiti (and some more pleasurable murals), and we suffered a number of break-ins at night by youngsters looking for money. We even had to call the police out on Christmas Day in 1992 to investigate. By late 1991 just two shops remained open—ours and Griffiths y Glo (a coal merchant). For some years we had searched but found that alternative premises for rental were very expensive and in short supply. The possibility of building a new shop on land adjacent to the Alfred Place Baptist Church building itself was not seriously considered, as on an earlier investigation we had been advised that this would be rejected. However, a new application was made and was successful in 1992. At a members' meeting on February 5, 1992, it was resolved to proceed with this new building project and to start looking to Christian people for the necessary funds. In fact, the foundations were dug in March 1992.

Under the heading "The First Purpose-Built Evangelical Bookshop Opens in Wales," a summer 1994 issue of the *Evangelical Magazine of Wales* described the first phase of the shop, then continued,

> The new shop took longer to complete than we had imagined, so for two more years the Western Parade shop remained open. In June 1994 the stock, shelves and counter were transported across to the new premises and the new shop in Alfred Place began its life on June 6. We believe it may be the first purpose-built Christian Bookshop for the sale of evangelical books ever to be opened in Wales.
>
> Aberystwyth is a good centre for such an enterprise: a recent *Western Mail* contained a special feature on the town: "Grey heads are in a minority on the town's streets, outnumbered by other shades of hair—including pink and green—because Aberystwyth attracts surprising numbers of young people who shun the bright lights in favour of life in this small and isolated town." Aberystwyth is to Wales what Alice Springs is to Australia it announced. But does Alice Springs have a Christian Bookshop?

We expected the new shop to cost in the region of £25,000, and as 1992 was the centenary year of the death of Charles Haddon Spurgeon, we observed then that a mark of inflation was that the expected cost of the bookshop was almost the same as Spurgeon's congregation had to raise to build the first Metropolitan Tabernacle some 131 years before! In the event, our shop costs have been in the region of £40,000, but with generous gifts and loans plus the successful trading of the shop since 1994, the monies were all met by April 2000.

Even unbelievers have commented favorably on the design of the new shop, and the way the windows and perspective harmonize with the adjacent chapel building, whose Victorian upright elegance has dominated the tiny street called Alfred Place (the origin of the name is unknown) since the chapel's construction in 1870. Craftsmen's use of wood is striking in an age of plastic, from the hardwood windows with their semi-circular tops to the internal shelves and cupboards. Our new location is adjacent to the town library at present, though that Carnegie building is frequently the subject of plans to relocate. The main shops in the town itself are now much closer, and the local Eastgate shops are improving: the tourist information bureau is nearby, and summer visitors usually find us easily.

One may read about the bookshop on the internet, and that is itself surely a token of an impending trend away from buildings to the "virtual Christian bookshop" of the next millennium—we hope to be part of that, though the very feel of the paper and binding of a sound Christian hardback will remain important and will need the existence of physical buildings like ours for people to browse and choose.

Sound Books

The important precursor of our shop was the bookstall in the vestibule of the church, begun in the mid-1960s soon after the call of Geoff Thomas to be the minister. A young student deacon was the catalyst. Books were obtained from what at that time numbered half a dozen Christian bookshops around Wales run by the Evangelical Movement of Wales, but some of them have had to close. The one in the arcade in Wrexham supplied the books to us by means of a parcel delivery service using the Crosville country buses. This continued in the 1970s with books supplied such as *Truth Unchanged, Unchanging* (Lloyd-Jones, five shillings), *Welsh Revival of 1904* (Eifion Evans, twelve shillings and six pence), and *What's Wrong with Preaching Today*? (Al Martin, one shilling and six pence).

Our convictions over sound books meant that those produced by the Banner of Truth Trust were top of our list, followed closely by the growing value of the Evangelical Press and many titles from Presbyterian and Reformed. In 1974 when the bookshop started, British currency had changed to pounds and pence, but prices sound strange in today's equivalents: *Life in the Spirit*, Lloyd-Jones, £2.50;

God Made Them Great, Tallach, £1.25; *The Reformed Pastor*, Baxter, £0.65. The Banner title *John Elias* had just been published (at £2.10), and *Banner* magazines were £0.10 each!

Over these last twenty-five years, the number of publishers we stock has remained constant at around sixty. The volume of evangelical books published is staggering, and selection for a small shop of no more than two thousand volumes is exceedingly difficult. But taking the best, and what riches are available over the centuries in such authors as Calvin, Bunyan, Owen, Whitefield, Berkhof, Ryle, Spurgeon, Pink, Lloyd-Jones, Henriksen, Murray (several!), and many, many more. But add to these the helpful works by John Blanchard, Faith Cook, Jerry Bridges, Stuart Olyott, Roger Ellsworth, Elisabeth Elliot, and again many, many more. Good children's books with Christian teaching and biblical accuracy are especially important for children growing up in our contemporary society, and we endeavor to stock titles that will help young readers come to faith in Christ and grow to love and serve Him throughout their lives. But the best book to read is still the Bible: whether text, reference, study, large print, leather, zip, yap, thumb indexed, or William Morgan (in Welsh). "*Llusern yw dy air i'm traed, a llewyrch i'm llwybr*" (Salm 119:105): "Your word is a lamp to my feet and a light to my path" (Ps. 119:105).

Do sound bookshops lead to sound authors? In our case, yes, they can indeed do so. I have a photo taken outside Western Parade in spring 1975 showing a theological student doing a Saturday stint opening the shop. After a faithful ministry in Belfast, Derek Thomas, a former deacon in Alfred Place Baptist Church, is still preaching, writing, pastoring, and lecturing in the United States, and we always stock his most valuable books.

A Dedicated Staff

The drive and enthusiasm of our young pastor, Geoff Thomas, was responsible for the start of this work. The link to a sound gospel church with a dedicated membership and many regular attenders swelled in number by the students in the university and colleges of

Aberystwyth made a Christian bookshop possible, even in a tiny town serving little more than a population of twenty thousand.

The volunteers who started the work were soon joined by the Welsh-language sister congregation, the Welsh Evangelical Church, and students such as Derek and Rosemary Thomas, who served in the mid-1970s, have had many dedicated successors. In fact, we are now seeing the children of some of these students helping in our work, so one generation's faithfulness has led to another's.

I remember the day Geoff and I drove on a return trip to London to purchase an initial stock of books from a wholesaler in Bromley and a visit a few months later with Eric Taylor to a supplier in Treorchy. In a typical year about 250 consignments of books must be selected, ordered, received, unpacked, checked, priced, shelved, arranged, displayed, and finally, paid for. In addition, there are the many customer requests to trace and obtain. And, as a small business, there are expenses and maintenance to cover, as well as annual accounts. These tasks are faithfully done in a corner of a room in someone's home.

Bud Mort, who is himself deaf and has the office of pastor to the deaf (using sign language), is an example of someone who was brought to Reformed convictions by seeing and then buying and reading sound books from the church bookstall before the shop began. Regarding the start of the bookshop, he comments,

> I had always longed and prayed for a Christian bookshop for Aberystwyth, and the event of its opening was a culmination of prayer, faith, and "make do and mend" because finance and resources were scarce. At that time I was helping to dismantle an old primary school in Llanon and noticed the wide floorboards were hardwood, which would make good shelves. They did appear a little dirty, but possessing some carpentry skills, the "clerk of works" (the late Ron Loosley) said that with planing and sanding they would be like new. The "supervisor of refurbishing" (the late Aubrey Davies) said that "they would look better with a coat of paint," and the shelves were finally installed for use.

> I then joined the list of volunteers to staff the shop one morning and one afternoon per week. The location near the old station bus stop brought a lot of curious folk inside, some to shelter out of the rain while they waited for their bus. Requests varied from "Do you sell party balloons with Bible verses on?" to "Have you books on the Baha'i faith?" Then there was an elderly man who came in weekly from Lampeter, trying to persuade me that my teaching on original sin was "all wrong" and to accept "universal redemption." Balmy days!

Paid staffing was experimented with on a part-time basis for several years during the 1977 to 1979 period, but turnover never generated enough income to continue this scheme. A student has been paid each summer for six weeks, giving the regular staff an invaluable break during that time.

How many people have been involved in running the shop? I wish we had kept records of this. Just the last five years has involved thirty-three people that I can readily remember, so over the twenty-five years, it is likely to have totaled nearly one hundred volunteers. I wish we could thank them all. Some have gone to glory, of course: Harry Thomas, Geoff's father, used to go to the bank for us regularly and always had a cheerful word to say as he came into the shop and opened the safe. Stephen Olyott, a church deacon, was always most supportive and helped in his area of work with our accounting and tax payments. Staffing has always attracted more women than men, but so many have freely given their time so often that the bookshop has become a part of the lives of many of us.

Faithful Customers

The dearth of good books and greetings cards in the secular shops of the town has provided us with many diverse regular customers: children, young people, students, pensioners, men, women, and friends from overseas. We supply Sunday school materials and Bible reading aids to many in the town and the surrounding country area. However, it may well be the shop staff who buy the most!

In the summer, visiting Christians encourage us with their custom and often with their complimentary comments. The annual conferences of the Evangelical Movement of Wales are always held here, and to have almost two thousand people over the two conference weeks makes it our busiest and nicest time in the shop, especially when the main conference speaker is also an author.

For several years we attempted an evangelistic bookstall at the local agricultural show, where our tent was in some contrast to the selling of tractors and the parading of Welsh Cob ponies and majestic Shire horses. But we have the majestic Savior to parade before men, do we not?

Now that we can no longer find a suitable place to preach in the open at the annual November fair days in the town, a bookstall is taken there, and has been well received and supported. And at least one customer has discovered our shop and church by our presence on the internet.

Thanksgiving to God

The four ingredients of a bookshop project like ours are only sufficient if it is all done in total dependence on God and trust in His Son, our Savior, as we believe it has. When discussing the start of the shop in an early church meeting, we said how important it was for the shop to maintain its witness to biblical Christianity, even if the church departed from it (and vice versa). Happily, neither has departed, and we aim to do everything in submission to Christ, His gospel, and to the whole Word of God.

Ministering to Help the Unborn Child

In 1979, an influential book and film series appeared entitled *Whatever Happened to the Human Race?* written by Francis A. Schaeffer and C. Everett Koop, MD. Dr. Schaeffer was a US evangelical missionary to Switzerland, and Dr. Koop was a pioneering pediatric surgeon from Philadelphia who later became the US surgeon general. The book and film series sounded an alarm against the growing acceptance of abortion, infanticide, and euthanasia. The first three chapters reviewed current attitudes to those practices, often linking them with the inhuman and genocidal policies of Nazi Germany. Then the causes of the modern malaise were examined and attributed to the spread of secular humanism and moral relativism in recent centuries and the weakness of the professing church's response to that. A godless rationalism had set its course to this ultimate immorality. The Bible, according to Schaeffer, is "God's propositional communication to mankind" and therefore, "God gives the pages, and thus God gives the answers about the nature of reality and man's proper response to it."[1] The book is a heartfelt plea to show greater reverence for God's inestimable gift of human life. Abortion is the one act of violence that BBC television refuses to show.

The year after the book appeared, the film series was shown over five consecutive Friday nights on the campus of the University in Aberystwyth. It was presented by a member of Alfred Place Baptist Church, my friend Dr. John R. Ling, who was for many years a deacon in the church. From 1976 to 2001 he was a lecturer in biochemistry and bioethics at the Institute of Biological Sciences at the university.

Those films not only educated but also challenged. We were rattled. But what to do? As a consequence of his influence and with the backing of his congregation, Dr. Ling became the founding chairman of the Aberystwyth LIFE Group and cofounder of Evangelicals for LIFE, a specialist grouping within the UK's foremost pro-life organization, LIFE. Hundreds of other UK evangelical Christians gladly found solace and a pro-life outlet by volunteering for LIFE. And that action continues today, with many as counselors, chairpersons, fundraisers, educators, trustees, and so on in LIFE and in other pro-life groups. Indeed, *Whatever Happened to the Human Race?* was a landmark project that also brought about a pro-life stance among UK evangelical publishers, magazines, organizations, and of course, churches. In Aberystwyth, we sought the threefold aims of LIFE by educating the townspeople and students about the truths

1. Francis A. Schaeffer and C. Everett Koop, *Whatever Happened to the Human Race?* (Old Tappan, N.J.: Fleming H. Revell, 1979), 152.

of abortion, helping both practically and emotionally people with unexpected and problem pregnancies, and exerting some political impact. John has held various honorary positions in LIFE and has lectured, debated, broadcast, and written about bioethical issues for the last forty or so years. He has taught internationally and throughout the UK including the London Seminary.

After his retirement from the university, he wrote some notable books on bioethical issues, one with that very title: *Bioethical Issues: Understanding and Responding to the Culture of Death, When Does Human Life Begin?*, and *The Edge of Life: Dying, Death and Euthanasia*. He also maintains a relevant website, www.johnling.co.uk.

How could any Christian—any person—kill a living, unborn child? Yet since the 1967 legalization of killing babies in their mothers' wombs, over ten million abortions have taken place in England, Wales, and Scotland. During 2019 over two hundred thousand abortions occurred in these nations. This is not just a big-city problem—in Aberystwyth, abortions regularly take place in our local hospital. There is also the sadness and guilt attached to such statistics on so many levels. But there is also a merciful God to all who seek His forgiveness. None can say, "But not for what I have done"; His mercy is greater than our greatest transgressions.

Ministering to Those with Learning Difficulties

Alfred Place Baptist Church opened a home for those who have learning disabilities. In the November 1973 edition of *The Evangelical Times,* an article appeared with a spread over several pages entitled "Cause for Concern" written by David Potter. It told the story of David and his wife's ten-year-old daughter, Rachel, who had Down syndrome. She lived for some years in a Christian residential school near Edinburgh, but apart from that school, there was almost no tangible Christian response to people with learning difficulties. In addition, scores of Christian parents were desperate to find such a home that would provide a secure Christian environment for their learning-disabled children.

Much interest in the issue was generated in the UK by the article, but particularly so in our church. The reason for that was the presence in the congregation of two such young people. Bud and Phyllis Mort had a daughter, Linda, who was around ten years of age, and then newly married Eric and Sonia Taylor's firstborn child, Matthew, was quite severely disabled.

We were having our usual midweek meeting, and Phyllis Mort spoke very movingly of this article and the need for such a home even in Aberystwyth. Why not? Someone gave £5 (I don't remember who), and the person chairing the meeting told us that it would go toward the need of such a home. I confess to being a little perplexed. Where were we going with this issue? Were we going to establish in Aberystwyth such a home? Where would we get the money to erect or purchase one such building and change it so that it would be fit for a dozen people with disabilities? What a task! My faith was weak.

In the weeks ahead, in both church officers' meetings and members' meetings we all hung together. The Welsh Evangelical Church supported us, and we brought together our two congregations to pray for God's guidance and blessing. David Potter himself came to Aberystwyth and answered many questions, and a dawning awareness came over the congregation that this was God's will for us. A solicitor friend of mine had the power of attorney to determine how a substantial legacy of one of his clients should be spent. A large house and its grounds called Plas Lluest came on the market for £38,000. It had been the home of the first principal of the Presbyterian Theological College and then the meeting place for the first Welsh-language school in Wales. We made an offer for it. The money came in through the giving of Christians and the legacy, and so it was purchased.

One of our members who was an architect designed the interior and rebuilt it so that all the necessary fire precautions were put in place. Then the equipment for a home for sixteen people—kitchen, laundry, bedrooms—was all purchased and put into place until the house was ready for the young men and women to move in. The money always came in at the needed time. George Muller's experience in seeing God's provision for his home in Bristol was not unique.

Hudson Taylor famously said, "God's work done in God's way will never lack God's supply."

We had superb readymade houseparents in the congregation in Bud and Phyllis Mort, and they did a great job in all the challenging early years as staff was appointed and the whole enterprise took off. The residents' happy arrival in church on Sunday brought a smile to our faces.

The home still exists, though the residents are older. Finding suitable staff is always challenging, but the leaders have been people who know God. It is still the home of Linda Mort, who was one of the prime catalysts for receiving the light burden from the Lord and the energy given to take the first steps. Matthew Taylor is still alive, but the home is not suitable for someone with his special needs; he is lovingly cared for elsewhere.

The enterprise was referred to as "Cause for Concern" for many years, but it is a much-used phrase, and so now the work is called "Livability" and spread across a number of locations in the United Kingdom.

Epilogue

Regrets and Rejoicing

What minister at the end of his allotted span is not in danger of drowning in regrets, aware of the chasm between what he is still learning of how a preacher-pastor should live, should have been, and should have known and what he actually was and is yet. The combustible material of disappointment can suddenly flare up from the heart of the preacher at the end of his days, lit by the fiery darts. Alas, there are lots of memories in the tinderbox of our lives, such as follies and hurtful words even to those we love the most. Yet still, with this consciousness of our sinfulness and the hurt our folly has caused, we are vain! Why is it so hard to pour contempt on all one's pride? Such a response should be instinctive. What phantoms we are! What do we have that we did not initially receive from God? What pathetic stewards we have been. So, what about this rodomontade? Vanity of vanities; it is all vanity. An autobiography! Come on! Every page I have written needs divine pity. But even God's weaklings, who only gave a cup of cold water to someone, did what they did because God was with them.

Prayer? If you want to humble a minister, ask him about his prayer life. Did I ever pray in private with a commensurate breathtaking awareness that the Creator of heaven and earth was listening to me? When I struggle to pray, I can fall before God and say, "I wish it weren't me. Mercy, mercy, mercy." Only this must I remember—whenever I have worked, it is I who worked, but when I prayed, I looked at the workings of God. "Hallowed be Thy name."

Every pastor acknowledges and even glories in his limitations. If anything was to be accomplished, then only the grace of God could do it. God placed me in a certain place, and He kept me there just as I was. I dared not leave, even in the face of occasional disapproval and pressures and the hostility of a few unhappy members. The Christian life moves from the challenging to the very difficult and from the very difficult to the impossible, and it is a poor Christian life if it is anything else. Yet it will never lack God's provision. Always grace will be more than sufficient. It will be super abundant.

How could I dismiss the exhortations for more discipline and harder work and striving to be a growing Christian with the excuse that I simply "was not gifted to do this or that sort of thing"? My sufficiency did not lie in my health and strength and IQ but in the fullness of the grace of my Savior. Expect great things from God. Attempt great things for God. The greatest is love, and it never fails.

How hard to accept utter and absolute divine forgiveness for all one's failures as a minister—sins of hypocrisy, pretense, laziness, and carnality and failures in pastoring and counseling, all as a self-declared servant of God! Can there be mercy for those who cleverly paraded themselves in the shadow instead of focusing exclusively on their Lord the rock? "For the chief of sinners grace abounds," God says. Take it, sinner. You preach it to others. Take it yourself. Take mercy. Take abounding forgiveness.

I believe that I never preached enough and in the right spirit on the doctrine of the divine judgment that will come upon wickedness. I am talking about the hell that my Savior talked about. What faith, righteousness, love, tears, and courage that takes!

Yet the great truths of the Christian faith found in the Bible I still believe and preach—that is, those reflected in the early church in the Chalcedonian statement and in the *solas* of the Reformation; in the Thirty-Nine Articles of the Anglicans and in the Heidelberg Catechism; in the *Body of Divinity* of the Puritan Thomas Watson, the Confessions of Faith of the Presbyterians, and the teachings of the Congregationalists and Baptists of the seventeenth century; in the truths preached by George Whitefield, Daniel Rowland, and Jonathan Edwards in the eighteenth century; in the 1823 Welsh Calvinistic Confession, in the preaching of C. H. Spurgeon and Robert Murray M'Cheyne, and in the teachings of Charles Hodge, Robert Lewis Dabney, and James Henley Thornwell in the nineteenth century; and in the twentieth century in the teaching of Vos, Machen, John Murray, Van Til, Lloyd-Jones, Iain Murray, Joel Beeke, and Kenneth A. Macrae of Stornoway. The truths these men confessed I, too, have believed for sixty-five years. I have spoken to God, and He has heard me and answered my prayers. In all my spoonfuls of regrets, I have been given a vast and abundant reservoir of blessings. God has not dealt with me as I deserved, and He has hidden my sins from those whom I fear most to hurt. Whatever the future will bring me, the past has brought me gold.

The only reason that all people should believe in Jesus Christ is that Christianity is true. Our Lord rose from the dead, and it is true, but truth has been sacrificed for modernist dogma in the twentieth century, and now in the twenty-first-century tolerance is yielding to tyranny. Minds, both in the professing church and outside it, are closing against the utter reliability of the gospel and the reality of new life in Christ. So, we have a duty to speak inconvenient truths and stand up against the last gasps of denominational power—whatever the cost.

Retirement

In the summer of 2016, I gave a series of sermons on 2 Timothy, the old apostle's exhortations and concluding counsels addressed to younger Timothy. Once that was complete, I retired and then attended the ordination service of my grandson Rhodri Brady, who followed me to Alfred Place. That was my goodbye. Who can say what benefits would have come to the church if I had left earlier? Some of my friends have had blessed short-term pastorates. They must have been confident with every call they accepted that it was not God's will that they continue for many years in a single pulpit. I never had a call to another church. Alfred Place was stuck with me!

So, the church helped me one Saturday as I moved down the hill eighty yards to the apartment where once Dad and Mam had lived. The rest of the furniture and books were put into storage where they still are. Iola was taken ill the very next Sunday and spent the next six weeks in hospital unable to eat, growing weaker in the last stages of Alzheimer's disease. She died on October 19, 2016.

Barbara Homrighausen

Remarriage

Iola and I had known and loved Barbara Homrighausen (originally from Germany) for almost forty years. She had a property in Aberystwyth and loved to visit and worship in Alfred Place, and it was natural in the next months that as we talked together we grew closer, and in 2018 we got married. She was born the same year as Iola, and our memories and journeys in British evangelicalism have been in parallel. She had been

With my daughters

a member of Westminster Chapel in London and had sat under Dr. Martyn Lloyd-Jones in his final years. I had the blessing of my daughters upon my choice of a wife. I don't think I could have married without that. We all miss Iola—we cannot say how much—but to have a godly, fair companion at this time in my life is breathtaking grace from God.

All my family in 2020 enjoying a picnic in a park in Cardiff. Since that occasion two more great grandchildren have been born.

Relocation

Barbara has lived in London for nearly sixty years. I needed to get away from Aberystwyth for several reasons, including to leave the new pastor, Rhodri Brady, in his first church without my intrusions in the life of the congregation and to go somewhere new and do something fresh. I was invited to preach for one Sunday in Twickenham, London, in Amyand Park Chapel in early 2018. I have subsequently joined the church and highly appreciate the ministry of Gerard Hemmings, my pastor, and the church eldership, the congregation's life of prayer, and the evangelism of the church. Some people, it is said, because of the delightfully relentless pressing concern from the pulpit on all the congregation to turn from sin and receive Jesus Christ into their lives, have taken offense and moved away to other evangelical churches that were less "offensively" evangelistic. If only that evangelistic concern was as prominent in many other gospel churches! It is a privilege not only to be a member there but to be able to preach in congregations all over the United Kingdom and in many places in the world. Now I write letters, lectures, articles, and books. I love the parks of London, the Thames, the buses, the tube, the old buildings, the classical music concerts. One of my daughters, her husband (who is one of my closest friends), and the youngest of their five sons live twenty minutes away. I am a blessed man.

I miss Wales, my old friends, my doctor, my dentist, my optician, and Aberystwyth promenade on a summer's evening. I especially miss the close proximity of my sister-in-law, Rhiain, and her husband, Keith, but I still have my apartment there and try to go back once a month. But I am loosing myself from earthly ties and launching out. I am seeking to prepare myself now for my next final move, for the extraordinary sight of the face of Jesus Christ and the metamorphosis of glorification, when I shall be transfigured and be made like Him. I also look forward to the breathless reunion with those of my loved ones and those I have known or read about who died in Christ and have gone before me, who are waiting for me.

Finally, there is the blissful vocation spreading out and out before me of serving the Lord in a new heavens and earth, my works following me. That will be the glory to be revealed that we have not yet seen, but what has been plainly told us is the final destination of all the people of God, for whom the Savior gave Himself as an offering for their sin, that this indeed will be our blessed future—"with the Lord." Until then, I echo the words of the psalmist:

> The lines have fallen to me in pleasant places;
> Yes, I have a good inheritance.
> I bless the LORD who has given me counsel;
> My heart instructs me in the night seasons.
> I have set the LORD always before me;
> Because He is at my right hand I shall not be moved.
> Therefore my heart is glad, and my glory rejoices;
> My flesh also will rest in hope.
> For You will not leave my soul in Sheol,
> Nor will You allow Your Holy One to see corruption.
> You will show me the path of life;
> In Your presence is fullness of joy;
> At Your right hand are pleasures forevermore.
> (Ps. 16:6–11)

~~~

> Only one life, a few brief years
> Each with its burdens, hopes and fears;
> Each with its days I must fulfill
> Living for self or in His will
> Only one life, 'twill soon be past.
> Only what's done for Christ will last.
> —C. T. Studd

MY EPITAPH:
GOD CREATED ME
SIN RUINED ME
GRACE RESTORED ME
~~~